The Expositor's Bible:
Ecclesiastes
By Samuel Cox, D.D.
Edited by Anthony Uyl

Woodstock, Ontario, 2017

The Expositor's Bible: Ecclesiastes
The Expositor's Bible: Ecclesiastes
By Samuel Cox, D.D.
Edited by Anthony Uyl
With a new translation by Samuel Cox, D.D.,
Author of commentaries on Job, Ruth, etc.
Originally edited by The Rev. W. Robertson Nicoli, M.A., LL.D.,
Editor of "The Expositor."

"Omnia vanitas, præter amare Deum, et illi soli servire."
   --St. Augustine.

Toronto: Willard Tract Depository and Bible Depot, Corner of Yonge and Temperance Streets. 1890.

The text of The Expositor's Bible: Ecclesiastes is all in the Public Domain. This edition is published by Devoted Publishing a division of 2165467 Ontario Inc.

What kind of philosophies do you have?
Let us know!

Contact us at: devotedpub@hotmail.com
Visit us on Facebook: Devoted Publishing
Get more products via our website: www.devotedpublishing.com
Published in Woodstock, Ontario, Canada 2017.

For bulk educational rates, please contact us at the above email address.

ISBN: 978-1-988297-94-1

Samuel Cox, D.D.

Table of Contents

PREFACE 4
   Footnote: 5
INTRODUCTION 6
   Footnotes: 20
THE PROLOGUE 23
   Footnote: 23
FIRST SECTION 24
SECOND SECTION 26
THIRD SECTION 28
FOURTH SECTION 31
THE EPILOGUE 34
EXPOSITION 35
   THE PROLOGUE 35
   Footnotes: 38
   FIRST SECTION 39
   Footnotes: 42
   SECOND SECTION 43
   Footnotes: 54
   THIRD SECTION 55
   Footnotes: 65
   FOURTH SECTION 66
   Footnotes: 76
   THE EPILOGUE 78
   Footnotes: 91

PREFACE

The Lectures on which this book is founded were delivered five-and-twenty years ago, and were published in A.D. 1867.[1] For more than twenty years the book has been out of print, a large first edition having been speedily sold out. No other edition was issued owing to the fact that my publisher soon passed into another profession. I have often been asked to reprint it, but have always felt that, before reprinting, I must rewrite it. Till of late, however, I could not command leisure for the task. But when, at the commencement of this year, the Editor of The Expositor's Bible did me the honour to ask permission to reprint it, that he might include it in this excellent series, I had leisure at command, and cheerfully devoted it to the revision of my work. Among the more recent commentaries I have read with this purpose in view, those which I have found most helpful and suggestive were that of Delitzsch, that by Dr. Wright, that of Dean Plumptre, and the fine fragment contributed to The Expositor by Dr. Perowne, the Dean of Peterborough. In the preface to the former edition I dwelt on my indebtedness to the commentary of Dr. Ginsburg, published in A.D. 1861. In my judgment it still remains by far the best, the most thorough and the most sound. It has but one serious defect; it is addressed to scholars, and so abounds in learning and erudition that it can never come into popular use. Indeed even now, although during the last twenty years there has been an immense advance in the study and exposition of Holy Writ, and many able and learned men have devoted themselves to the service of the general public, I know of no commentary on this Scripture which really meets the wants of the unlettered. I cannot but hope, therefore, that the Quest of the Chief Good may still serve a useful purpose, and that, in its revised form, it may be found helpful to those who most need help.

In rewriting the book I have retained as much as I could of its earlier form, lest the vivacity of a first exposition of the Scripture should be lost. And, indeed, the alterations I have had to make are but slight for the most part, though I have in many places altered, and, I hope, amended both the translation and the commentary: but there are one or two additions--they will be found on pages 20-26, and, again, in certain modifications of the exposition of Chapter XII., verses 9-12, on pages 279-305; dealing mainly with the structure of Ecclesiastes--which may, I trust, be found useful not to the general reader alone. Since the original edition appeared I have had to study the Book of Job, most of the Psalms, many of the Prophetical writings, and some of the Proverbs; and it was inevitable that in the course of these pleasant studies I should arrive at clearer and more definite conceptions on the structure of Hebrew poetry. These I now place at the service of my readers, and submit to the judgment of scholars and critics.

Another and much more important result of these subsequent studies has been that I can now speak with a more assured confidence of the theme of this Scripture, and of its handling by the Author. None of the scholars who have recently commented on the Book doubt that it is the quest of the chief good which it sets forth; and though some of them arrange and divide it differently, yet, on the whole and in the main, they are agreed that this quest is urged in Wisdom, in Pleasure, in Devotion to Public Affairs, in Wealth and in the Golden Mean; and that it ends and rests in the large noble conclusion, that only as men reverence God, and keep his commandments, and trust in his love, do they touch their true ideal, and find a good that will satisfy and sustain them under all changes, even to the last. The assent to this view of the Book was by no means general a quarter of a century ago; but it is so wide now, and is sanctioned by the authority of so many schools of learning, that I think no reader of the following pages need be disturbed by misgivings as to the accuracy of the main lines of thought here set forth.

Few Scriptures of the Old Testament are so familiar to the general reader as Ecclesiastes; and that mainly, I think, because it addresses itself to a problem which is "yours, mine, every man's." Many more quotations from it have entered into our current speech than have been taken from Job, for example, although Job is both a much larger and a much finer poem than this--"the finest poem," as a great living poet has said, "whether of the modern or of the antique world." It is a Book which can never lose its interest for men until the last conflict in the long strife of doubt has led in the final victory of faith; and seems, in especial, to adapt itself to the conditions and wants of the present age. It deals with the very questions which are in all our minds, and offers a solution of them, and, so far as I know, the only solution, in which those who have "eternity in their hearts" can rest. May all who study it, with such help as the following pages afford, find rest to their souls, and be drawn from the heat and strife of thought into the calm and hallowed sanctuary which it throws open to our erring feet.

Samuel Cox, D.D.

The Holme, Hastings, October 1890.

Footnote:

1. The Quest of the Chief Good. A Popular Commentary on the book Ecclesiastes, with a New Translation. By Samuel Cox. London: Arthur Miall.

INTRODUCTION

§ 1. ON THE AUTHORSHIP, FORM, DESIGN, AND CONTENTS OF THE BOOK.

Those who raise the question, "Is life worth living?" answer it by--living on; for no man lives simply to proclaim what a worthless and wretched creature he is. But for the most part the question is mooted in a merely academical and not very sincere spirit. And to the dainty and fastidious pessimist who goes about to imply his own superiority by declaring that the world which contents his fellows is not good enough for him, there still seems no better reply than the rough but rousing and wholesome rebuke which Epictetus gave to such as he some nineteen centuries ago, reminding them that there were many exits from the theatre of life, and advising them, if they disliked the "show", to retire from it by the nearest door of escape, and to make room for spectators of a more modest and grateful spirit.

Of the pessimists of his time he demands, "Was it not God who brought you here? And as what did He bring you? Was it not as a mortal? Was it not as one who was to live with a little portion of flesh upon the earth, and to witness his administration--to behold the great spectacle around you for a little while? After you have beheld the solemn and august spectacle as long as is permitted you, will you not depart when He leads you out, adoring and thankful for what you have heard and seen? For you the solemnity is over. Go away, then, like a modest and grateful person. Make room for others."

"But why," urges the pessimist, "did He bring me into the world on these hard terms?"

"Oh!" replies Epictetus, "if you don't like the terms, it is always in your power to leave them. He has no need of a discontented spectator. He will not miss you much, nor we either."

But if any man lift the question into a more sincere and noble form by asking, "How may life be made worth living, or best worth living?"--in other words, "What is the true ideal, and what the chief good, of man?"--he will find no nobler answer to it, and none more convincingly and persuasively put, than that contained in this Scripture, which modern pessimists are apt to quote whenever they want to "approve" their melancholy hypothesis "with a text." From Schopenhauer downward, this Book is constantly cited by them as if it confirmed the conclusion for which they contend, Taubert even going so far as to find "a catechism of pessimism" in it. Their assumption, however, is based on a total misapprehension of the design and drift of Ecclesiastes of which no scholar should have been guilty, and of which it is hard to see how any scholar could have been guilty had he studied it as a whole, instead of carrying away from it only what he wanted. So far from lending any countenance to their conclusion of despair, it frankly traverses it--as I hope to show, and as many have shown before me-- and lands us in its very opposite; the conclusion of the whole matter with the Hebrew Preacher being, that whoso cultivates the virtues of charity, diligence, and cheerfulness, because God is in heaven and rules over all, he will not only find life well worth living, but will pursue its loftiest ideal and touch its true blessedness.

When scholars and "philosophers" have fallen into a mistake so radical and profound, it is not surprising that the unlettered should have followed their leaders into the ditch, and taken this Scripture to be the most melancholy in the Sacred Canon, instead of one of the most consolatory and inspiriting, for want of apprehending its true aim. Beyond all doubt, there is a prevailing ground-tone of sadness in the Book; for through by far the larger part of its course it has to deal with some of the saddest facts of human life--with the errors which divert men from their true aim, and plunge them into a various and growing misery. But the voice which sinks so often into this tone of sadness is the voice of a most brave and cheerful spirit, a spirit whose counsels can only depress us if we are seeking our chief good where it cannot be found. For the Preacher, as we shall see, does not condemn the wisdom or the mirth, the devotion to business or the acquisition of wealth, in which most men find "the chief good and market of their time," as in themselves vanities. He approves of them; he shows us how we may so pursue and so use them as to find them very pleasant and wholesome; how we may so dispense with them, if they prove beyond our reach, as none the less to enjoy a very true and abiding content. His constant and recurring moral is that we are to enjoy our brief day on earth; that God meant us to enjoy it; that we are to be up and doing, with a heart for any strife, or toil, or pleasure; not to sit still and weep over broken illusions and defeated hopes. Our lower aims and possessions become vanities to us only when we seek in them that supreme satisfaction which He who has "put eternity into our hearts" designed us to find gesture, might provoke the most terrible outrages (viii. 3, 4; x. 4). The true relation between the sexes was violated; the ruling classes crowded their harems with concubines, and even the wiser sort of men took to themselves any woman they desired; while, with cynical injustice, they first degraded women, and then condemned them as alike and altogether bad, their hands chains, their love a snare (vii. 26, 28; ix. 9). The oppressions of the time were so constant, so cruel, and life grew so dark beneath them, that those who died long ago were counted happier than those who were still alive; while happier than either were those who had not been born to see the intolerable evils on which the sun looked calmly down day by day (iv. 1-3). In fine, the whole fabric of the State was fast falling into ruin and decay, through the greed and sloth of rulers who taxed the people to the uttermost in order to supply their wasteful luxury (x. 18, 19); while yet, so dreadful was their tyranny and their spies so ubiquitous, that no man dared to breathe a word against them even to the wife of his bosom and in the secrecy of the bed-chamber (x. 20); the only consolation of the oppressed was the grim hope that a time of retribution would overtake their tyrants, from which neither their power nor their craft should be able to save them (viii. 5-8).

Nothing would be more difficult than to accept this as a picture of the social and political features of the Hebrew commonwealth during the reign of Solomon, or even during those later years of his reign in which his rule grew hard and despotic. Nothing can well be more incredible than that this should be intended as a picture of his reign, save that it should be a picture drawn by his own hand! To suppose Solomon the author of this Scripture is to suppose that the wisest of kings and of men was base enough to pen a deliberate and malignant libel on himself, his time, and his realm! On the other hand, the description, dark and lurid as it is, exactly accords with all we know of the terrible condition of the Jews who wept in captivity by the waters of Babylon under the later Persian rule, or were ground under the heels of the Persian satraps after their return to the land of their fathers. In all probability, therefore, as our most competent authorities are agreed, the Book is a poem rather than a chronicle, written by an unknown Hebrew author, during the Captivity or shortly after the Return, certainly not before B.C. 500, and probably somewhat later. [3]

Nor is this inference, drawn from the style and general contents of the Book, unsupported by verses in it which at first sight seem altogether opposed to such an inference. All the special and direct indications of authorship are to be found either in the first or in the last chapter.

The very first verse runs, "The words of the Preacher, son of David, King in Jerusalem." Now, David had only one son who was King in Jerusalem, viz. Solomon; the verse, therefore, seems to fix the authorship on Solomon beyond dispute. Nevertheless, the conclusion is untenable. For (1) in his known and admitted works the Wise King distinctly claims to be their author. The Book of Proverbs commences with "The Proverbs of Solomon," and the Canticles with "The Song of Songs, which is Solomon's." But the book Ecclesiastes does not once mention his name, though it speaks of a "son of David," i.e. one of David's descendants. Instead of calling this son of David Solomon, it calls him "Coheleth," or, as we translate the word, "The Preacher." Now, the word Coheleth [4] is not a masculine noun, as the name of a man should be, but the feminine participle of an unused conjugation of a Hebrew verb which means "to collect," or "to call together." It denotes, not an actual man, but an abstraction, a personification, and is probably intended to denote one who calls a congregation round him, i.e. a preacher, any preacher, preacher in the abstract. (2) This "son of David," we are told, was "King in Jerusalem;" and the phrase implies that the Book was written at a time when there either were or had been kings out of Jerusalem, when Jerusalem was not the only site of a Hebrew throne, and therefore after the disruption of Solomon's realm into the rival kingdoms of Israel and Judah. (3) Again, we find Coheleth affirming (i. 12), "I was King over Israel in Jerusalem," and (i. 16), "I acquired greater wisdom than all (all kings, i.e., say the critics) who were before me in Jerusalem." But to say nothing of the questionable modesty of the latter sentence if it fell from the pen of Solomon, he was only the second occupant of the throne in Jerusalem; for Jebus, or Jerusalem, was only conquered from a Philistine clan by his father David. And if there had been only one, how could he speak of "all" who preceded him? (4) And still further, the tense of the verb in "I was King over Israel" can only carry the sense "I was King, but am King no more." Yet we know that Solomon reigned over Israel to the day of his death, that there never was a day on which he could have strictly used such a tense as this. So clear and undisputed is the force of this tense that the rabbis, who held Solomon to be the author of Ecclesiastes, were obliged to invent a fable or tradition to account for it. They said, "When King Solomon was sitting on the throne of his kingdom, his heart was greatly lifted up within him by his prosperity, and he transgressed the commandments of God, gathering to him many horses, and chariots, and riders, amassing much gold and silver, and marrying many wives of foreign extraction. Wherefore the anger of the Lord was kindled against him, and He sent against him Ashmodai, the ruler of the demons; and he drave him from the throne of his kingdom, and took away the ring from his hand (Solomon's ring is famous for its marvellous powers in all Oriental fable), and sent him forth to wander about the world. And he went through the villages and cities, with a staff in his hand, weeping and lamenting, and saying, 'I am Coheleth; I was beforetime Solomon, and reigned over Israel in Jerusalem; but now I rule over only this staff.'" It is a pretty and pathetic fable, but it is a fable; and though it proves nothing else, we may fairly only in Him and in serving Him. If we love and serve Him, if we gratefully acknowledge Him to be the Author of "every good gift and every perfect boon," if we seek first his kingdom and righteousness; in fine, if we are Christian in more than name, the study of this Book should not make us sad. We should find in it a confirmation of our most intimate convictions, and incentives to act upon them. But if we do not hold our wisdom, our mirth, our labour, our wealth as the gifts and ordinances of God for our good, if we permit them to usurp his seat and become as gods to us, then indeed this Book will be sad enough for us, but no whit sadder than our lives. It will be sad, and will make us sad, yet only that it may lead us to repentance, and through repentance to a true and lasting joy.

***

It is to be feared that the popular misconception of this singular and most instructive Scripture goes much farther than this, and extends to questions much more superficial than that of the temper or spirit it breathes. If, for example, the average reader of the Bible were asked, Who wrote this Scripture? when was it written? to whom was it addressed? what is its general scope and design? his answer, I suppose, would be: "Solomon wrote this Book; of course, therefore, it was written in his lifetime, and addressed to the men over whom he ruled; and his design in writing it was to reveal his own experience of life for their instruction." And yet in all probability no one of these answers is true, or anywhere near the truth. According to the most competent judges, the Book Ecclesiastes was not written by Solomon, nor for centuries after his death; it was addressed to a generation of feeble and oppressed captives, who had been carried away into exile, or had lately returned from it, and not to the free prosperous nation which rose to its highest pitch in the reign of the Wise King. It is a dramatic representation of the experience of a Jewish sage, who deliberately set himself to discover and pursue the chief good of man in all the provinces and along all the avenues in which it is commonly sought, eked out by what he supposed or tradition reported Solomon's experience to have been; and its design was to comfort men who were groaning under the heaviest wrongs of Time with the bright hope of Immortality.

To scholars versed in the niceties of the Oriental languages, the most convincing proof of the comparatively modern date and authorship of the Book is to be found in its words, and idioms, and style. The base forms of Hebrew and the large intermixture of foreign terms, phrases, and turns of speech which characterize it--these, with the absence of the nobler rhythmic forms of Hebrew poetry, are held to be a conclusive demonstration that it was written during the Rabbinical period, at a time long subsequent to the Augustan age in which Solomon lived and wrote. The critics and commentators whose names stand highest [2] tell us that it would be just as easy for them to believe that Hooker wrote Blair's Sermons, or that Shakespeare wrote the plays of Sheridan Knowles, as to believe that Solomon wrote Ecclesiastes. And of course on such questions as these we can only defer to the verdict of men who have made them the study of their lives.

But with all our deference for learning, we have so often seen the conclusions of the ripest scholars modified or reversed by their successors, and we all know "questions of words" to be capable of so many different interpretations, that probably we should still hold our judgment in suspense, were there no arguments against the traditional hypothesis such as plain men use and can understand. There are many such arguments, however, and arguments that seem to be of a conclusive force.

As, for instance, this: The whole social state described in this Book is utterly unlike what we know to have been the condition of the Hebrews during the reign of Solomon, but exactly accords with the condition of the captive Israelites, who, at the disruption of the Hebrew monarchies, were carried away into Babylonia. Under Solomon the Hebrew State touched its highest point. His throne was surrounded by statesmen of tried sagacity; his judges were incorrupt. Commerce grew and prospered, till gold became as common as silver had been, and silver as common as brass. Literature flourished, and produced its most perfect fruits. And the people, though heavily taxed during the later years of his reign, enjoyed a security, a freedom, an abundance unknown whether to their fathers or to their children. "Judah and Israel were many in number as the sands by the sea, eating, drinking, and making merry.... And Judah and Israel dwelt safely, every man under his vine and under his fig-tree, from Dan even to Beersheba, all the days of Solomon" (1 Kings iv. 20, 25). But as we read this Book we gather from it the picture of a social state in which kings were childish, and princes addicted to revelry and drunkenness (x. 16); great fools were lifted to high places and rode on stately horses, while nobles were degraded and had to tramp through the mire (x. 6, 7); the race was not to the swift, nor the battle to the strong, nor riches to the intelligent, nor favour to the learned (ix. 11). The most eminent public services were suffered to pass unrewarded, and were forgotten the moment the need for them was passed (ix. 14, 15). Property was so insecure that to amass wealth was only to multiply extortions, and to fall a prey to the cupidity of princes and judges, insomuch that the sluggard who folded his hands, so long as he had bread to eat, was esteemed wiser than the diligent merchant who applied himself to the labours and anxieties of traffic (iv. 5, 6). Life was as insecure as property, and stood at the caprice of men who were slaves to their own lusts; a hasty word spoken in the divan of any one of the satraps, or even a resentful infer from it that, even in the judgment of the rabbis, the book Ecclesiastes must, on its own showing, have been written after Solomon had ceased to be King, i.e. after he had ceased to live.

In the Epilogue (xii. 9-12) the Author of the Book lifts the dramatic mask from his face, and permits us to see who he really is; a mask, let me add, somewhat carelessly worn, since we see nothing of it in the last ten chapters of the Book. Although he has written in a feigned name, and, without asserting it, has so moulded his phrases, at least in the earlier chapters of his work, as to suggest to his readers that he is, if not Solomon himself, at least Solomon's mouthpiece, attributing the garnered results of his experience to one greater than himself, that they may carry the more weight--just as Browning speaks in the name of Rabbi Ben Ezra, for instance, or Fra Lippo Lippi, or Abt Vogler, borrowing what he can of outward circumstance from the age and class to which they belong, and yet really uttering his own thought and emotion through their lips--he now confesses that he is no king of an age long past, but a rabbi, a sage, a teacher, a master, who has both made some proverbs of his own and collected the wise sayings of others who had gone before him, in order that he might carry some little light and comfort to the sorely bested men of his own generation and blood. [5] In short, he has exercised his right as a poet, or "maker," to embody the results of his wide and varied experience of life in a dramatic form, but is careful to let us know, before he takes leave of us, that it is a fictitious or dramatic Solomon, and not Solomon himself, to whom we have been listening throughout.

So that all the phrases in the Book which are indicative of its authorship confirm the inference drawn from its style and its historical contents; viz. that it was not written by Solomon, nor in his reign, but by an unknown sage of a long-subsequent period, who, by a dramatic impersonation of the characteristic experiences of the son of David, or rather of his own experiences blended with the Solomonic traditions and poured into their moulds, sought to console and instruct his oppressed fellow-countrymen.

But perhaps the most convincing argument in favour of this conclusion is that, when once we think of it, we cannot possibly accept the Solomon set before us in Ecclesiastes as the Solomon depicted in the historical books of Scripture. Solomon the son of David, with all his wisdom, played the fool. The foremost man and Hebrew of his time, he gave his heart to "strange women," and to gods whose ritual was not only idolatrous, but cruel, dark, impure. In his pursuit of science, unless the whole East belie him, he ran into secret magical arts, incantations, divinations, an occult intercourse with the powers of ill. In all ways he departed from the God who had enriched him with the choicest gifts, and sank, through luxury, extravagance, and excess, first into a premature old age, [6] and then into a death so unrelieved by any sign of penitence, or any promise of amendment, that from that day to this rabbis and divines have discussed his final doom, many of them leaning to the darker alternative. This

"uxorious king, whose heart, though large,
Beguiled by fair idolatresses, fell
To idols foul,"

is the Solomon of history. But the Solomon of Ecclesiastes is a sage who represents himself as conducting a series of moral experiments for the good of mankind, in order that, with all the weight of manifold experience, he may teach men what is that good and right way which alone leads to peace. However hardly we may think of the Wise King who was guilty of so many follies, we can scarcely think of him as such a fool that he did not know his sins to be sins, or as such a knave that he deliberately endeavoured to palm them off on other ages, not as transgressions of the Divine Law, but as a series of delicate philosophic experiments which he was good enough to conduct for the benefit of the race.

On the whole, then, we conclude that in this Book Solomon is taken as the Hebrew type of wisdom, the wisdom which is based on large and varied experience; and that this experience is here dramatized, in so far as the writer could conceive it, for the instruction of a race which from first to last, from the fable of Jotham to the parables of our Lord, were accustomed to receive instruction in fictitious and dramatic forms. Its author was not Solomon, but one of "the wise" whose name can no longer be recovered; it was written, not in the time of Solomon, i.e. about 1000 B.C., but some five or six centuries later: and it was addressed not to the wealthy and peaceful citizens whose king held his court in Jerusalem, but to their degenerate and enfeebled descendants during the period of the Persian supremacy. [7]

***

Doubtless many of the prevailing misapprehensions of the meaning, authorship, and animating spirit of the Book are due, in some measure, to the singular form into which it is thrown. It belongs to what is known as the Chokma, i.e. the Gnomic school, as opposed to the Lyrical school of Hebrew poetry. The Jewish, like Oriental literature in general, early assumed this form, which seems to have a natural affinity with the Eastern mind. Grave men, who made a study of life or who devoted themselves to a life of study, were likely to be sententious, to compress much thought into few words, especially in the ages in which writing was a somewhat rare accomplishment, or in which, as in the Hebrew schools, instruction was given by a living voice. No doubt they began with coining sage or witty aphorisms, generally lit up with a happy metaphor, each of which was complete in itself. Such sayings, as memorable and portable, no less than as striking for beauty and "matterful" for meditation, would commend themselves to an age in which books were few and scarce. They are to be found in abundance in the proverbs of all ancient races, and in the Book of Proverbs which bears the name of Solomon, and many of the more didactic and elaborate Psalms; while the Book of Job preserves many of the sayings current among the Arabs and the Egyptians. But with the Hebrews this literary mode took what is, so far as I am aware, a singular and unparalleled development, from the time of Solomon onwards, rising to its highest pitch in the Book of Job, and sinking to its lowest--within the limits of the Canon at least--in the cramping over-ingenuities of the acrostic Psalms, and in such proverbs as those attributed to Agur the son of Jakeh.

This development has not as yet, I think, attracted the attention it deserves; at least I have nowhere met with any formal recognition of it. Yet, undoubtedly, while at first the Hebrew sages were content to compress much wit or wisdom into the small compass of a gnome, which they polished like a gem, leaving each to shine by its own lustre and to make its own unaided impression, there rose in process of time men who saw new and great capacities in this ancient literary form, and set themselves to string their gems together, to arrange their own or other men's proverbs so aptly and artistically that they enhanced each other's beauty, while at the same time they compelled them to carry a logical and continuous stream of thought, to paint an elaborate picture, to build up a lofty yet breathing personification (that of Wisdom, for example, in Proverbs viii.), to describe a lengthened and varied ethical experience (as in Ecclesiastes), and even to weave them into a large and sublime poem, like that of Job, which has never been excelled. The reluctance with which this form lends itself to the nobler functions of literature, the immense difficulty of the instrument which many of the Hebrew poets wielded, will become apparent to any one who should try the experiment. We have a goodly collection of proverbs, drawn from many sources, foreign as well as native, in the English tongue. Let any man endeavour so to set or arrange them, or a selection from them, as to produce a fine poem on a lofty theme, and he at least will not underrate the difficulty of the task, even though we should concede to him the right to make proverbs where he could not find them to his mind. Yet to many of the finest Hebrew poets the very restrictions of this form seem to have possessed a charm such as the far less rigid and encumbering laws of the sonnet, or even of the triolet and other fanciful poetic wares of modern times, have exerted on the minds of many of our own poets. [8] A careful student of the Chokma school might even, I believe, trace the growth of this art, from its small beginnings in the earlier gnomic sayings of the Wise, to its culmination in the Book of Job; and, in so doing, would confer a boon on all students of Holy Writ. [9]

It is to this school that the Preacher belongs, as he himself informs us in the Epilogue to his fine Poem. He set himself, he says, "to compose, to collect, and to arrange many proverbs" (xii. 9), rejecting any that were not "words of truth," preferring, as was natural in a time so dark, such as were "words of comfort" (xii. 10), and seeking his sayings both from the sages who stood by the old ways and those who looked for the new (xii. 11). And, of course, the arranging of his awkward and inelastic material was far more difficult than composing it--arranging it so as to compel it to tell his story, and carry his argument to its lofty close. It is Story, the sculptor and poet, I believe, who says that "the best part of every work of art is unseen," unexpressed, inexpressible in tones, or verse, or colours: it is that invisible something which lends it dignity, spirit, life, that "style" which, in this case, is in very deed the man. And the best part of Coheleth's noble work is this art of arranging his gnomic sayings in the best order, the order in which they illuminate each other most brightly and contribute most effectively to the total impression. Hence, both in translating and in endeavouring to interpret him, whenever I have had to choose between rival renderings or meanings, I have made it a rule to prefer that which most conduced to the logical sequence of his work or carried the finer sense, deeming that at least so much as this was due to so great a master, and entertaining no fear that I could invent any meaning which would outrun his intention.

In fine, if I were to gather up into a few sentences the impression which "much study" of this Scripture has left on my mind as to the manner in which the author worked upon it, I should say: that Coheleth, a man of much of Solomon's original "largeness of heart" and a great lover of wisdom, set himself to collect the scattered sayings of the sages who were before him. He took the traditional story of Solomon as the ground and framework of his poem, at least at the outset, though he seems to have soon laid it aside, and endeavoured so to assort and arrange the proverbs he had collected that each would lead up to the next; while each group of them would describe some of the ways in which men commonly pursued the chief good, ways in most of which Solomon was at least reputed to have travelled far. Finding gaps which could not be well filled up from his large and various collection, he bridged them over with proverbs of his own composing, till he had got a sufficient account of each of the main adventures of that Quest. And, then, he put adventure after adventure together in the order in which they best led up to his great conclusion.

In all this I have said nothing, it is true, of that "inspiration of the Almighty" which alone gives man understanding of spiritual things. But why should not "He who worketh all," and has deigned to use every form of literary art by which men teach their fellows, move and inspire a lover of wisdom to collect and arrange the sayings of the Wise, if by these he could carry truth and comfort to those who were in sore need of both? And where, save from heaven and from Him who rules in heaven, could Coheleth have learned the great secret--the secret of a retributive life beyond the grave? Even the best and wisest of the Hebrews saw that life only "as through a glass, darkly;" and even their fitful and imperfect conception of it seems always to have been--as in the case of David, Job, Isaiah--an immediate gift from God, and a gift so large that even their hands of faith could hardly grasp it. No one need doubt the inspiration of a Scripture which affirms, not only that God is always with us, passing a present and effective judgment on all we do, but also that, when this life is over, He will bring every deed and every secret thing into judgment, whether it be good or whether it be bad. That was not an everyday thought with the Jewish mind. We find it only in men who were moved by the Holy Ghost to accept the teaching of his providence or the revelation of his grace.

***

As for the design of the Book, no one now doubts that it sets before us the search for the summum bonum, the quest of the Chief Good. Its main immediate intention was to deliver the exiled Jews from the misleading ethical theories and habits into which they had fallen, from the sensualism and the scepticism occasioned by their imperfect conception of the Divine ways, by showing them that the true good of life is not to be secured by philosophy, by the pursuit of pleasure, by devotion to traffic or public affairs, by amassing wealth; but that it results from a temperate and thankful enjoyment of the gifts of the Divine bounty, and a cheerful endurance of toil and calamity, combined with a sincere service of God and a steadfast faith in that future life in which all wrongs will be righted and all the problems which now task and afflict us will receive a triumphant solution. Availing himself of the historical and traditional records of Solomon's life, he depicts, under that disguise, the moral experiments which he has conducted; depicts himself as having put the claims of wisdom, mirth, business, wealth, to a searching test, and found them incompetent to satisfy the cravings of the soul; as attaining no rest nor peace until he had learned a simple enjoyment of simple pleasures, a patient constancy under heavy trials, heartfelt devotion to the service of God, and an unwavering faith in the life to come.

***

The contents of the Poem are, or may be, distributed into a Prologue, Four Acts or Sections, and an Epilogue.

In the Prologue (chap. i., vv. 1-11), Coheleth states the Problem to be solved.

In the First Section (chap. i., ver. 12--chap. ii., ver. 26), he depicts the endeavour to solve it by seeking the Chief Good in Wisdom and in Pleasure.

In the Second Section (chap. iii., ver. 1--chap. v., ver. 20), the Quest is pursued in Traffic and Political Life.

In the Third Section (chap. vi., ver. 1--chap. viii., ver. 15), the Quest is carried into Wealth and the Golden Mean.

In the Fourth Section (chap. viii., ver. 16--chap. xii., ver. 7), the Quest is achieved, and the Chief Good found to consist in a tranquil and cheerful enjoyment of the present, combined with a cordial faith in the future, life.

And in the Epilogue (chap. xii., vv. 8-14) he summarises and emphatically repeats this solution of the Problem.

***

It was very natural that the Problem here discussed should fill a large space in Hebrew thought and literature; that it should be the theme of many of the Psalms and of many of the prophetic "burdens", as well as of the Books Ecclesiastes and Job. For the Mosaic revelation did teach that virtue and vice would meet suitable rewards now, in this present time. At the giving of the Law Jehovah announced that He would show mercy to the thousands of those who kept his commandments, and that He would visit the iniquities of the disobedient upon them. The Law that came by Moses is crowded with promises of temporal good to the righteous, and with threatenings of temporal evil to the unrighteous. The fulfilment of these threatenings and promises is carefully marked in the Hebrew chronicles; it is the supplication which breathes through the recorded prayers of the Hebrew race, and the theme of their noblest songs; it is their hope and consolation under the heaviest calamities. What, then, could be more bewildering to a godly and reflective Jew than to discover that this fundamental article of his faith was questionable, nay, that it was contradicted by the commonest facts of human life as life grew more complex and involved? When he saw the righteous driven before the blasts of adversity like a withered leaf, while the wicked lived out all their days in mirth and affluence; when he saw the only nation that attempted obedience to the Law groaning under the miseries of a captivity embittered by the cruel caprices of rulers who could not even rule themselves, and unrelieved by any hope of deliverance, while heathen races revelled in the lusts of sense and power unrebuked: when this seemed to be the rule of providence, the law of the Divine administration, and not that better rule revealed in his Scriptures, is it any wonder that, forgetting all corrective and balancing facts, he was racked with torments of perplexity; that, while some of his fellows plunged into the base relief of sensualism, he should be plagued with doubts and fears, and search eagerly through all avenues of thought for some solution of the mystery?

Nor, indeed, is this problem without interest for us; for we as persistently misinterpret the New Testament as the Hebrews did the Old. We read that "whatsoever a man soweth, that shall he also reap;" we read that "the meek shall inherit the earth;" we read that for every act of service done to Christ we shall receive "a hundredfold now, in this present time;" and we are very prompt with the gross, careless interpretation which makes such passages mean that if we are good we shall have the good things of this life, while its evil things shall be reserved for the evil. Indeed, we are trained--or, perhaps I should say, until recently we were trained--in this interpretation from our earliest years. Our very spelling-books are full of it, and are framed on the model of "Johnny was a good boy, and he got plum-cake; but Tommy was a bad boy, and he got the stick." Nearly all our story-books have a similar moral: it is always, or almost always, the good young man who gets the beautiful wife and large estate, while the bad young man comes to a bad end. Our proverbs are full of it, and axioms such as "Honesty is the best policy," a pernicious half-truth, are for ever on our lips. Our art, in so far as it is ours, is in the same conspiracy. In Hogarth, for instance, as Thackeray has pointed out, it is always Francis Goodchild who comes to be Lord Mayor and poor Jem Scapegrace who comes to the gallows. And when, as life passes on, we discover that it is the bad boy who often gets the plum-cake, and the good boy who goes to the rod; that bad men often have beautiful wives and large estates, while good men fail of both; when we find the knave rising to place and authority, and honest Goodchild in the workhouse or the Gazette, then there rise up in our hearts the very doubts and perplexities and eager painful questions which of old time troubled the Psalmist and the Prophet. We cry out with Job--

"It is all one--therefore will I say it,
The guilty and the guiltless He treateth alike;
The deceiver and the deceived both are his;"

or we say with the Preacher,--

"This is the greatest evil of all that is done under the sun
That there is one fate for all;
The same fate befalleth to the righteous and to the wicked,
To the good and pure and to the impure,
To him that sacrificeth and to him that sacrificeth not:
As is the good so is the sinner,
And he that sweareth as he that feareth an oath."

And it is well for us if, like the Hebrew poet, we can resist this cruel temptation, and hold fast the integrity of our faith; if we can rest in the assurance that, after all and when all is done, "the little that a righteous man hath is better than the riches of many wicked;" that God has something better than wealth and lucky haps for the good, and merciful correctives of a more sovereign potency than penury and mishaps for the wicked. If we have this faith, our study of Ecclesiastes can hardly fail to deepen and confirm it; if we are not so happy as to have it, Coheleth will give us sound reasons for embracing it.

Samuel Cox, D.D.

§ 2. ON THE HISTORY OF THE CAPTIVITY.

If we may now assume the Book Ecclesiastes to have been written, not in the time of Solomon, but during, or soon after, the Babylonian Captivity, our next duty is to learn what we can of the social, political, and religious conditions of the two races among whom the Jews were thrown when they were carried away from the land of their fathers. That they learned much, as well as suffered much, while they sat by the waters of Babylon; that they emerged from their long exile with a profound attachment to the Word of God, such as their fathers had never known, and with many precious additions to that Word, is beyond a doubt. As plants grow fastest by night, so men make their most rapid growth in knowledge and in faith when times are dark and troubled. And all students of this period are at one in affirming that during the Captivity a radical and most happy change passed upon the Hebrew mind. They came out of it with a hatred of idolatry, a faith in the life beyond the grave, a pride in their national Law, a hope in the advent of the great Deliverer and Redeemer, with which the elder Psalmists and Prophets had failed to inspire them, but which henceforth they never wholly relinquished. With the religious there was blended an intellectual advance. Books and teachers were sought and honoured as never heretofore. Schools and synagogues grew up in every town and village in which they dwelt. "Of making of many books there was no end." Education was compulsory. Study was regarded as more meritorious than sacrifice, a scholar as greater than a prophet, a teacher as greater than a king, if at least we may trust proverbs which were current among them. Before the Captivity one of the least literate of nations--noble as their national literature was, at its close the Jews were distinguished by their zeal for culture and education.

To trace the progress of this marvellous revival of letters and religion--a renaissance and a reformation in one--would be a most welcome task, had we the materials for it and the skill to use them. But even the scanty materials that exist lie scattered through the historical and literary remains of many different races--in the cylinders, sculptures, paintings, inscriptions, tombs, shrines of Nineveh, Babylon, Behistun, and Persepolis, in the Zendavesta, in the pages of Herodotus and the earlier Greek historians, in Josephus, in the Apocrypha, in the Talmud, and in at least a dozen of the Old Testament books; and some of these "sources" are very far as yet from having been explored and mastered. Hence the history of this period still remains to be written, and will probably be largely conjectural whenever, if ever, it is written. Yet what period is of graver interest to the student of the Bible? If we could recover its history, it would throw a new and most welcome light on well-nigh one-half of the Old Testament Scriptures, if not on all.

Happily, a brief sketch of it, such as is well within any man's reach, will suffice to show how, from their contact with the Babylonian and Persian races, the Jews received literary and religious impulses which go far to account for the marvellous changes which swept over them, and enable us to read the Preacher intelligently, and see how his social and political allusions exactly correspond with what we know of the time. [10]

***

About a hundred and twenty years after the destruction of the kingdom of Israel by Shalmaneser, King of Assyria (B.C. 719), the kingdom of Judah fell before Nebuchadnezzar, King of Babylon (B.C. 598-596). The city, palace, and temple of Jerusalem were levelled in a common ruin; the nobles, priests, merchants, and skilled artisans, all the pith and manhood of Judah, were carried away captive; only a few of the most abject of the people were left to mourn and starve amid the ravaged fields. Nothing could present a more striking contrast to their native land than the region to which the Jews were deported. Instead of a small picturesque mountain-country, with its little cities set on hills or on the brink of precipitous ravines, they entered on a vast plain, fertile beyond all precedent indeed, and abounding in streams, but with nothing to break the monotony of level flats save the high walls and lofty towers of one enormous city. For Babylonia proper was simply an immense plain, lying between the Arabian Desert and the Tigris, and of an extent somewhat under that of Ireland. But though of a limited area as compared with the vast empire of which it was the centre, by its amazing fertility it was capable of sustaining a crowded population. It was watered not only by the great rivers Tigris and Euphrates, but by their numerous affluents, many of which were themselves considerable streams; it was "a land of brooks and fountains." On this rich alluvial plain, amply supplied with water, and under the fierce heat of the sun, wheat and barley, with all kinds of grain, yielded a return far beyond all modern parallel. The capital city of this fertile province was the largest and the most magnificent of the ancient world, standing on both sides of the Euphrates, as London stands on both sides of the Thames, and covering at least a hundred square miles.

In this country and city (for "Babylon" stands for both in the Bible), so unlike the sunny cliffs and scattered villages of their native home, the Jews, who, like all hill-races, cherished a passionate affection for the land of their fathers, spent many bitter years. On the broad featureless plain they pined for "the mountains" of Judea (Ezekiel xxxvi.; Psalm cxxxvii.); they sat down by the waters and wept as they remembered "the hill of the Lord." They do not seem, however, to have been handled with exceptional harshness by their captors. They were treated as colonists rather than as slaves. They were allowed to live together in considerable numbers, and to observe their own religious rites. They took the advice of the prophet Jeremiah (xxix. 4-7), who had warned them that their exile would extend over many years, and built houses, planted gardens, married wives, and brought up children; they "sought the peace of the city" in which they were captives, "and prayed for it," knowing that in its peace they would have peace. If many of them had to labour gratuitously on the great public works--and this labour was exacted of most of the conquered races--many rose, by fidelity, thrift, diligence, to places of trust, and amassed considerable wealth. Among those who filled high posts in the household or administration of the successive monarchs of Babylon were Daniel, Hananiah, Mishael, and Azariah; Zerubbabel, Ezra, Nehemiah, and Mordecai; Tobit--if indeed Tobit be a real and not a fictitious person--and his nephew Achiacharus.

But who were the people, and what were the social and political conditions of the people, among whom the Hebrew captives lived? The two leading races with whom they were brought in contact were the Babylonians--an offshoot from the ancient Chaldean stock--and the Persians. The history of the Captivity divides itself into two main periods, therefore, the Persian and the Babylonian, at each of which we must glance.

***

1. The Babylonian Period.--For more than fifty years after they were carried away captive, the Jews served a Chaldean race, and were governed by Assyrian despots, of whom Nebuchadnezzar [11] was by far the greatest whether in peace or war. It is hardly too much to say that but for him the Babylonians would have had no place in history. A great soldier, a great statesman, a great builder and engineer, he knew how to consolidate and adorn his vast empire, an empire which is said to have "extended from the Atlantic to the Caspian, and from Caucasus to the Great Sahara." We owe our best conception of the personal character and public life of this great despot to the Book of Daniel. Daniel, although a Jew and a captive, was the vizier of the Babylonian monarch, and retained his post until the Persian conquest, when he became the first of "the three presidents" of the new empire. He therefore paints Nebuchadnezzar from the life. And in his Book we see the great King at the head of a magnificent court, surrounded by "princes, governors, and captains, judges, treasurers, councillors, and sheriffs," waited on by "well-favoured" eunuchs, attended by a crowd of astrologers and "wise men" who interpret to him the will of Heaven. He wields an absolute power, and disposes with a word of the lives and fortunes of his subjects, even the highest and most princely. All offices are in his gift. He can raise a slave to the second place in his kingdom (Daniel, to wit), and impose a foreigner (again, Daniel) on the priestly college as its head. Of so enormous a wealth that he makes an image of pure gold ninety feet high and nine feet broad, he lavishes it on public works--on temples, gardens, canals, fortifications--rather than on personal indulgence. Religious after a fashion, he wavers between "the God of the Jews" and the deity after whom he was named and whom he calls his god. In temper he is hasty and violent, but not obstinate; he suddenly repents of his sudden resolves; he is capable of bursts of gratitude and devotion no less than of fierce accesses of fury, and displays at times a piety and self-abasement astonishing in an Oriental despot. His successors--Evil-Merodach, Neriglissar, Laborosoarchod, Nabonadius, and Belshazzar--need not detain us. Little is known of them, and, with one exception, their reigns were very short; and their main task seems to have been the erection of vast and sumptuous structures such as Nebuchadnezzar had been wont to rear. Probably none of the Babylonian monarchs save Nebuchadnezzar made any deep impression on the Hebrew mind.

And, indeed, the people of Babylon were much more likely than their despots to influence the Hebrew captives; for with them they would be brought into daily contact. Now the Babylonians were marked by a singular intellectual ability. Keen to know, patient to observe, exact and laborious in their researches, they could hardly fail to teach much to subject races, and to inspire them with some desire for knowledge. They had carried the sciences of mathematics and astronomy to a high pitch of perfection. They are said to have determined, within two seconds, the exact length of the solar year, and not to have been far wrong in the distances at which they computed the sun, moon and planets from the earth; and they compiled a serviceable catalogue of the fixed stars. The Hebrew prophets often refer to their "wisdom and learning." They excelled in architecture. Two of their vast works, the walls of Babylon, and the hanging gardens, were reckoned among "the seven wonders" of the ancient world. Their skill in manufacturing and arranging enamelled bricks has never yet been equalled. [12] In all mechanical arts, indeed, such as cutting stones and gems, casting gold and silver, blowing glass, modelling vases and ware, weaving carpets and muslins and linen, they take a very high place among the nations of antiquity. With manufacturing and artistic skill they combined the spirit of enterprise and adventure which leads to commerce. They were addicted to maritime pursuits; the "cry," or joy, "of the

Chaldeans is in their ships," says Isaiah (xliii. 14); and Ezekiel (xvii. 4) calls Babylonia "a land of traffic," and its chief city "a city of merchants."

But a larger, and probably the largest, class of the people must have busied themselves with the toils of agriculture; the broad Chaldean plain being famous, from the time of the Patriarchs to the present day, for an amazing and almost incredible fertility. Wheat, barley, millet, and sesame, all flourished with astonishing luxuriance, the ground commonly yielding a hundredfold, two hundredfold, and even ampler rewards for the toil of the husbandman.

With these abundant sources of wealth at their command, the people naturally grew luxurious and dissolute. "The daughter of the Chaldeans," says Isaiah (xlvii. 1-8), "is tender and delicate," given to pleasures, apt to live carelessly; her young men, says Ezekiel (xxiii. 15), are dandies, "exceeding in dyed attire," painting their faces, and wearing earrings. Chastity, in our modern sense of the term, was unknown. [13] The pleasures of the table and of the couch were carried to excess. Yet, like many other Eastern races, the Babylonians hid under their soft luxurious exterior a fierceness very formidable to their foes. The Hebrew Prophets (Hab. i. 6-8; Isaiah xiv. 16) describe them as "a bitter and hasty," a "terrible and dreadful" people, "fiercer than the evening wolves," a people whose tramp "made the earth tremble, and did shake kingdoms;" and all the historians of the time charge them with a thirst for blood which often took the most savage and inhuman forms.

Of the horrible licence and cruelty of the worship of Bel, Merodach, and Nebo, which did much to foster the fierce and cruel temper of the people, it is not necessary, it is hardly possible, to speak. Roughly taken, it was the service of the great forces of Nature by a wanton indulgence of the worst passions of man. It is enough to know that in Babylon idolatry took forms which made all forms of idolatry henceforth intolerable to the Jews; that now, once for all, they renounced that worship of strange gods to which they and their fathers had always hitherto been prone. This of itself was an immense advance, a great gain. Nor was it their only gain; for if by contact with the idolatrous Babylonians the Jews were driven back on their own Law and Scripture, their intercourse with a people of so active an intellect and a learning so deep and wide led them to study the Word of Jehovah in a new and more intelligent spirit.

Nor is it less obvious that in the social and political conditions of the Babylonians we have a key to many of the allusions to public life contained in Ecclesiastes. The great empire, indeed, presents precisely those elements which, in degenerate times and under feebler despots, must inevitably develop into the disorder, and misery, and crime which Coheleth depicts.

***

2. The Persian Period.--The conquest of Babylon by the Persians, led by the heroic Cyrus, is, thanks to Daniel, one of the most familiar incidents of ancient history, so familiar that I need not recount it. By this conquest Cyrus--"the Shepherd, the Messiah, of the Lord," as Isaiah (xliv. 28; xlv. 1) terms him--became the undisputed master of well-nigh the whole known world of the time. Nor does he seem to have been unworthy of his extraordinary position. Of all ancient Oriental monarchs, out of the Hebrew pale, he bears the highest repute. Even the Greek authors, for the most part, represent him as energetic and patient, magnanimous and modest, and of a religious mind. Æschylus calls him "kindly" or "generous." Xenophon selected him as a model prince for all races. Plutarch says that "in wisdom, and virtue, and greatness of soul he appears to have been in advance of all kings." Diodorus makes one of his speakers say that Cyrus gained his ascendency by his self-command and good-feeling and gentleness. Simple in his habits, brave, and of a most just, humane, and clement spirit, he hated the cruel and lascivious idols of the East, and worshipped one only God, "the God of heaven." There is none like him in the antique world, none at least among the kings and princes of that world. And when, at the conquest of Babylon, he discovered in the captive Jews a race that also hated idols, and served one Lord, and knew a law of life as pure as his own, or even purer, we need feel no surprise either that he broke their bands in sunder and set them free to return to their native land, or that they saw in this pure and noble nature, this virtuous and religious prince, "a servant of Jehovah," and even a partial and shadowy resemblance to that Divine Deliverer and Redeemer for whose advent they had been taught to look.

Cyrus was sixty years of age when he took Babylon (B.C. 539), and died ten years after his conquest. He was succeeded by men utterly unlike himself, so unlike that the Persian nobles revolted from them, and placed Darius Hystaspes, the heir of an ancient dynasty, on the throne. As Cyrus was the soldier of the Persians, so Darius was their statesman. He it was who founded the "satrapial" form of administration; i.e. instead of governing the various provinces of his empire through native princes, he placed Persian satraps over them, these satraps being charged with the collection of the public revenue, the maintenance of order, and the administration of justice; in fact, he governed the whole Eastern world very much as we govern India. The internal organization of his vast unwieldy empire was the great work of Darius through his long reign of six-and-thirty years; but the event by which he is best remembered, and which proved to be fruitful in the most disastrous results to the State, was the opening of that fatal war with Greece, which at last, and under his feeble and degenerate successors, Xerxes, Artaxerxes, and the rest, reached its close in the downfall of the Persian empire. We need not linger over the details of the story. It will be enough, for our purpose, to say that from the accession of Xerxes down to the conquest of the Persian empire by Alexander the Great--a stretch of a hundred and fifty years--that empire was declining to its fall. Its history towards the end was a mere succession of intrigues and insurrections, conspiracies and revolts. "Battle, murder, and sudden death" are its staple. The restraints of law and order grew ever weaker. The satraps were practically supreme in their several provinces, and used their power to extort enormous wealth from their miserable subjects. Eunuchs and concubines ruled in the palace. Manliness died out; the Persians were no longer taught "to ride, to draw the bow, and to speak the truth;" cunning and treachery took its place. The scene grows more and more pitiful, till at last the welcome darkness rushes down, and hides the ignoble agony of perhaps the vastest and wealthiest empire the world has seen.

***

But we must turn from the despots and their adventures to form some slight acquaintance with the people, the Persian people who, by the conquest of Cyrus, became the ruling class in the empire, always remembering, however, that the Babylonians must have remained by myriads both in the capital and in the provinces, and would continue to exert their influence on Hebrew thought and activity.

In all moral and religious qualities the Persians were far in advance of the Chaldeans, though they were probably behind them in many civilized arts and crafts. They were famous for their truthfulness and valour. The Greeks [14] confessed the Persians to be their equals in "boldness and warlike spirit"-- Æschylus [15] calls them "a valiant-minded people"--while they are lavish in praise of the Persian veracity, a virtue in which they themselves were notably deficient. To the Persians God was "the Father of all truth;" to lie was shameful and irreligious. They disliked traffic because of its haggling, equivocation, and dishonest shifts. "Their chief faults," and even these were not developed till they became masters of the world, "were an addiction to self-indulgence and luxury, a passionate abandon to the feeling of the hour whatever it might be, and a tameness and subservience in all their relations toward their princes which seem to moderns incompatible with self-respect and manliness." Patriotism came to mean mere loyalty to the monarch; the habit of unquestioning submission to his will, and even to his caprice, became a second nature to them. The despotic humour natural in "a ruling person" was thus nourished till it ran to the wildest excess. "He was their lord and master, absolute disposer of their lives, liberties, and property, the sole fountain of law and right, incapable himself of doing wrong, irresponsible, irresistible--a sort of God upon earth; one whose favour was happiness, at whose frown men trembled, before whom all bowed themselves down with the lowest and humblest obeisance." No subject could enter his presence save by special permission, or without a prostration like that of worship. To come unbidden was to be cut down by the royal guards, unless, as a sign of grace, he extended his golden sceptre to the culprit. To tread on the king's carpet was a grave offence; to sit, even unwittingly, on his seat a capital crime. So slavish was the submission both of nobles and of people that we are required on good authority to accredit such stories as these: wretches bastinadoed by the king's order declared themselves delighted that his majesty had condescended to remember them; a father, whose innocent son was shot by the despot in pure wantonness, had to crush down his natural indignation and grief, and to compliment the royal archer on the accuracy of his aim.

Despising trade and commerce as menial and degrading, the ruling caste of a vast empire, with a monopoly of office and boundless means of wealth at their command, accustomed to lord it over subject races, of a high spirit and a faith comparatively pure, their very prosperity was their ruin, as it has been that of many a great nation. In their earlier times, they were noted for their sobriety and temperance. Content with simple diet, their only drink was water from the pure mountain streams; their garb was plain, their habits homely and hardy. But their temperance soon gave place to an immoderate luxury.[16] They acquired the Babylonian vices, and adopted at least the licence of the Babylonian rites. They filled their harems with wives and concubines. From the time of Xerxes onwards they grew nice and curious of appetite, eager for pleasure, effeminate, dissolute.

With the growth of luxury on the part of the nobles and the people, the fear of the despot, at whose mercy all their acquisitions stood, grew more intense, more harassing, more degrading. Xerxes and his successors were utterly reckless in their exercise of the absolute power conceded to them, and delegated it to favourites as reckless as themselves. No noble however eminent, no servant of the State however faithful or distinguished, could be sure that he might not at any moment incur a displeasure which would strip him of all he possessed, even if it did not also condemn him to a cruel and lingering death. Out of mere sport and wantonness, to relieve the tedium of a weary hour, the despot might slay him with his own hand. For the crime, or assumed crime, of one person a whole family, or class, or race might be cut off unheard. Of the lengths to which this cruelty and caprice might go we have a sufficient example in the Book of Esther. The Ahasuerus of that singular narrative was, there can hardly be any doubt, the Xerxes of secular history--the very names, unlike as they sound, are the same name differently pronounced by two different races. [17] And all that the Book of Esther relates of the despot who repudiates a wife because she will not expose herself to the drunken admiration of a crowd of revellers, who raises a servant to the highest honours one day and hangs him the next, who commands the massacre of an entire race and then bids them inflict a horrible carnage on those who execute his decree, exactly accords with the Greek narratives which depict him as scourging the sea for having broken down his bridge over the Hellespont, beheading the engineers whose work was swept away by a storm, wantonly putting to death the sons of Pythias, his oldest friend, before their father's eyes; as first giving to his mistress the splendid robe presented to him by his queen, and then giving up to the queen's barbarous vengeance the mother of his mistress; as shamefully misusing the body of the heroic Leonidas, and, after his defeat by the Greeks, giving himself up to a criminal voluptuousness and offering a reward to the inventor of any new pleasure.

***

The Book Ecclesiastes was written certainly not before the reign of Xerxes (B.C. 486-465), and probably many years after it, a period in which, bad as were the conditions of his time, the times grew ever more lawless, the despotism more intolerable, the violence and licentiousness of the subordinate officials more unblushing. But at whatever period within these limits we may place it, all we have learned of the Babylonians and the Persians during the later years of the Captivity and the earlier years of the Exile (during which the Jews were still under the Persian rule) is in entire correspondence with the social and political state depicted by the Preacher. The abler and more kindly despots--as Cyrus, Darius, Artaxerxes--showed a singular favour to the Jews. Cyrus published a decree authorizing them to return to Jerusalem and rebuild their temple, and enjoining the officials of the empire to further them in their enterprise; Darius confirmed that decree, despite the malignant misrepresentations of the Samaritan colonists; Artaxerxes held Ezra and Nehemiah in high esteem, and sent them to restore order and prosperity to the city of their fathers and its inhabitants. But a large number, apparently even a large majority, of the Jews, unable or disinclined to return, remained in the various provinces of the great empire, and were of course subject to the violence and injustice from which the Persians themselves were not exempt. "Vanity of vanities, vanity of vanities, all is vanity!" cries the Preacher till we grow weary of the mournful refrain. Might he not well take that tone in a time so out of joint, so lowering, so dark?

The Book is full of allusions to the Persian luxury, to the Persian forms of administration, above all, to the corruptions of the later years of the Persian empire, and the miseries they bred. Coheleth's elaborate description (ii. 4-8) of the infinite variety of means by which he sought to allure his heart unto mirth--his palaces, vineyards, paradises, with their reservoirs and fountains, crowds of attendants, treasures of gold and silver, the harem full of beauties of all races--seems taken direct from the ample state of some luxurious Persian grandee. His picture of the public administration (v. 8, 9), in which "superior watcheth over superior, and superiors again watch over them," is a graphic sketch of the satrapial system, with its official hierarchy rising grade above grade, which was the work of Darius. [18] When the animating and controlling spirit of that system was taken away, when weak foolish despots sat on the throne, and despots just as foolish and weak ruled in every provincial divan, there ensued precisely that political state to which Coheleth perpetually refers. [19] Iniquity sat in the place of judgment, and in the place of equity there was iniquity (iii. 16); kings grew childish, and princes spent their days in revelry (x. 16); fools were lifted to high place, while nobles were degraded; and slaves rode on horses, while their quondam masters tramped through the mire (x. 6, 7). There was no fair reward for faithful service (ix. 11). Death brooded in the air, and might fall suddenly and unforeseen on any head, however high (ix. 12). To correct a public abuse was like pulling down a wall: some of the stones were sure to fall on the reformer's feet, from some cranny a serpent was sure to start out and bite him (x. 8, 9). To breathe a word against a ruler, even in the strictest privacy, was to run the hazard of destruction (x. 20). A resentful gesture, much more a rebellious word, in the divan was enough to ensure outrage. In short, the whole political fabric was fast falling into disrepair and decay, the rain leaking through the rotting roof, while the miserable people were ground down with ruinous exactions, in order that their rulers might revel on undisturbed (x. 18, 19). It is under such a pernicious and ominous maladministration of public affairs, and the appalling miseries it breeds, that there springs up in the hearts of men that fatalistic and hopeless temper to which Coheleth gives frequent expression. Better never to have been born than to live a life so cramped and thwarted, so full of perils and fears! Better to snatch at every pleasure, however poor and brief, than seek, by self-denial, by virtue, by integrity, to accumulate a store which the first petty tyrant who gets wind of it will sweep off, or a reputation for wisdom and goodness which will be no protection from, which will be only too likely to provoke, the despotic humours of men "dressed in a little brief authority."

The Expositor's Bible: Ecclesiastes

If even Shakespeare,[20] in an unrestful and despairing mood strangely foreign to his serene temperament, beheld

> *"desert a beggar born,*
> *And needy nothing trimmed in jollity,*
> *And purest faith unhappy forsworn,*
> *And gilded honour shamefully misplaced,*
> *And maiden virtue rudely strumpeted,*
> *And right perfection wrongfully disgraced,*
> *And strength by limping sway disabled,*
> *And art made tongue-tied by authority,*
> *And folly, doctor-like, controlling skill,*
> *And simple truth miscall'd simplicity,*
> *And captive good attending captain ill;"*

if, "tired with all these," he cried for "restful death," we can hardly wonder that the Preacher, who had fallen on times so evil that, compared with his, Shakespeare's were good, should prefer death to life.

***

But there is another side to this sad story of the Captivity, another and a nobler side. If the Jews suffered much from Persian misrule, they learned much and gained much from the Persian faith. In its earlier form the religious creed whose documents Zoroaster afterwards collected and enlarged in the Zendavesta was probably the purest of the ancient heathen world; and even when it was corrupted by the baser additions of later times, its purer form was still preserved in songs (Gâthâs) and traditions. There can be no reasonable doubt that it largely affected the subsequent faith of the Hebrews, not indeed teaching them any truth they had not been taught before, but constraining them to recognize truths in their Scriptures which hitherto they had passed over or neglected.

In its inception the Persian creed and practice were a revolt against the sensuous and sensual worship of the great forces of Nature into which most Eastern religions, often pure enough, in their primitive forms, had degenerated, and, in especial, from the base forms into which the Hindus had degraded that primitive faith which is still to be recovered from the Rig-Veda. It acknowledged persons, real spiritual intelligences, in place of mere natural powers; and it drew moral distinctions between them, dividing these ruling intelligences into good and bad, pure and impure, benignant and malevolent,--an immense advance on the mere admiration of whatever was strong. Nay, in some sense, the Persian faith affirmed monotheism against polytheism; for it asserted that one Great Intelligence ruled over all other intelligences, and through them over the universe. This Supreme Intelligence, which the Persians called Ahura-mazda (Ormazd), is the true Creator, Preserver, Governor, of all spirits, all men, all worlds. He is "good," "holy," "pure," "true," "the Father of all truth," "the best Being of all," "the Master of Purity," "the Source and Fountain of all good." On the righteous He bestows "the good mind" and everlasting happiness; while He punishes and afflicts the evil. His worshippers were to the last degree intolerant of idolatry. They suffered no image to profane their temples; their earliest symbol of Deity is almost as pure and abstract as a mathematical sign, a circle with wings; the circle to denote the eternity of God, and the wings his omnipresence. Under this Supreme Lord, "the God of heaven," they admitted inferior beings, angels and archangels, whose names mark them out as personified Divine attributes, or as faithful servants who administer some province of the Divine empire.

To win the favour of the God of heaven it was requisite to cultivate the virtues of purity, truthfulness, industry, and a pious sense of the Divine presence; and these virtues must spring from the heart, and cover thought as well as word and deed. His worship consisted in the frequent offering of prayer, praise, and thanksgiving; in the reiteration of certain sacred hymns; in the occasional sacrifice of animals which, after being presented before Ormazd, furnished forth a feast for priest and worshipper; and in the performance of a mystic ceremony (the Soma), the gist of which seems to have lain in a grateful acknowledgment that the fruits of the earth, typified by the intoxicating juice of the Homa plant, were to be received as the gift of Heaven. A sentence or two from one of the hymns[21] of which there are many in the Zendavesta, will show better than many words to how high a pitch Divine worship was carried by the Persians: "We worship Thee, Ahura-mazda, the pure, the master of purity. We praise all good thoughts, all good words, all good deeds which are or shall be; and we likewise keep clean and pure all that is good. O Ahura-mazda, thou true happy Being! We strive to think, to speak, and to do only such things as may be best fitted to promote the two lives" (i.e. the life of the body and the life of the soul).

In this course of well-doing the faithful were animated and confirmed by a devout belief in the immortality of the soul and a conscious future existence. They were taught that at death the souls of men, both good and bad, travelled along an appointed path to a narrow bridge which led to Paradise; over this bridge only pious souls could pass, the wicked falling from it into an awful gulf in which they received the due reward of their deeds. The happy souls of the good were helped across the long narrow arch by an angel, [22] and as they entered Paradise a great archangel rose from his throne to greet each of them with the words, "How happy art thou, who hast come to us from mortality to immortality!"

This wonderfully pure creed was, however, in process of time, corrupted in many ways. First of all, "the sad antithesis of human life," the conflict between light and darkness, good and evil--the standing puzzle of the world--led the votaries of Ormazd to dualism. Ormazd loved and created only the good. The evil in man, and in the world, must be the work of an enemy. This enemy, Ahriman (Augrô-maniyus), has been seeking from eternity to undo, to mar and blast, the fair work of the God of heaven. He is the baleful author of all evil, and under him are spirits as malignant as himself. Between these good and evil powers there is incessant conflict, which extends to every soul and every world. It will never cease until the great Deliverer arise--for even of Him the Persians had some dim prevision--who shall conquer and destroy evil at its source, all things then rounding to their final goal of good.

Another corrupting influence had its origin in a too literal interpretation of the names given to the Divine Being, or the qualities ascribed to Him, by the founders of the faith. Ormazd, for example, had been described as "true, lucid, shining, the originator of all the best things, of the spirit in nature and of the growth in nature, of the luminaries and of the self-shining brightness which is in the luminaries." From these epithets and ascriptions there sprang in later days the worship of the sun, then of fire, as a type of God--a worship still maintained by the disciples of Zoroaster, the Ghebers and the Parsees. And from this point onward the old sad story repeats itself; once more we have to trace a pure and lofty primitive faith along the grades through which it declines to the low, base level of a sensuous idolatry. The Magians, always the bitter enemies of Zoroastrianism, held that the four elements--fire, air, earth, and water--were the only proper objects of human reverence. It was not difficult for them to persuade those who already worshipped fire, and were beginning to forget of Whom fire was the symbol, to include in their homage air, water, and earth. Divination, incantations, the interpretation of dreams and omens soon followed, with all the dark shadows which science and religion cast behind them. And then came the lowest deep of all, that worship of the gods by sensual indulgence to which idolatry gravitates, as by a law.

Nevertheless, we must remember that, even at their worst, the Persians preserved the sacred records of their earlier faith, and that their best men steadily refused to accept the base additions to it which the Magians proposed. Corrupt as in many respects many of them became, the conquest of Babylon was the death-blow to the sensual idol-worship which had reigned for twenty centuries on the Chaldean plain; it never wholly recovered from it, though it survived it for a time. From that date it declined to its fall: "Bel bowed down; Nebo stooped; Merodach was broken in pieces" (Isa. xlvi. 1; Jer. l. 2). The nobler monarchs of Persia were true disciples of the primitive creed of their race. It was similarity of creed which won their favour for the Hebrew captives. In the decree which enfranchised them (Ezra i. 2, 3) Cyrus expressly identifies Ormazd, "the God of heaven," with Jehovah, the God of Israel; he says, "The Lord God of heaven hath given me all the kingdoms of the earth, and He hath charged me to build Him a house at Jerusalem." Nor was this belief in one God, whose temple was to be defiled by no image even of Himself, the only point in common between the better Persians, such as Cyrus and Darius, and the better Jews. There were many such points. Both believed in an evil spirit tempting and accusing men; in myriads of angels, all the host of heaven, who formed the armies of God and did his pleasure; in a tree of life and a tree of knowledge, and a serpent the enemy of man; both shared the hope of a coming Deliverer from evil, the belief in an immortal and retributive life beyond the grave, and a happy Paradise in which all righteous souls would find a home and see their Father's face. These common faiths and hopes would all be points of sympathy and attachment between the two races; and it is to this agreement in religious doctrine and practice that we must ascribe the striking facts that the Persians, ordinarily the most intolerant of men, never persecuted the Jews; and that the Jews, ordinarily so impatient of foreign domination, never made a single attempt to cast off the Persian yoke, but stood by the declining empire even when the Greeks were thundering at its gates.

On one question all competent historians and commentators are agreed; viz. that the Jews gained immensely in the clearness and compass of their religious faith during the Captivity. That, which was the punishment, was also the term, of their idolatry; into that sin they never afterwards fell. Now first, too, they began to understand that the bond of their unity was not local, not national even, but spiritual and religious; they were spread over every province of a foreign empire, yet they were one people, and a sacred people, in virtue of their common service of Jehovah and their common hope of Messiah's advent. This hope had been vaguely felt before, and just previous to the Captivity Isaiah had arrayed it in an unrivalled splendour of imagery; now it sank into the popular mind, which needed it so sorely, and became a deep and ardent longing of the national heart. From this period, moreover, the immortality of the soul and the life beyond death entered distinctly and prominently into the Hebrew creed. Always latent in their Scriptures, these truths disclosed themselves to the Jews as they came into contact with the Persian doctrines of judgment and future rewards. Hitherto they had thought mainly, if not exclusively, of the temporal rewards and punishments by which the Mosaic law enforced its precepts. Henceforth they saw that, in time and on earth, human actions are not carried to their final and due results; they looked forward to a judgment in which all wrongs should be righted, all unpunished sins receive their recompense, and all the sufferings of the good be transmuted into joy and peace.

Now this, as we shall see, is the very moral of the Book Ecclesiastes, the triumphant climax to which it mounts. The endeavour of Coheleth is to show how evil and good were blended in the human lot, evil so largely preponderating in the lot of many of the good as to make life a curse unless it were sustained by hope; to give hope by assuring the Hebrew captives that "God takes cognizance of all things," and "will bring every work to judgment," good or bad; and to urge on them, as the conclusion of his Quest, and as the whole duty of man, to prepare for that supreme audit by fearing God and keeping his commandments. This was the light he was commissioned to carry into their great darkness; and if the lamp and the oil were of God, it is hardly too much to say that the spark which kindled the lamp was taken from the Persian fire, since that too was of God. Or, to vary the figure, and make it more accurate, we may say that the truths of the future life lay hidden in the Hebrew Scriptures, and that it was by the light of the Persian doctrine of the future that the Jews, stimulated by the mental culture and activity acquired in Babylon, discovered them in the Word.

It is thus, indeed, that God has taught men in all ages. The Word remains ever the same, but our conditions change, our mental posture varies, and with our posture the angle at which the light of Heaven falls on the sacred page. We are brought into contact with new races, new ideas, new forms of culture, new discoveries of science, and the familiar Word forthwith teems with new meanings, with new adaptations to our needs; truths unseen before, though they were always there, come to view, deep truths rise to the surface, mysterious truths grow simple and plain, truths that jangled on the ear melt into harmony; our new needs stretch out lame hands of faith, and find an unexpected but ample supply; and we are rapt in wonder and admiration as we afresh discover the Bible to be the Book for all races and for all ages, an inexhaustible fountain of truth and comfort and grace.

Footnotes:

2. Rosenmüller, Ewald, Knobel, De Wette, Delitzsch, Ginsburg, with many other competent judges, are agreed on this point; and even those who in part differ from them differ only in assigning the Book to a date still farther removed from the time of Solomon. There are but few scholars who now contend for the Solomonic authorship, and hardly any of these are, I think, in the first rank.

3. The fourth century B.C. is, I think, its most probable date. In his recent exposition of Ecclesiastes, the Dean of Wells attempts to bring the date down to about B.C. 240. But his arguments are so curious and fanciful, and his conclusion is based so largely on conjecture, and on dubious similarities of phrase in the language of the Hebrew Preacher, and of some of the later philosophers of Greece, that I suspect very little weight will be attached to his gallant attempt to breathe new life into the moribund hypothesis of the ingenious Mr. Tyler. Delitzsch, for example, a high and recognized authority, declares that there is "not a trace of Greek influence" in this Scripture, though Dr. Plumptre finds so many. But though neither his hypothesis nor his confessedly conjectural biography of the unknown author carries the force of "sober criticism," there is much in his Commentary which will be found very helpful.

4. Plumptre writes the word Koheleth, and Perowne Quoheleth. Which of the three initial letters should be used is of little consequence, and hence I retain the form in most common use. Ecclesiastes is simply its Greek equivalent.

5. See the commentary on these verses for a fuller exposition of his real claims and position.

6. Solomon could not have been more than sixty years of age when he died, yet it was not till he was "old" that his wives "turned away his heart from the Lord his God" (1 Kings xi. 4).

7. "It may be regarded as beyond doubt that it was written under the Persian domination" (Delitzsch).

8. The nearest analogy in English literature to this triumphant use of the proverb of which I can think is Pope's use of the couplet--in every way a much lesser feat, however; while its burlesque or caricature may be found in Tupper's Proverbial Philosophy.

9. In the Book of Proverbs, for instance, he would find, in addition to the incomparable personification of Wisdom to which I have already referred, many examples of the proverb proper, many detached sayings whose underlying thought is illustrated by a stroke of imagination; such as that (chap. xxv. 11) in which the enhanced beauty of an appropriate word when spoken at the opportune moment is compared with the golden fruit of the orange when set in its frame of silver blooms (Expositions, vol. iv.). He would also find some of those small picturesque descriptions produced by an artistic sequence of proverbs--the same theme being sometimes worked over by different artists, in different ages, one and the same moral being enforced by wholly different designs; as, for instance,

Samuel Cox, D.D.

where Solomon (chap. vi. 6-11) enforces the duty of a forethoughtful industry by a picture of the ant and her prudent ways; while an unknown sage of a later date (chap. xxiv. 30-34) appends precisely the same moral, expressed in the same words, to his graphic picture of the Sluggard's garden (The Expositor, Second Series, vol. vi.). Moreover, if he turn to chapter xxx. he will see how this form of art, which once soared so high, was capable of sinking into a kind of puerile conundrum--with its three too wonderful things, and its four little things which yet are wise--while its moral tone remained pure and high. And, finally, in the exposition of the Epilogue to Ecclesiastes he will find how, after sinking so low, it rose once more, in the hands of the later rabbis, into many beautiful forms of fable, and exhortation, and parable.

10. For this sketch I am largely indebted to Rawlinson's Five Great Monarchies of the Ancient Eastern World, and his commentary on Herodotus.

11. Instead of Nebuchadnezzar Jeremiah and Ezekiel use the form Nebuchadrezzar, which is nearer to the original Nabu-Kuduri-utzur, i.e. "Nebo is the protector against misfortune."

12. There is a curious allusion to these enamelled bricks, and the admiration the Jews conceived for them, in Ezekiel xxiii. 14-16.

13. See Herodotus, book i., chap. 199; Strabo, xvi., p. 1058; and the Book of Baruch, vi. 43.

14. Herodotus, ix. 62.

15. Æschyl., Pers., 94.

16. "There is no nation which so readily adopts foreign customs as the Persians.... As soon as they hear of any luxury they instantly make it their own.... Each of them has several wives, and a still larger number of concubines."--(Herodotus book i., chap. 135).

17. Their common root is the Sanscrit Kshatra, a king; in the Persepolitan inscriptions this word appears as Ksérshé, and from this both the Hebrew Achashuerash (Ahasuerus) and the Greek Xerxes would easily be formed.

18. "The political condition of the people which this Book presupposes is that in which they are placed under satraps" (Delitzsch).

19. It would be possible to collect from the Psalms of this date materials for a description of the wrongs and miseries inflicted on the Jews, and of their keen sense of them, quite as graphic and intense as that of the Preacher. Here are a few phrases hastily culled from them. The oppressors of Israel are described as being "clothed with cruelty as with a garment," as "returning evil for good, and hatred for good-will."

> "Lift up thyself, thou Judge of the earth;
> Render to the proud their desert.
> They prate, they speak arrogantly;
> All the workers of iniquity boast themselves.
> They break in pieces Thy people, O Lord,
> And afflict Thine heritage.
> They slay the widow and the stranger,
> And murder the fatherless.
> And they say, The Lord shall not see,
> Neither shall the God of Jacob consider" (xciv.).
> "I am bowed down and brought very low;
> I go mourning all the day long;
> Truly I am nigh unto falling,
> And my heaviness is ever before me" (xxxviii.).
> "My days consume away like smoke,
> And my bones are burned up like as a firebrand;
> My heart is smitten down and withered like grass,
> So that I forget to eat my bread" (cii.).
> "I am helpless and poor,

And my heart is wounded within me" (cix.). Most of the "imprecatory" Psalms belong to this period; and the terrible wrongs of the Captivity, though they may not justify, in large measure explain and excuse, that desire for vengeance which has given so much offence to some of our modern critics.

20. Sonnets, LXVI.

21. Haug's Essays, pp. 162-3, quoted by Rawlinson.

22. This helpful angel is by no means peculiar to the Persian faith. All the imaginative races of antiquity conceived of a being more divine than man, though originally not equal to the gods, who guided the departed soul on its lonely journey through the dark interspaces of death. Theut conducted the released spirit of the Egyptian to the judgment-seat. Hermes performed the same kind office for the Greeks, Mercury for the Romans. Yama was the nekropompos of the Hindus, and the Persians retained

the legend. The Rig-Veda represents him as the first man who passed through death to immortality, and as therefore the best guide of other men. Nor is it doubted that the Persians derived their belief in a future life from the primitive Hindu creed. If their faith was, as I have said, a revolt from the degenerate forms of Hindu worship, it was also a return to its more ancient forms, as religious reformations are apt to be. The fathers of the Aryan stock had an unwavering assurance of a future life. In his Essay on the Funeral Rites of the Brahmans, Max Müller cites a sort of liturgy with which the ancient Hindu used to bid farewell to his deceased friend while the body lay on the funeral pyre, which is, surely, very noble and pathetic: "Depart thou, depart thou by the ancient paths, to the place whither our fathers have departed. Meet with the ancient ones (the Pitrs); meet with the Lord of Death; obtain thy desires in heaven. Throw off thine imperfections; go to thy home. Become united with a body; clothe thyself in a shining form. Go ye; depart ye; hasten ye from hence" (Rig-Veda x. 14). To which, as choral responses, might be added, "Let him depart to those for whom flow the rivers of nectar. Let him depart to those who through meditation have obtained the victory, who by fixing their thoughts on the unseen have gone to heaven.... Let him depart to the mighty in battle, to the heroes who have laid down their lives for others, to those who have bestowed their goods on the poor" (Rig-Veda x. 154). As the body was consumed on the pyre the friends of the dead chanted a hymn in which, after having bidden his body return to the various elements from which it sprang, they prayed, "As for his unborn part, do Thou, Lord (Agni), quicken it with Thy heat; let Thy flame and Thy brightness kindle it: convey it to the world of the righteous." It was from this pure and lofty source that the Persians drew their faith in the better life to be. Max Müller also quotes as the prayer of a dying Hindu woman, "Place me, O Pure One, in that everlasting and unchanging world where light and glory are found. Make me immortal in the world in which joys, delights, and happiness abide, where the desires are obtained" (Atharda Veda xii. 3, 17). Cremation itself bore witness to the Hindu faith in immortality, since they held that "the fire which set free the spiritual element from the superincumbent clay, completed the third or heavenly birth," the second birth having been achieved when men set themselves to a faithful discharge of their religious duties.

Samuel Cox, D.D.

THE PROLOGUE

IN WHICH THE PROBLEM OF THE BOOK IS INDIRECTLY STATED.

Chap. I., vv. 1-11.

1 The words of the Preacher, son of David, king in Jerusalem. 2 Vanity of vanities, saith the Preacher; Vanity of vanities, all is vanity, 3 Since man hath no profit from all his labour Which he laboureth under the sun! [23] 4 One generation passeth, and another generation cometh; While the earth abideth for ever. 5 The sun also riseth, and the sun goeth down; And panteth toward the place at which it will rise again. 6 The wind goeth toward the south, and veereth to the north; It whirleth round and round; And the wind returneth on its course. 7 All the streams run into the sea, yet the sea is not full; To the place whence the streams came, thither they return again. 8 All things are weary with toil. Man cannot utter it. The eye can never be satisfied with seeing, Nor the ear with hearing. 9 What hath been will be, And that which is done is that which will be done; And there is no new thing under the sun. 10 If there be anything of which it is said, "Behold, this is new!" It hath been long ago, in the ages that were before us. 11 There is no remembrance of those who have been; Nor will there be any remembrance of men who are to come Among those that will live after them.

Footnote:

23. Just as we speak of this "sublunary world," so "under the sun" is the characteristic designation of the earth throughout this Book.

FIRST SECTION

THE QUEST OF THE CHIEF GOOD IN WISDOM AND IN PLEASURE.

Chap. I., v. 12, to Chap. II., v. 26.

The Quest in Wisdom. Ch. i., vv. 12-18.
    12 I, the Preacher, was King over Israel, in Jerusalem: 13 And I applied my heart to survey and search by wisdom Into all that is done under heaven: This sore task hath God given to the children of men, To exercise themselves therewith.
    Ver. 13. To survey and search into, etc. The verbs indicate the broad extent which his researches covered, and the depth to which they penetrated.
    14 I have considered all the works that are done under the sun, And, behold, they are all vanity and vexation of spirit.
    Ver. 14. Vexation of spirit. Literally, "striving after the wind." But the time-honoured phrase, "vexation of spirit," sufficiently expresses the writer's meaning; and it seems better to retain it than, with the Revised Version, to introduce the Hebrew metaphor, which has a somewhat novel and foreign sound.
    15 That which is crooked cannot be set straight, And that which is lacking cannot be made up. 16 Therefore I spake to my heart, saying, Lo, I have acquired greater wisdom Than all who were before me in Jerusalem, My heart having seen much wisdom and knowledge; 17 For I had given my heart to find knowledge and wisdom. I perceive that even this is vexation of spirit;
    Ver. 17. To find knowledge and wisdom. Both the Authorized and Revised Versions render "to know wisdom, and to know madness and folly." The latter clause, however, violates both the sense and the grammatical construction. The word translated "to know" is not an infinitive, but a noun, and should be rendered "knowledge;" the word translated "folly" means "prudence," and the word translated "madness" hardly means more than "folly." The text, too, seems corrupt. The sense of the passage is against it, I think, as it now stands; for the design of the Preacher is simply to show the insufficiency of wisdom and knowledge, not to prove folly foolish. On the whole, therefore, it seems better to follow the high authority which arranges the text as it is here rendered. The Hebraist will find the question fully discussed in Ginsburg.
    18 For in much wisdom is much sadness, And to multiply knowledge is to multiply sorrow.

The Quest in Pleasure. Ch ii., vv. 1-11.
    1 Then I said to my heart, Go to, now let me prove thee with mirth, And thou shalt see pleasure: And, lo, this too is vanity! 2 To mirth I said, Thou art mad! And to pleasure, What canst thou do? 3 I thought in my heart to cheer my body with pleasure, While my spirit guided it wisely, And to lay hold on folly, Till I should see what it is good for the sons of men to do under heaven, Through the brief day of their life. 4 I gave myself to great works; I built me houses; I planted me vineyards; 5 I made me gardens and parks, And I planted in them all manner of fruit-trees; 6 I made me tanks of water, From which to water the groves: 7 I bought me men-servants and maid-servants, And had servants born in my house. I had also many herds of oxen and sheep, More than all who were before me in Jerusalem: 8 I heaped up silver and gold, And the treasures of kings and of kingdoms: I got me men-singers and women-singers; And took delight in many fair concubines: 9 So that I surpassed all who were before me in Jerusalem, My wisdom abiding with me; 10 And nothing that my eyes desired did I withhold from them, I did not keep back my heart from any pleasure; For my heart took joy in all my toil, And this was my portion therefrom. 11 But when I turned to look on all the works which my hands had wrought, And at the labour which it cost me to accomplish them, Behold, all was vanity and vexation of spirit, And there was no profit under the sun.

Samuel Cox, D.D.

Wisdom and Pleasure compared. Ch. ii., vv. 12-23.

12 Then I turned to compare wisdom with madness and folly-- And what can he do that cometh after the king Whom they made king long ago?-- 13 And I saw that wisdom excelleth folly As far as light excelleth darkness: 14 The wise man's eyes are in his head, While the fool walketh blindly. Nevertheless I knew that the same fate will befall both. 15 Therefore I spake with my heart: "A fate like that of the fool will befall me, even me; To what end, then, am I wiser?" And I said to my heart: "This too is vanity, 16 For there is no more remembrance of the wise man than of the fool; For both will be forgotten, As in time past so also in days to come: And, alas, the wise man dieth even as the fool!" 17 So life became hateful to me, for a sore burden was upon me, Even the labour which I wrought under the sun; Since all is vanity and vexation of spirit: 18 Yea, I hated all the gain which I had gained under the sun, Because I must leave it to the man who shall come after me, 19 And who can tell whether he will be a wise man or a fool? Yet shall he have power over all my gain Which I have wisely gained under the sun: This too is vanity. 20 Then I turned and gave my heart up to despair Concerning all the gain which I had gained under the sun; 21 For here is a man who hath laboured wisely, and prudently, and dexterously, And he must leave it as a portion to one who hath not laboured therein: This also is vanity and a great evil; 22 For man hath nothing of all his heavy labour, And the vexation of his heart under the sun, 23 Since his task grieveth and vexeth him all his days, And even at night his heart hath no rest: This too is vanity.

The Conclusion. Ch. ii., vv. 24-26.

24 There is nothing better for a man than to eat and to drink, And to let his soul take pleasure in his labour. But even this, I saw, cometh from God; 25 For who can eat, And who enjoy himself, apart from Him? 26 For to the man who is good before Him, He giveth wisdom and knowledge and joy; But to the sinner He giveth the task to gather and to heap up, That he may leave it to him who is good before God: This also is vanity and vexation of spirit.

SECOND SECTION

THE QUEST OF THE CHIEF GOOD IN DEVOTION TO THE AFFAIRS OF BUSINESS.

Chap. III., v. 1, to Chap. V., v. 20.

The Quest obstructed by Divine Ordinances; Ch. iii., vv. 1-15.

1 There is a time for all things, And a season for every undertaking under heaven: 2 A time to be born, and a time to die; A time to plant, and a time to pluck up plants; 3 A time to kill, and a time to heal; A time to break down, and a time to build up; 4 A time to weep, and a time to laugh; A time to mourn, and a time to dance; 5 A time to cast stones, and a time to gather up stones; A time to embrace, and a time to refrain from embracing; 6 A time to get, and a time to lose; A time to keep, and a time to throw away; 7 A time to rend, and a time to sew; A time to be silent, and a time to speak; 8 A time to love, and a time to hate; A time for war, and a time for peace: 9 He who laboureth hath therefore no profit from his labours. 10 I have considered the task which God hath given to the sons of men, To exercise themselves withal: 11 He hath made everything beautiful in its season; He hath also put eternity into their heart; Only they understand not the work of God from beginning to end. 12 I found that there was no good for them but to rejoice, And to do themselves good all their life; 13 But also that, if a man eat and drink, And take pleasure in all his labour, It is a gift of God. 14 I found too that whatever God hath ordained continueth for ever; Nothing can be added to it, And nothing taken from it: And God hath so ordered it that men may fear before Him. 15 That which is hath been, And that which is to be was long ago; For God recalleth the past.

And by Human Injustice and Perversity. Ch. iii., v. 16. Ch. iv., v. 3.

16 Moreover, I saw under the sun That there was iniquity in the place of justice, And in the place of equity there was iniquity. 17 I said to mine heart: "God will judge the righteous and the wicked, For there is a time for everything and for every deed with Him." 18 Yet I said to my heart of the children of men: "God hath sifted them, To show that they, even they, are but as beasts. 19 For a mere chance is man, and the beast a mere chance, And they are both subject to the same chance; As is the death of the one, so is the death of the other; And both have the same spirit: And the man hath no advantage over the beast, For both are vanity: 20 Both go to the same place; Both sprang from dust, and both turn into dust: 21 And who knoweth whether the spirit of man goeth upward, Or the spirit of the beast goeth downward to the earth?"

Ver. 21. The question is here, as so often in Hebrew, the strongest form of negative. As in ver. 19 the Preacher affirms of man and beast that "both have the same spirit," and, in ver. 20, that "both go to the same place," so, in this verse, he emphatically denies that there is any difference in their destination at death.

22 Wherefore I saw that there is nothing better for man Than to rejoice in his labours; For this is his portion: And who shall give him to see what will be after him?

iv.

1 Then I turned to consider once more All the oppressions that are done under the sun: I beheld the tears of the oppressed, And they had no comforter; And their oppressors were violent, Yet had they no comforter: 2 And I accounted the dead who died long ago Happier than the living who are still alive; 3 While happier than either is he who hath not been born, Who hath not seen the evil which is done under the sun.

It is rendered hopeless by the base Origin of Human Industries. Ch. iv., vv. 4-8.

4 Then too I saw that all this toil, And all this dexterity in toil, Spring from man's rivalry with his neighbour: This also is vanity and vexation of spirit. 5 The sluggard foldeth his hands, Yet he eateth his meat: 6 Better a handful of quiet Than two handsful of labour with vexation of spirit. 7 And again I turned, and saw a vanity under the sun: 8 Here is a man who hath no one with him, Not even a son or a brother; And yet there is no end of all his labour, Neither are his eyes satisfied with riches: For whom, then, doth he labour and deny his soul any of his wealth? This too is vanity and an evil work.

Yet these are capable of a nobler Motive and Mode. Ch. iv., vv. 9-16.

Samuel Cox, D.D.

9 Two are better than one, Because they have a good reward for their labour: 10 For if one fall, the other will lift up his fellow; But woe to the lonely one who falleth And hath no fellow to lift him up! 11 Moreover, if two sleep together, they are warm; But he that is alone, how can he be warm? 12 And if an enemy assail the one, two will withstand him. And a threefold cord is not easily broken. 13 Happier is a poor and wise youth Than an old and foolish king Who even yet has not learned to take warning; 14 For he goeth forth from the prison to the throne, Although he was born a poor man in the kingdom. 15 I see all the living who walk under the sun Flocking to the youth who stood up in his stead; 16 There is no end to the multitude of the people over whom he ruleth: Nevertheless those who live after him will not rejoice in him; For even this is vanity and vexation of spirit.

***

So also a nobler and happier Mode of Worship is open to men: Ch. v., vv. 1-7.

1 Keep thy foot when thou goest to the House of God; For it is better to obey than to offer the sacrifice of fools, Who know not when they do evil. 2 Do not hurry on thy mouth, And do not force thy heart to utter words before God; For God is in heaven, and thou upon earth: Therefore let thy words be few. 3 For as a dream cometh through much occupation, So foolish talk through many words. 4 When thou vowest a vow unto God, Defer not to pay it; For he is a fool whose will is not steadfast. Pay that which thou hast vowed. 5 Better that thou shouldest not vow Than that thou shouldest vow and not pay. 6 Suffer not thy mouth to cause thy flesh to sin, And say not before the Angel, "It was an error:" For why should God be angry at thine idle talk And destroy the work of thy hands?

Ver. 6. Before the Angel. That is, before the Angel who, as the Hebrews thought, presided over the altar of worship, and who was present even when only two or three met for the study of the Law: to study the Law being in itself an act of worship.

7 For in many words, as in many dreams, there is vanity: But fear thou God.

***

And a more helpful and consolatory Trust in the Divine Providence. Ch. v., vv. 8-17.

8 If thou seest the oppression of the poor, And the perversion of justice in the State, Be not dismayed thereat; For superior watcheth superior, And superiors again watch over them: 9 And the advantage for the people is, that it extendeth to all, For even the king is servant to the field.

Ver. 9. Some commentators prefer another possible reading of this difficult verse: But the profit of a land is every way a king devoted to the field, i.e. a lover and promoter of good husbandry. This reading, however, does not, I think, harmonise so well with the context as that given above.

10 He that loveth silver is never satisfied with silver, Nor he that clingeth to riches with what they yield: This too is vanity; 11 For when riches increase they increase that consume them: What advantage then hath the owner thereof, Save the looking thereupon with his eyes? 12 Sweet is the sleep of the husbandman, Whether he eat little or much; While abundance suffereth not the rich to sleep. 13 There is a great evil which I have seen under the sun-- Riches hoarded up by the rich To the hurt of the owner thereof: 14 For the riches perish in some unlucky adventure, And he begetteth a son when he hath nothing in his hand: 15 As he cometh forth from the womb of his mother, Even as he cometh naked, So also he returneth again, And taketh nothing from his labour Which he may carry away in his hand. 16 This also is a great evil, That just as he came so he must go. For what profit hath he who laboureth for the wind? 17 Yet all his days he eateth in darkness, And is much perturbed, and hath vexation and grief.

The Conclusion. Ch. v., vv. 18-20.

18 Behold, that which I have said holds good,-- That it is well for man to eat and to drink And to enjoy the good of all his labour wherein he laboureth under the sun, Through the brief day of his life which God hath given him: For this is his portion. 19 And I have also said, That a man to whom God hath given riches and wealth, If He hath also enabled him to eat thereof, And to take his portion and to rejoice in his labour;-- This is a gift of God: 20 He doth not fret because the days of his life are not many, For God hath sanctioned the joy of his heart.

THIRD SECTION

THE QUEST IN WEALTH AND IN THE GOLDEN MEAN.

Chaps. VI., ver. 1, to VIII., ver. 15.

The Quest in Wealth. He who makes Riches his Chief Good is haunted by Fears and Perplexities: Ch. vi., vv. 1-6.

1 There is another evil which I have seen under the sun, And it weigheth heavily upon men: 2 Here is a man to whom God hath given riches and wealth and abundance, So that his soul lacketh nothing of all that it desireth; And God hath not given him the power to enjoy it, But a stranger enjoyeth it: This is vanity and a great evil. 3 Though one beget a hundred children, And live many years, Yea, however many the days of his years, Yet if his soul be not satisfied with good, Even though the grave did not wait for him, Better is an abortion than he: 4 For this cometh in nothingness and goeth in darkness, And its memory is shrouded in darkness; 5 It doth not even see and know the sun: It hath more rest than he. 6 And if he live twice a thousand years and see no good:-- Do not both go to the same place?

For God has put Eternity into his Heart; Ch. vi., vv. 7-10.

7 All the labour of this man is for his mouth; Therefore his soul cannot be satisfied: 8 For what advantage hath the wise man over the fool, Or what the poor man over the stately magnate?

Ver. 8. The magnate. Literally, "he who knoweth to walk before the living;" some "great person," some man of eminent station, who is much in the eye of the public.

9 It is better, indeed, to enjoy the good we have Than to crave a good beyond our reach: Yet even this is vanity and vexation of spirit.

Ver. 9. To enjoy the good we have, etc. Literally, "Better is that which is seen by the eyes (the present good) than that which is pursued by the soul (the distant and uncertain good)."

10 That which hath been was long since ordained; And it is very certain that even the greatest is but a man, And cannot contend with Him who is mightier than he.

And much that he gains only feeds Vanity;

11 Moreover there are many things which increase vanity: What advantage then hath man? Nor can he tell what will become of his Gains.

12 And who knoweth what is good for man in life, The brief day of his vain life which he spendeth as a shadow? And who can tell what shall be after him under the sun?

The Quest in the Golden Mean. The Method of the Man who pursues it. Ch. vii., vv. 1-14.

1 A good name is better than good nard, And the day of death better than the day of one's birth: 2 It is better to go to the house of mourning Than to the house of feasting, Because this is the end of every man, And the living should lay it to heart:

Ver. 2. "Because this is the end;" i.e. the death bewailed in the house of mourning.

3 Better is serious thought than wanton mirth, For by a sad countenance the heart is bettered: 4 The heart of the wise therefore is in the house of mourning, But in the house of mirth is the heart of fools. 5 It is better for a man to listen to the reproof of the wise Than to listen to the song of fools; 6 For the laughter of fools is like the crackling of thorns under a pot: This also is vanity.

Ver. 6. The laughter of fools, etc. There is a play on words in the original which cannot be reproduced in English. Dean Plumptre, following the lead of Delitzsch, proposes as the nearest equivalents, "As crackling nettles under kettles," or "As crackling stubble makes the pot bubble."

7 Wrong-doing maketh the wise man mad, As a bribe corrupteth the heart. 8 The end of a reproof is better than its beginning, And patience is better than pride; 9 Therefore hurry not on thy spirit to be angry: For anger is nursed in the bosom of fools. 10 Say not, "How is it that former days were better than these?" For that is not the part of wisdom. 11 Wisdom is as good as wealth, And hath an advantage over it for those who lead an active life:

Ver. 11. Those who lead an active life. Literally, "those who see the sun," i.e. those who are much in the sun, who lead a busy active life, are much occupied with traffic or public affairs.

Samuel Cox, D.D.

12 For wisdom is a shelter, And wealth is a shelter; But the advantage of wisdom is That it fortifieth the heart of them that have it.

Ver. 12. Fortifieth the heart; i.e. quickens life, a new life, a life which keeps the heart tranquil and serene under all chances and changes.

13 Consider moreover the work of God, Since no man can straighten that which He hath made crooked. 14 In the day of prosperity be thou content; And in the day of adversity Consider that God hath made this as well as that, In order that man should not be able to foresee that which is to come.

Ver. 14.: In the day of prosperity, etc. Literally, "in the day of good be in good." It may be rendered "in the good day be of good cheer." This as well as that; i.e. adversity as well as prosperity. God sends both in order that, not foreseeing what will come to pass, we may live in a constant and humble dependence on Him.

The Perils to which it exposes him. (1) He is likely to compromise Conscience: Ch. vii., vv. 15-20.

15 In my fleeting days I have seen Both the righteous die in his righteousness, And the wicked live long in his wickedness: 16 Be not too righteous therefore, Nor make thyself too wise lest thou be abandoned; 17 Be not very wicked, nor yet very foolish, Lest thou die before thy time: 18 It is better that thou shouldest lay hold of this And also not let go of that; For whoso feareth God will take hold on both.

Ver. 18. This ... and that. This refers to the folly and wickedness of ver. 17, and that to the wisdom and righteousness of ver. 16. Take hold on both. Literally, "go along with both."

19 This wisdom alone is greater strength to the wise Than an army to a beleaguered city;

Ver. 19. This wisdom: viz. the moderate common-sense view of life which has just been described. Than an army, etc. Literally, "Than ten (i.e. many) mighty men in a city."

20 For there is not a righteous man on earth Who doeth good and sinneth not.

(2) To be indifferent to Censure: Ch. vii., vv. 21, 22.

21 Moreover seek not to know all that is said of thee, Lest thou hear thy servant speak evil of thee;

Ver. 21. Seek not to know, etc. Literally, "Give not thy heart (even if thy ears) to all words that are uttered."

22 For thou knowest in thine heart That thou also hast many times spoken evil of others. 23 All this wisdom have I tried; I desired a higher wisdom, but it was far from me; 24 That which was far off remaineth far off, And deep remaineth deep: Who can find it out?

(3) To despise Women; Ch. vii., vv. 25-29.

25 Then I and my heart turned to know this wisdom And diligently examine it-- To discover the cause of wickedness, vice, And that folly which is madness: 26 And I found woman more bitter than death; She is a net; Her heart is a snare, and her hands are chains: Whoso is good before God shall escape her, But the sinner shall be taken by her. 27 Behold, what I have found, saith the Preacher-- Taking things one by one to reach the result-- 28 I have found one man among a thousand, But in all that number a woman have I not found: 29 Lo, this only have I found, That God made man upright, But that they seek out many devices.

(4) And to be indifferent to Public Wrongs. Ch. viii., vv. 1-13.

1 Who is like the wise man? And who like him that understandeth the interpretation of this saying? The wisdom of this man maketh his face bright, And his rude features are refined.

Ver. 1. This saying: i.e. that which follows. And his rude features, etc. Culture lends an air of refinement to the face, carriage, manners.

2 I say then, Obey the king's commandment, And the rather because of the oath of fealty: 8?

Ver. 2. The oath of fealty. Literally, "the oath by God." The Babylonian and Persian despots exacted an oath of loyalty from conquered races. Each had to swear by the god he worshipped.

3 Do not throw off thine allegiance, Nor resent an evil word, For he can do whatsoever he please;

Ver. 3. Do not throw off, etc. Literally, "Do not hurry from his presence, or even stand up because of an evil word." To stand up in the divan of an Eastern despot is a sign of resentment; to rush from it a sign of disloyalty and rebellion.

4 For the word of a king is mighty; And who shall say to him, "What doest thou?" 5 Whoso keepeth his commandment will know no evil. Moreover the heart of the wise man foreseeth a time of retribution-- 6 For there is a time of retribution for all things-- When the tyranny of man is heavy upon him: 7 Because he knoweth not what will be, And because no one can tell him when it will be.

Ver. 7. Because he knoweth not; i.e. the tyrant does not know. The sense seems to be: Retribution is all the more certain because, in his infatuation, the despot does not foresee the disastrous results of his tyranny, and because no one can tell him when or how they will disclose themselves.

8 No man is ruler over his own spirit, To retain the spirit, Nor has he any power over the day of

his death; And there is no furlough in this war, And no craft will save the wicked. 9 All this have I seen, Having applied my heart to all that is done under the sun.

Ver. 9.: All this have I seen; i.e. all this retribution on tyrants and the consequent deliverance of the oppressed.

10 But there is a time when a man ruleth over men to their hurt. Thus I have seen wicked men buried, And come again; And those who did right depart from the place of the holy, And be forgotten in the city: This also is vanity.

Ver. 10.: But the Preacher has also seen times when retributive justice did not overtake the oppressors, when they came again in the persons of children as wicked and tyrannical as themselves.

11 Because sentence against an evil deed is not executed forthwith, The heart of the sons of men is set in them to do evil.

Ver. 11.: Because sentence, etc. "God does not always pay on Saturdays," says an old Italian proverb.

12 Though a sinner do evil a hundred years, And groweth old therein, Yet I know that it shall be well with those who fear God, Who truly fear before Him; 13 And it shall not be well with the wicked, But, like a shadow, he shall not prolong his days, Because he doth not fear before God.

Therefore the Preacher condemns this View of Human Life.

14 Nevertheless, this vanity doth happen on the earth, That there are righteous men who have a wage like that of the wicked, And there are wicked men who have a wage like that of the righteous: This too, I said, is vanity. 15 And I commended mirth, Because there is nothing better for man under the sun Than to eat, and to drink, and to be merry; For this will go with him to his work Through the days of his life, Which God giveth him under the sun.

Ver. 15.: "And this will go with him:" viz. this clear enjoying temper, than which, as yet, the Preacher has found "nothing better."

Samuel Cox, D.D.

FOURTH SECTION

THE QUEST OF THE CHIEF GOOD ACHIEVED.

Chap. VIII., ver. 16, to Chap. XII., ver. 7.

The Chief Good not to be found in Wisdom: Ch. viii., v. 16.-Ch. ix., v. 6.
    16 As then I applied my heart to acquire wisdom, And to see the work which is done under the sun-- And such a one seeth no sleep with his eyes by day or by night: 17 I saw that man cannot find out all the work of God Which is done under the sun; Though man labour to discover it, He cannot find it out; And though the wise may say he understandeth it Nevertheless he hath not found it out.
    Ver. 17.: To illustrate this verse Dean Plumptre happily quotes Hooker's noble and familiar words: "Dangerous it were for the feeble brain of man to wade far into the doings of the Most High; whom although to know be life, and joy to make mention of His name, yet our soundest knowledge is to know that we know Him not as indeed He is, neither can know Him, and our safest eloquence concerning Him is our silence, when we confess without confession that His glory is inexplicable, his greatness above our capacity and reach."

ix.
    1 For all this have I taken to heart and explored, That the righteous, and the wise, and their labours are in the hand of God: They know not whether they shall meet love or hatred; All lies before them. All are treated alike;
    Ver. 1.: They know not whether they shall meet love or hatred may mean that even the wisest cannot tell whether they shall meet (1) the love or the enmity of God, as shown in adverse or favourable providences; or (2) the things which they love or hate; or (3) the love or the hatred of their fellows. The last of the three seems the most likely.
    All lies before them; i.e. all possible chances, changes, events.
    Only God can determine or foresee what is coming to meet them.
    2 The same fate befalleth to the righteous and to the wicked, To the good and pure and to the impure, To him that sacrificeth and to him that sacrificeth not; As with the good so is it with the sinner, With him that sweareth as with him who feareth an oath. 3 This is the greatest evil of all that is done under the sun, That there is one fate for all: And that, although the heart of the sons of men is full of evil, And madness is in their hearts through life, Yet, after it, they go to the dead;
    Ver. 3.: The words of this verse do not, as they stand, seem to carry on the logical sequence of thought. The Preacher's complaint is that even the wise and the good are not exempted from the common fate, not that the foolish and reckless are exposed to it. The text may be corrupt; but Ginsburg is content with it. A good reading of
    it, however, is still wanting.
    4 For who is exempted? To all the living there is hope, For a living dog is better than a dead lion; 5 For the living know that they shall die, But the dead know not anything; And there is no more any compensation to them, For the very memory of them is gone: 6 Their love, too, no less than their hatred and rivalry, hath perished; And there is no part for them in ought that is done under the sun.

Nor in Pleasure: Ch. ix., vv. 7-12.
    7 Go, then, eat thy bread with gladness, And drink thy wine with a merry heart, Since God hath accepted thy works: 8 Let thy garments be always white; Let no perfume be lacking to thy head: 9 And enjoy thyself with any woman whom thou lovest All the days of thy life Which He giveth thee under the sun, All thy fleeting days: For this is thy portion in life, And in the labour which thou labourest under the sun.
    Ver. 9.: "Enjoy thyself with any woman." The word here rendered "woman" does not mean "wife." And as the Hebrew Preacher is here speaking under the mask of the lover of pleasure, this immoral maxim is at least consistent with the part he plays. More than one good critic, however, read "a wife" for "any woman."
    10 Whatsoever thine hand findeth to do, Do it whilst thou art able; For there is no work, nor

The Expositor's Bible: Ecclesiastes

device, nor knowledge, nor wisdom in Hades, Whither thou goest. 11 Then I turned and saw under the sun, That the race is not to the swift, Nor the battle to the strong; Nor yet bread to the wise, Nor riches to the intelligent, Nor favour to the learned; 12 But time and chance happen to all, And that man doth not even know his time: Like fish taken in a fatal net, And like birds caught in a snare, So are the sons of men entrapped in the time of their calamity, When it falleth suddenly upon them.

Nor in Devotion to Public Affairs and its Rewards: Ch. ix., v. 13-Ch. x. v. 20.

13 This wisdom also have I seen under the sun, And it seemed great to me-- 14 There was a little city, And few men in it, And a great king came against it and besieged it, And threw up a military causeway against it: 15 Now there was found in it a poor wise man, And he saved that city by his wisdom; Yet no one remembered this same poor man. 16 Therefore say I, Though wisdom is better than strength, Yet the wisdom of the poor is despised, And his words are not listened to: 17 Though the quiet words of the wise have much advantage Over the vociferations of a fool of fools, And wisdom is better than weapons of war, Yet one fool destroyeth much good:

x.

1 As a dead fly maketh sweet ointment to stink, So a little folly overpowereth (much) wisdom and honour. 2 Nevertheless the mind of the wise man turns toward his right hand, But the mind of the fool to his left; 3 For so soon as the fool setteth his foot in the street He betrayeth his lack of understanding; Yet he saith of every one (he meeteth), "He is a fool!"

Ver. 3.: Setteth his foot in the street. Literally, "walketh in the road." The sentence seems to be a proverb used to denote the extreme stupidity of the fool who, the very moment he leaves his house, is bewildered, cannot even find his way from one familiar spot to another, and sees his own folly in every face he meets.

4 If the anger of thy ruler be kindled against thee, Resent it not: Patience will avert a graver wrong.

Ver. 4.: Resent it not. Literally, "Quit not thy place."--See note on chapter viii., ver. 3.

5 There is an evil which I have seen under the sun, An outrage which only a ruler can commit: 6 A great fool is lifted to high place, While the noble sit degraded: 7 I have seen servants upon horses, And masters walking like servants on the ground.

Ver. 7.: To ride upon a horse is still a mark of distinction in many Eastern States. In Turkish cities, till of late, no Christian was permitted to ride any nobler beast than an ass or a mule: so neither were the Jews, in the Middle Ages, in any Christian city.

8 Yet he that diggeth a pit shall fall into it; And whoso breaketh down a wall a serpent shall bite him; 9 He who pulleth down stones shall be hurt therewith; And whoso cleaveth logs shall be cut. 10 If the axe be blunt, and he do not whet the edge, He must put on more strength; But wisdom should teach him to sharpen it.

Ver. 10.: Ginsburg renders this difficult and much-disputed passage thus: "If the axe be blunt, and he do not sharpen it beforehand, he shall only increase the army; the advantage of repairing hath wisdom," and explains it as meaning: "If any insulted subject lift a blunt axe against the trunk of despotism, he will only make the tyrant increase his army, and thereby augment his own sufferings; but it is the prerogative of wisdom to repair the mischief which such precipitate folly occasions." I have offered what seems a simpler explanation in the comment on this passage, and have tried to give a simpler, yet not less accurate, rendering in the text. But there are almost as many readings of this difficult verse as there are critics; and it is impossible to do more than make a hesitating choice among them.

11 If the serpent bite because it is not charmed, There is no advantage to the charmer.

Ver. 11.: The charmer. Literally, "the master of the tongue." The allusion of the phrase is of course to the subtle cantillations by which the charmer drew, or was thought to draw, serpents from their "lurk," and to render them harmless.

12 The words of the wise man's mouth win him grace; But the lips of a fool swallow him up, 13 For the words of his mouth are folly at the beginning, And end in malignant madness. 14 The fool is full of words, Though no man knoweth what shall be, Either here or hereafter: And who can tell him? 15 The work of a fool wearieth him, For he cannot even find his way to the city.

Ver. 15.: He cannot even find his way to the city; a proverbial saying. It denotes the fool who has not wit enough even to keep a high road, to walk in the beaten path which leads to a capital city. The thought was evidently familiar to Jewish literature; for Isaiah (xxxv. 8) speaks of the way of holiness as a highway in which "wayfaring men, though fools, shall not err."

16 Woe to thee, O land, when thy king is a child, And thy princes feast in the morning! 17 Happy art thou, O land, when thy king is noble, And thy princes eat at due hours, For strength and not for revelry! 18 Through slothful hands the roof falleth in, And through lazy hands the house lets in the rain.

Vers. 18, 19.: And money pays for all; i.e. the money of the people. The slothful prodigal rulers,

Samuel Cox, D.D.

under whose mal-administration the whole fabric of the State was fast falling into decay, extorted the means for their profligate revelry from their toil-worn and oppressed subjects. It is significant of the caution induced by the extreme tyranny of the time, that the whole description of its political condition is conveyed in proverbs more enigmatical than usual, and capable of being interpreted in more senses than one.

19 They turn bread, and wine, which cheereth life, into revelry; And money has to pay for all. 20 Nevertheless revile not the king even in thy thoughts, Nor a prince even in thy bed-chamber, Lest the bird of the air carry the report, And the winged tribes tell the story.

But in a wise Use and a wise Enjoyment of the Present Life; Ch. xi., vv. 1-8.

1 Cast thy bread upon the waters, For in time thou mayest find the good of it; 2 Give a portion to seven, and even to eight, For thou knowest not what calamity may come upon the earth. 3 When the clouds are full of rain, They empty it upon the earth; And when the tree falleth, toward south or north, In the place where the tree falleth there will it lie. 4 Whoso watcheth the wind shall not sow, And he who observeth the clouds shall not reap; 5 As thou knowest the course of the wind As little as that of the embryo in the womb of the pregnant, So thou knowest not the work of God, Who worketh all things. 6 Sow, then, thy seed in the morning, And slack not thy hand in the evening, Since thou knowest not which shall prosper, this or that, Or whether both shall prove good: 7 And the light shall be sweet to thee, And it shall be pleasant to thine eyes to behold the sun: 8 For even if a man should live many years, He ought to rejoice in them all, And to remember that there will be many dark days; Yea, that all that cometh is vanity.

Combined with a stedfast Faith in the Life to come. Ch. xi., v. 9-Ch. xii., v. 7.

9 Rejoice, O young man, in thy youth, And let thy heart cheer thee in the days of thy youth; And pursue the ways of thine heart, And that which thine eyes desire; And know that for all these God will bring thee into judgment: 10 Banish, therefore, care from thy mind, And put away sadness from thy flesh, For youth and manhood are vanity.

xii.

And remember thy Creator in the days of thy youth, Before the evil days come, And the years approach of which thou shalt say, "I have no pleasure in them;" 2 Before the sun groweth dark, And the light, and the moon, and the stars; And the clouds return after the rain: 3 When the keepers of the house shall quake, And the men of power crouch down; When the grinding-maids shall stop because so few are left, And the women who look out of the lattices will be shrouded in darkness, And the door shall be closed on the street:

Ver. 3.: The women who look out of the lattices; i.e. the luxurious ladies of the harem looking through their windows to see what is going on outside. Compare Judges v. 28; 2 Samuel vi. 16; and 2 Kings ix. 30.

4 When the sound of the mills shall cease, And the swallow fly shrieking to and fro, And all the song-birds drop silently into their nests.

Ver. 4.: The swallow, etc. Literally, "the bird shall arise for a noise," i.e. the bird which flies abroad and makes a noise at the approach of a tempest: viz. the swallow. All the songbirds. Literally, "all the daughters of song," a Hebraism for birds.

5 There shall be terror at that which cometh from the height, And fear shall beset the highway: The almond also shall be rejected, And the locust be loathed, And the caper-berry provoke no appetite; Because man goeth to his long home, And the mourners pace up and down the street;--

Ver. 5.: From the height, i.e. from heaven. The locust be loathed. It is commonly assumed that the locust was only eaten by the poor; but Aristotle (Hist. Anim., v. 30) names them as a delicacy, and Ginsburg affirms that they are still considered so by the cultivated and well-to-do Arabs. His long home. Literally, "his eternal home," the domus æterna of the early Christian tombs.

6 Before the silver cord snappeth asunder, And the golden bowl escapeth; Before the pitcher be shattered at the fountain, And the wheel is broken at the well; 7 And the body is cast into the earth from which it came, And the spirit returneth to God who gave it.

THE EPILOGUE

IN WHICH THE PROBLEM OF THE BOOK IS CONCLUSIVELY SOLVED.

Chap. XII., vv. 8-14.
   8 Vanity of vanities, saith the Preacher, All is vanity! 9 And not only was the Preacher a wise man; He also taught the people wisdom, And compared, collected, and arranged many proverbs. 10 The Preacher sought out words of comfort, And wrote down in uprightness words of truth. 11 The words of the Wise are like goads, And those of the Masters of the Assemblies like spikes driven home, Given out by the same Shepherd. 12 And of what is more than these, my son, beware; For of making of many books there is no end, And much study is a weariness to the flesh. 13 The conclusion of the matter is this;-- That God taketh cognisance of all things: Fear Him, therefore, and keep his commandments, For this it behoveth every man to do,
   Ver. 13.: God taketh cognisance of all things. Literally, "Everything is noted" or "heard," i.e. by God the Judge. Ginsburg conjectures, not without reason, as I think, that the Sacred Name was omitted from this clause of the verse simply because the Author wished to reserve it for the more emphatic clause which follows it. Many good scholars, however, read the clause as meaning simply, "The conclusion of the matter, when all has been heard," i.e. which even the Sages can adduce.
   14 Since God will bring every deed to the judgment Appointed for every secret thing, Whether it be good or whether it be bad.

Samuel Cox, D.D.

EXPOSITION

THE PROLOGUE

IN WHICH THE PROBLEM OF THE BOOK IS INDIRECTLY STATED.

Chap. I., vv. 1-11.

The search for the summum bonum, the quest of the Chief Good, is the theme of the Book Ecclesiastes. Naturally we look to find this theme, problem, this "riddle of the painful earth," distinctly stated in the opening verses of the Book. It is stated, but not distinctly. For the Book is an autobiographical poem, the journal of the Preacher's inward life set forth in a dramatic form. "A man of ripe wisdom and mature experience, he takes us into his confidence. He unclasps the secret volume, and invites us to read it with him. He lays before us what he has been, what he has thought and done, what he has seen and felt and suffered; and then he asks us to listen to the judgment which he has deliberately formed on a review of the whole." [24] But that he may the more reservedly lay bare his heart to us, he uses the Poet's privilege, and presents himself to us under a mask and wrapped in Solomon's ample mantle. And a dramatic poet conveys his conceptions of human character and circumstance and action, not by direct picturesque descriptions, but, placing men before us "in their habit as they lived," he makes them speak to us, and leaves us to infer their character and condition from their words.

In accordance with the rules of his art, the dramatic Preacher brings himself on the stage of his poem, permits us to hear his most penetrating and characteristic utterances, confesses his own most secret and inward experiences, and thus enables us to conceive and to judge him. He is true to his artistic canons from the outset. His prologue, unlike that of the Book of Job, is cast in the dramatic form. Instead of giving us a clear statement of the moral problem he is about to discuss, he opens with the characteristic utterances of the man who, wearied with many futile endeavours, gathers up his remaining strength to recount the experiments he has tried and the conclusion he has reached. Like Browning, one of the most dramatic of modern poets, he plunges abruptly into his theme, and speaks to us from the first through "feigned lips." Just as in reading the Soliloquy of the Spanish Cloister, or the Epistle of Karshish, the Arab Physician, or a score other of Browning's Poems, we have first to glance through it in order to collect the scattered hints which indicate the speaker and the time, and then laboriously to think ourselves back, by their help, into the time and conditions of the speaker, so also with this Hebrew poem. It opens abruptly with "words of the Preacher," who is at once the author and the hero of the drama. "Who is he," we ask, "and what?" "When did he live, and what place did he fill?" And at present we can only reply, He is the voice of one crying in the wilderness of Oriental antiquity, and saying, "Vanity of vanities! all is vanity!" [25] For what intent, then, does his voice break the long silence? Of what ethical mood is this pathetic note the expression? What prompts his despairing cry?

It is the old contrast--old as literature, old as man--between the ordered steadfastness of nature and the disorder and brevity of human life. The Preacher gazes on the universe above and around him. The ancient earth is firm and strong beneath his feet. The sun runs his race with joy, sinks exhausted into its ocean bed, but rises on the morrow, like a giant refreshed with old wine, to renew its course. The variable and inconstant wind, which bloweth where it listeth, blows from the same quarters, runs through the very circuit which was its haunt in the time of the world's grey fathers. The streams which ebb and flow, which go and come, run along time-worn beds and are fed from their ancient source. But man, "to one point constant never," shifts from change to change. As compared with the calm uniformity of nature, his life is a mere phantasy, passing for ever through a tedious and limited range of forms, each of which is as unsubstantial as the fabric of a vision, many of which are as base and sordid as they are unreal, and all of which, for ever in a flux, elude the grasp of those who pursue them, or disappoint those who hold them in their hands. "All is vanity; for man has no profit," no adequate and enduring reward, "for all his labour;" literally, "no balance, no surplus, on the balance-sheet of life:" less happy, because less stable, than the earth on which he dwells, he comes and goes, while the earth goes on for ever (vv. 2-4).

This painful contrast between the ordered stability of nature and the changeful and profitless disorder of human life is emphasized by a detailed reference to the large natural forces which rule the world, and which abide unchanged, although to us they seem the very types of change. The figure of ver. 5 is, of course, that of the racer. The sun rises every morning to run its course, pursues it through the day, "pants," as one well-nigh breathless, toward its goal, and sinks at night into its subterraneous bed in the sea; but, though exhausted and breathless at night, it rises on the morrow refreshed, and eager, like a strong, swift man, to renew its daily race. In ver. 6 the wind is represented as having a regular law and circuit, though it now blows South, and now veers round to the North. The East and West are not mentioned, probably because they are tacitly referred to in the rising and setting sun of the previous verse: all the four quarters are included between the two. In ver. 7 the streams are described as returning on their sources; but there is no allusion here, as we might suppose, to the tides,--and indeed tidal rivers are comparatively rare,--or to the rain which brings back the water evaporated from the surface of the streams and of the sea. The reference is, rather, to an ancient conception of the physical order of nature held by the Hebrew as by other races, according to which the ocean, fed by the streams, sent back a constant supply through subterraneous passages and channels, in which the salt was filtered out of it; through these they supposed the rivers to return to the place whence they came. The ruling sentiment of these verses is that, while all the natural elements and forces, even the most variable and inconstant, renew their strength and return upon their course, for frail man there is no return; permanence and uniformity characterise them, while transitoriness and instability mark him for their own. They seem to vanish and disappear; the sun sinks, the winds lull, the streams run dry; but they all come back again: for him there is no coming back; once gone, he is gone for ever.

But it is vain to talk of these or other instances of the weary yet restless activity of the universe; "man cannot utter it." For, besides these elemental illustrations, the world is crowded with illustrations of incessant change, which yet move within narrow bounds and do nothing to relieve its sameliness. So numerous are they, so innumerable, that the curious eye and inquisitive ear of man would be worn out before they had completed the tale of them: and if eye and ear could never be satisfied with hearing and seeing, how much less the slower tongue with speaking (ver. 8)? All through the universe what hath been still is and will be; what was done is done still and always will be done; the sun still running the same race, the winds still blowing from the same points, the streams still flowing between the same banks and returning by the same channels. If any man suppose that he has discovered new phenomena, any natural fact which has not been repeating itself from the beginning, it is only because he is ignorant of that which has been from of old (vv. 9, 10). [26] Yet, while in nature all things return on their course and abide for ever, man's day is soon spent, his force soon exhausted. He does not return; nay, he is not so much as remembered by those who come after him. Just as we have forgotten those who were before us, so those who live after us will forget us (ver. 11). The burden of all this unintelligible world lies heavily on the Preacher's soul. He is weary of the world's "everlasting sameness." The miseries and confusions of the human lot baffle and oppress his thoughts. Above all, the contrast between Nature and Man, between its massive and stately permanence and the frailty and brevity of our existence, breeds in him the despairing mood of which we have the keynote in his cry, "Vanity of vanities, vanity of vanities, all is vanity!"

Yet this is not the only, not the inevitable, mood of the mind as it ponders that great contrast. We have learned to look upon it with other, perhaps with wider, eyes. We say, How grand, how soothing, how hopeful is the spectacle of nature's uniformity! How it lifts us above the fluctuations of inward thought, and gladdens us with a sense of stability and repose! As we see the ancient inviolable laws working out into the same gracious and beautiful results day after day and year by year, and reflect that "what has been will be," we are redeemed from our bondage to vanity and corruption; we look up with composed and reverent trust to Him who is our God and Father, and onward to the stable and glorious immortality we are to spend with Him; we argue with Habakkuk (chap. i. ver. 12), "Art not Thou from everlasting, O Lord our God, our Holy One? We shall not die," but live.

But if we did not know the Ruler of the universe to be our God and Father; if our thoughts had still to "jump the life to come" or to leap at it with a mere guess; if we had to cross the gulf of death on no more solid bridge than a Peradventure; if, in short, our life were infinitely more troubled and uncertain than it is, and the true good of life and its bright sustaining hope were still to seek, how would it be with us then? Then, like the Preacher, we might feel the steadfastness and uniformity of nature as an affront to our vanity and weakness. In place of drinking in hope and composure from the fair visage and unbroken order of the universe, we might deem its face to be darkened with a frown or its eye to be glancing on us with bitter irony. Instead of finding in its inevitable order and permanence a hopeful prophecy of our recovery into an unbroken order and an enduring peace, we might passionately demand why, on an abiding earth and under an unchanging heaven, we should die and be forgotten; why, more inconstant than the variable wind, more evanescent than the parching stream, one generation should go never to return, and another generation come to enjoy the gains of those who were before them, and to blot their memory from the earth.

This, indeed, has been the impassioned protest and outcry of every age. Literature is full of it. The contrast between the tranquil unchanging sky, with its myriads of pure lustrous stars, which are always

Samuel Cox, D.D.

there and always in a happy concert, and the frailty of man rushing blindly through his brief and perturbed course has lent its ground-tones to the poetry of every race. We meet it everywhere. It is the oldest of old songs. In all the many languages of the divided earth we hear how the generations of men pass swiftly and stormfully across its bosom, "searching the serene heavens with the inquest of their beseeching looks," but winning no response; asking always, and always in vain, "Why are we thus? why are we thus? frail as the moth, and of few days like the flower?" It is this contrast between the serenity and the stability of nature and the frailty and turbulence of man which afflicts Coheleth and drives him to conclusions of despair. Here is man, "so noble in reason, so infinite in faculty, in apprehension so like a god," longing with an ardent intensity for the peace which results from the equipoise and happy occupation of his various powers; and yet his whole life is wasted in labours and tumults, in perplexity and strife; he goes to his grave with his cravings unsatisfied, his powers untrained, unharmonised, knowing no rest till he lies in the narrow bed from which is no uprising! What wonder if to such an one as he "this goodly frame, the earth, seems but a sterile promontory" stretching out a little space into the dark, infinite void; "this most excellent canopy, the air ... this brave o'erhanging firmament, this majestical roof fretted with golden fire," nothing but "a foul, pestilential congregation of vapours"? What wonder if, for him, the very beauty of nature should turn into a repulsive hideousness, and its steadfast, unchanging order be held a satire on the disorder and vanity of his life?

Solomon, moreover,--and Solomon in his premature old age, sated and weary, is the mask under which the Preacher conceals his natural face,--had had a large experience of life, had tried its ambitions, its lusts, its pursuits and pleasures; he had tested every promise of good which it held forth, and found them all illusory; he had drunk of every stream, and found no pure living water with which he could slake his thirst. And men such as he, sated but not satisfied, jaded with voluptuous delights and without the peace of faith, commonly look out on the world with haggard eyes. They feed their despair on the natural order and purity which they feel to be a rebuke to the impurity of their own restless and perturbed hearts. Many of us have, no doubt, stood on Richmond Hill, and looked with softening eyes on the rich pastures dotted with cattle, and broken with clumps of trees through which shoot up village spires, while the full, placid Thames winds in many a curve through pasture and wood. It is not a grand or romantic scene; but on a quiet evening, in the long level rays of the setting sun, it is a scene to inspire content and thankful, peaceful thoughts. Wilberforce tells us that he once stood in the balcony of a villa looking down on this scene. Beside him stood the owner of the villa, a duke notorious for his profligacy in a profligate age; and as they looked across the stream, the duke cried out, "O that river! there it runs, on and on, and I so weary of it!" And there you have the very mood of this Prologue; the mood for which the fair, smiling heavens and the gracious, bountiful earth carry no benediction of peace, because they are reflected from a heart all tossed into crossing and impure waves.

All things depend on the heart we bring to them. This very contrast between Nature and Man has no despair in it, breeds no dispeace or anger in the heart at leisure from itself and at peace with God. Tennyson, for instance, makes a merry musical brook sing to us on this very theme.

> "I come from haunts of coot and hern,
> I make a sudden sally
> And sparkle out among the fern,
> To bicker down a valley.
> "I chatter over stony ways
> In little sharps and trebles,
> I bubble into eddying bays,
> I babble on the pebbles.
> "I chatter, chatter as I flow
> To join the brimming river;
> For men may come and men may go,
> But I go on for ever.
> "I steal by lawns and grassy plots,
> I slide by hazel covers;
> I move the sweet forget-me-nots
> That grow for happy lovers.
> "I slip, I slide, I gloom, I glance
> Among my skimming swallows;
> I make the netted sunbeams dance
> Against my sanded shallows.
> "I murmur under moon and stars
> In brambly wildernesses;
> I linger by my shingly bars;
> I loiter round my cresses.

The Expositor's Bible: Ecclesiastes
> *"And out again I curve and flow*
> *To join the brimming river;*
> *For men may come and men may go*
> *But I go on for ever."*

It is the very plaint of the Preacher set to sweet music. He murmurs, "One generation passeth, and another generation cometh, but the earth abideth for ever;" while the refrain of the Brook is,--

> *"For men may come and men may go,*
> *But I go on for ever."*

Yet we do not feel that the Song of the Brook should feed any mood of grief and despair. The tune that it sings to the sleeping woods all night is "a cheerful tune." By some subtle process we are made to share us bright, tender hilarity, though we too are of the men that come and go. Into what a fume would the Hebrew Preacher have been thrown had any little "babbling brook" dared to sing this saucy song to him. He would have felt it as an insult, and have assumed that the merry, innocent creature was "crowing" over the swiftly passing generations of men. But, for the Christian Poet, the Brook sings a song whose blithe dulcet strain attunes the heart to the quiet harmonies of peace and good-will.

Again I say all depends on the heart we turn to nature. It was because his heart was heavy with the memory of many sins and many failures, because too the lofty Christian hopes were beyond his reach, that this "son of David" grew mournful and bitter in her presence.

This, then, is the mood in which the Preacher commences his quest of the Chief Good. He is driven to it by the need of finding that in which he can rest. As a rule, it is only on the most stringent compulsions that we any of us undertake this high Quest. Of their profound need of a Chief Good most men are but seldom and faintly conscious; but to the favoured few, who are to lead and mould the public thought, it comes with a force they cannot resist. It was thus with Coheleth. He could not endure to think that those who have "all things put under their feet" should lie at the mercy of accidents from which their realm is exempt; that they should be the mere fools of change, while that abides unchanged for ever. And, therefore, he set out to discover the conditions on which they might become partakers of the order and stability and peace of nature; the conditions on which, raised above all the tides and storms of change, they might sit calm and serene even though the heavens should be folded as a scroll and the earth be shaken from its foundations. This, and only this, will he recognise as the Chief Good, the Good appropriate to the nature of man, because capable of satisfying all his cravings and supplying all his wants.

Footnotes:

24. Dean Perowne, in The Expositor, First Series, vol. ix.
25. Compare Horace (Od. iv. 7, 9): Pulvis et umbra sumus.
26. So Marcus Aurelius (Meditt., xi. 1): "They that come after us will see nothing new; and they who went before saw nothing more than we have seen."

Samuel Cox, D.D.

FIRST SECTION

THE QUEST OF THE CHIEF GOOD IN WISDOM AND IN PLEASURE.

Chap. I., Ver. 12, to Chap. II., Ver. 26.

Oppressed by his profound sense of the vanity of the life which man lives amid the play of permanent natural forces, Coheleth sets out on the search for that true and supreme Good which it will be well for the sons of men to pursue through their brief day; the good which will sustain them under all their toils, and be "a portion" so large and enduring as to satisfy even their vast desires.

The Quest in Wisdom. Ch. i., vv. 12-18.

1. And, as was natural in so wise a man, he turns first to Wisdom. He gives himself diligently to inquire into all the actions and toils of men. He will ascertain whether a larger acquaintance with their conditions, a deeper insight into the facts, a more just and complete estimate of their lot, will remove the depression which weighs upon his heart. He devotes himself earnestly to this Quest, and acquires a "greater wisdom than all who were before him."

This wisdom, however, is not a scientific knowledge of facts or of social and political laws, nor is it the result of philosophical speculations on "the first good or the first fair," or on the nature and constitution of man. It is the wisdom that is born of wide and varied experience, not of abstract study. He acquaints himself with the facts of human life, with the circumstances, thoughts, feelings, hopes, and aims of all sorts and conditions of men. He is fain to know "all that men do under the sun," "all that is done under heaven." Like the Arabian Caliph, "the good Haroun Alraschid," we may suppose that Coheleth goes forth in disguise to visit all quarters of the city; to talk with barbers, druggists, calenders, porters, with merchants and mariners, husbandmen and tradesmen, mechanics and artizans; to try conclusions with travellers and with the blunt wits of home-keeping men. He will look with his own eyes and learn for himself what their lives are like, how they conceive of the human lot, and what, if any, are the mysteries which sadden and perplex them. He will ascertain whether they have any key that will unlock his perplexities, any wisdom that will solve his problems or help him to bear his burden with a more cheerful heart. Because his depression was fed by every fresh contemplation of the order of the universe, he turns from nature to "the proper study of mankind."

But this also he finds a heavy and disappointing task. After a wide and dispassionate scrutiny, when he has "seen much wisdom and knowledge," he concludes that man has no fair reward "for all his labour that he laboureth under the sun," that no wisdom avails to set straight that which is crooked in human affairs, or to supply that which is lacking in them. The sense of vanity bred by his contemplation of the stedfast round of nature only grows more profound and more painful as he reflects on the numberless and manifold disorders which afflict humanity. And hence, before he ventures on a new experiment, he makes a pathetic appeal to the heart which he had so earnestly applied to the search, and in which he had stored up so large and various a knowledge, and confesses that "even this is vexation of spirit," that "in much wisdom is much sadness," and that "to multiply knowledge is to multiply sorrow."

And whether we consider the nature of the case or the conditions of the time in which this Book was written, we shall not be surprised at the mournful conclusion to which he comes. For the time was full of cruel oppressions and wrongs. Life was insecure. To acquire property was to court extortion. The Hebrews, and even the conquering race which ruled them, were slaves to the caprice of satraps and magistrates whose days were wasted in revelry and in the unbridled indulgence of their lusts. And to go among the various conditions of men groaning under a despotism like that of the Turk, whose foot strikes with barrenness every spot on which it treads; to see all the fair rewards of honest toil withheld, the noble degraded and the foolish exalted, the righteous trodden down by the feet of the wicked; all this was not likely to quicken cheerful thoughts in a wise man's heart: instead of solving, it could but complicate and darken the problems over which he was already brooding in despair.

And, apart from the special wrongs and oppressions of the time, it is inevitable that the thoughtful student of men and manners should become a sadder as he becomes a wiser man. To multiply knowledge, at least of this kind, is to multiply sorrow. We need not be cynics and leave our tub only to reflect on the dishonesty of our neighbours, we need only go through the world with open and observant eyes in order to learn that "in much wisdom is much sadness." Recall the wisest of modern times, those who have had the most intimate acquaintance with man and men, Goethe and Carlyle for example; are they not all touched with a profound sadness? [27] Do they not look with some scorn on the common life of the mass of men, with its base passions and pleasures, struggles and rewards? and, in proportion as they have the spirit of Christ, is not their very scorn kindly, springing from a pity which lies deeper than itself? Did not even the Master Himself, though full of ruth and grace, share their feeling as He saw publicans growing rich by extortion, hypocrites mounting to Moses' chair, subtle, cruel foxes couched on thrones, scribes hiding the key of knowledge, and the blind multitude following their blind leaders into the ditch?

Nay, if we look out on the world of to-day, can we say that even the majority of men are wise and pure? Is it always the swift who win the race, and the strong who carry off the honours of the battle? Do none of our "intelligent lack bread," nor any of the learned favour? Are there no fools lifted to high places to show with how little wisdom the world is governed, and no brave and noble breasts dinted by the blows of hostile circumstances or wounded by "the slings and arrows of outrageous fortune"? Are all our workmen diligent and all our masters fair? Are no false measures and balances known in our markets, and no frauds on our exchanges? Are none of our homes dungeons, with fathers and husbands for jailors? Do we never hear, as we stand without, the sound of cruel blows and the shrieks of tortured captives? Are there no hypocrites in our Churches "that with devotion's visage sugar o'er" a corrupt heart? And do the best men always gain the highest place and honour? Are there none in our midst who have to bear--

"The whips and scorns of time,
The oppressor's wrong, the proud man's contumely,
The pangs of despised love, the laws delay.
The insolence of office, and the spurns
That patient merit of the unworthy takes"?

Alas, if we think to find the true Good in a wide and varied knowledge of the conditions of men, their hopes and fears, their struggles and successes, their loves and hates, their rights and wrongs, their pleasures and their pains, we shall but share the defeat of the Preacher, and repeat his bitter cry, "Vanity of vanities, vanity of vanities, all is vanity!" For, as he himself implies at the very outset (ver. 13), "this sore task," this eternal quest of a wisdom which will solve the problems and remove the inequalities of human life, is God's gift to the children of men,--this search for a solution they never reach. Age after age, unwarned by the failure of those who took this road before them, they renew the hopeless quest.

The Quest in Pleasure. Ch. ii., vv. 1-11.

2. But if we cannot reach the object of our Quest in Wisdom, we may, perchance, find it in Pleasure. This experiment also the Preacher has tried, tried on the largest scale and under the most auspicious conditions. Wisdom failing to satisfy the large desires of his soul, or even to lift it from its depression, he turns to mirth. [28] Once more, as he forthwith announces, he is disappointed in the result. He pronounces mirth a brief madness; in itself, like wisdom, a good, it is not the Chief Good; to make it supreme is to rob it of its natural charm.

Not content with this general verdict, however, he recounts the details of his experiment, that he may deter us from repeating it. Speaking in the person of Solomon and utilising the facts of his experience, Coheleth claims to have started in the quest with the greatest advantages; for "what can he do who cometh after the king whom they made king long ago?" He surrounded himself with all the luxuries of an Oriental prince, not out of any vulgar love of show and ostentation, nor out of any strong sensual addictions, but that he might discover wherein the secret and fascination of pleasure lay, and what it could do for a man who pursued it wisely. He built himself new, costly palaces, as the Sultan of Turkey used to do almost every year. He laid out paradises, planted them with vines and fruit-trees of every sort, and large shady groves to screen off and attemper the heat of the sun. [29] He dug great tanks and reservoirs of water, and cut channels which carried the cool vital stream through the gardens and to the roots of the trees. He bought men and maids, and surrounded himself with the retinue of servants and slaves requisite to keep his palaces and paradises in order, to serve his sumptuous tables, to swell his pomp: i.e. he gathered together such a train of ministers, attendants, domestics, indoor and outdoor slaves, as is still thought necessary to the dignity of an Oriental "lord." His herds of flocks, a main source of Oriental wealth, were of finer strain and larger in number than had been known before. He amassed enormous treasures of silver and gold, the common Oriental hoard. He collected the peculiar treasures "of kings and of the kingdoms;" whatever special commodity was yielded by any foreign land was caught up for his use by his officers or presented to him by his allies. [30] He hired famous musicians and singers, and gave himself to those delights of harmony which have had a peculiar charm for the Hebrews of all ages. He crowded his harem with the beauties both of his own and of foreign lands. He withheld nothing from them that his eyes desired, and kept not his heart from any pleasure. He set himself seriously and intelligently to make happiness his portion; and, while cherishing or cheering his body with pleasures, he did not rush into them with the blind eagerness "whose violent property foredoes itself" and defeats its own ends. His "mind guided him wisely" amid his delights; his "wisdom helped him" to select, and combine, and vary them, to enhance and prolong their sweetness by a certain art and temperance in me enjoyment of them.

> "He built his soul a lordly pleasure-house,
> Wherein at ease for aye to dwell;
> He said, 'Oh Soul, make merry and carouse,
> Dear Soul, for all is well!'"

Alas, all was not well, though he took much pains to make and think it well. Even his choice delights soon palled upon his taste, and brought on conclusions of disgust. Even in his lordly pleasure-house he was haunted by the grim, menacing spectres which troubled him before it was built. In the harem, in the paradise he had planted, under the groves, beside the fountains, at the sumptuous banquet,--a bursting bubble, a falling leaf, an empty wine cup, a passing blush, sufficed to bring back the thought of the brevity and the emptiness of life. When he had run the full career of pleasure, and turned to contemplate his delights and the labour they had cost him, he found that these also were vanity and vexation of spirit, that there was no "profit" in them, that they could not satisfy the deep, incessant craving of the soul for a true and lasting Good.

Is not his sad verdict as true as it is sad? We have not his wealth of resources. Nevertheless there may have been a time when our hearts were as intent on pleasure as was his. We may have pursued whatever sensuous, intellectual, or aesthetic excitements were open to us with a growing eagerness till we have lived in a whirl of craving and stimulating desire and indulgence, in which the claims of duty have been neglected and the rebukes of conscience unheeded. And if we have passed through this experience, if we have been carried for a time into this giddying round, have we not come out of it jaded, exhausted, despising ourselves for our folly, disgusted with what once seemed the very top and crown of delight? Do we not mourn, our after life through, over energies wasted and opportunities lost? Are we not sadder, if wiser, men for our brief frenzy? As we return to the sober duties and simple joys of life, do not we say to Mirth, "Thou art mad!" and to Pleasure, "What canst thou do for us?" Yes, our verdict is that of the Preacher, "Lo, this too is vanity!" Non enim hilaritate, nec lascivia, nec visu, aut joco, comite levitatis, sed sæpe etiam tristes firmitate, et constantia sunt beati. [31]

Wisdom and Mirth compared. Ch. ii., vv. 12-23.

It is characteristic of the philosophic temper of our Author, I think, that, after pronouncing Wisdom and Mirth vanities in which the true Good is not to be found, he does not at once proceed to try a new experiment, but pauses to compare these two "vanities," and to reason out his preference of one over the other. His vanity is wisdom. For it is only in one respect that he puts mirth and wisdom on an equality, viz. that they neither of them are, or lead up to, the supreme Good. In all other respects he affirms wisdom to be as much better than pleasure as light is better than darkness, as much better as it is to have eyes that see the light than to be blind and walk in a constant gloom (vv. 12-14). It is because wisdom is a light and enables men to see that he accords it his preference. It is by the light of wisdom that he has learned the vanity of mirth, nay, the insufficiency of wisdom itself. But for that light he might still be pursuing pleasures which could not satisfy, or laboriously acquiring a knowledge which would only deepen his sadness. Wisdom had opened his eyes to see that he must seek the Good which gives rest and peace in other regions. He no longer goes on his Quest in utter blindness, with all the world before him where to choose, but with no indication of the course he should, or should not, take. He has already learned that two large provinces of human life will not yield him what he seeks, that he must expend no more of his brief day and failing energies on these.

Therefore wisdom is better than mirth. Nevertheless it is not best, nor can it remove the dejections of a thoughtful heart. Somewhere there is, there must be, that which is better still. For wisdom cannot explain to him why the same fate should befall both the sage and the fool (ver. 15), nor can it abate the anger that burns within him against an injustice so obvious and flagrant. Wisdom cannot even explain why, even if the sage must die no less than the fool, both must be forgotten wellnigh as soon as they are gone (vv. 16, 17); nor can it soften the hatred of life and its labours which this lesser yet patent injustice has kindled in his heart. Nay, wisdom, for all so brightly as it shines, throws no light on an injustice which, if of lower degree, frets and perplexes his mind,--why a man who has laboured prudently and dexterously and has acquired great gains should, when he dies, leave all to one who has not laboured therein, without even the poor consolation of knowing whether he will be a wise man or an idiot (vv. 19-21). In short, the whole skein of life is in a dismal tangle which wisdom itself, dearly as he loves it, cannot unravel; and the tangle is that man has no fair "profit" from his labours, "since his task grieveth and vexeth him all his days, and even at night his heart hath no rest;" and when he dies he loses all his gains, such as they are, for ever, and cannot so much as be sure that his heir will be any the better for

The Expositor's Bible: Ecclesiastes
them. "This also is vanity" (vv. 22, 23).

The Conclusion. Ch. ii. vv. 24-26.
And yet, good things are surely good, and there is a wise and gracious enjoyment of earthly delights. It is right that a man should eat and drink, and take a natural pleasure in his toils and gains. Who, indeed, has a stronger claim than the labourer himself to eat and enjoy the fruit of his labours? Still, even this natural enjoyment is the gift of God; apart from his blessing the heaviest toils will produce but a scanty harvest, and the faculty of enjoying that harvest may be lacking. It is lacking to the sinner; his task is to heap up gains which the good will inherit. But he that is good before God will have the gains of the sinner added to his own, with wisdom to enjoy both. [32] This, whatever appearances may sometimes suggest, is the law of God's giving: that the good shall have abundance, while the bad lack; that more shall be given to him who has wisdom to use what he has aright, while from him who is destitute of this wisdom, even that which he hath shall be taken away. Nevertheless even this wise use and enjoyment of temporal good does not and cannot satisfy the craving heart of man; even this, when it is made the ruling aim and chief good of life, is vexation of spirit.

***

Thus the First Act of the Drama closes with a negative. The moral problem is as far from being solved as at the outset. All we have learned is that one or two avenues along which we urge the Quest will not lead us to the end we seek. As yet the Preacher has only the ad interim conclusion to offer us, that both Wisdom and Mirth are good, though neither, nor both combined, is the supreme Good; that we are therefore to acquire wisdom and knowledge, and to blend pleasure with our toils; that we are to believe pleasure and wisdom to be the gifts of God, to believe also that they are bestowed, not in caprice, but according to a law which deals out good to the good and evil to the evil. We shall have other opportunities of weighing and appraising his counsel--it is often repeated--and of seeing how it works into and forms part of Coheleth's final solution of the painful riddle of the earth, the baffling mystery of life.

Footnotes:

27. Père Lacordaire has a fine passage on this theme. "Weak and little minds find here below a nourishment which suffices for their intellect and satisfies their love. They do not discover the emptiness of visible things because they are incapable of sounding them to the bottom. But a soul which God has drawn nearer to the Infinite very soon feels the narrow limits within which it is pent; it experiences moments of inexpressible sadness, the cause of which for a long time remains a mystery; it even seems as though some strange concurrence of events must have chanced in order thus to disturb its life; and all the while the trouble comes from a higher source. In reading the lives of the Saints, we find that nearly all of them have felt that sweet melancholy of which the ancients said that there was no genius without it. In fact, melancholy is inseparable from every mind that looks below the surface and every heart that feels profoundly. Not that we should take complacency in it, for it is a malady that enervates when we do not shake it off; and it has but two remedies--Death or God." Elsewhere, still quite in the spirit of the Preacher, he says: "Every day I feel more and more that all is vanity. I cannot leave my heart in this heap of mud."

28. So Goethe's Faust, after having failed to solve the insoluble problems of life by study and research, "plunges deep in pleasure," that he "may thus still the burning thirst of passionate desire."

29. "One such pleasaunce as this there was at Etam, Solomon's Belvedere, as Josephus informs us (Antiq., VIII. 7, 3). Thither it was the custom of the king, he says, to resort when he made his morning excursions from the city, clad in a white garment, and driving his chariot, surrounded by his body-guard of young men in the flower of their age, clad in Tyrian purple, and with gold dust strewed upon their hair, so that their whole head sparkled when the sun shone upon it, and mounted upon horses from the royal stables, famed for their beauty and fleetness."--Dr. Perowne, The Expositor, First Series, vol. x.

30. In speaking of the Persian revenue, Rawlinson says that besides a definite money payment, "a payment, the nature and amount of which were also fixed, had to be made in kind, each province being required to furnish that commodity, or those commodities, for which it was most celebrated,"--as, for example, grain, sheep, cattle, mules, fine breeds of horses, beautiful slaves. The Five Great Monarchies, vol. iv., chap. vii., p. 421.

31. Cicero, De Fin., Lib. II., Cap. 20.

32. This affirmation, so surprising at first sight, is also made by Job (chap. xxvii., vv. 15, 16), "This is the doom of the wicked man from God.... Though he heap up silver like dust, and gather robes as mire, that which he hath gathered shall the righteous wear, and the innocent shall divide his silver."

Samuel Cox, D.D.

SECOND SECTION

THE QUEST OF THE CHIEF GOOD IN DEVOTION TO THE AFFAIRS OF BUSINESS.

Chap. III., Ver. 1, to Chap. V., Ver. 20.

I. If the true Good is not to be found in the School where Wisdom utters her voice, nor in the Garden in which Pleasure spreads her lures: may it not be found in the Market, in devotion to Business and Public Affairs? The Preacher will try this experiment also. He gives himself to study and consider it. But at the very outset he discovers that he is in the iron grip of immutable Divine ordinances, by which "seasons" are appointed for every undertaking under heaven (ver. 1), ordinances which derange man's best-laid schemes, and "shape his ends, rough-hew them how he will," that no one can do anything to purpose "apart from God," except by conforming to the ordinances, or laws, in which He has expressed His will (comp. chap, ii., vv. 24-26).

The Quest obstructed by Divine Ordinances; Ch. iii., vv. 1-15.

The time of birth, for instance, and the time of death, are ordained by a Power over which men have no control; they begin to be, and they cease to be, at hours whose stroke they can neither hasten nor retard. The season for sowing and the season for reaping are fixed without any reference to their wish; they must plant and gather in when the unchangeable laws of nature will permit (ver. 2). Even those violent deaths, and those narrow escapes from death, which seem most purely fortuitous, are predetermined; as are also the accidents which befall our abodes (ver. 3). So, again, if only because determined by these accidents, are the feelings with which we regard them, our weeping and our laughter, our mourning and our rejoicing (ver. 4). If we only clear a plot of ground from stones in order that we may cultivate it, or that we may fence it in with a wall; or if an enemy cast stones over our arable land to unfit it for uses of husbandry--a malignant act frequent in the East--and we have painfully to gather them out again: even this, which seems so purely within the scope of human free-will, is also within the scope of the Divine decrees--as are the very embraces we bestow on those dear to us, or withhold from them (ver. 5). The varying and unstable desires which prompt us to seek this object or that as earnestly as we afterwards carelessly cast it away, and the passions which impel us to rend our garments over our losses, and by-and-bye to sew up the rents not without some little wonder that we should ever have been so deeply moved by that which now sits so lightly on us; these passions and desires, which at one time strike us dumb with grief and so soon after make us voluble with joy, with all our fleeting and easily-moved hates and loves, strifes and reconciliations, move within the circle of law, although they wear so lawless a look, and are obsequious to the fixed canons of Heaven (vv. 6-8). They travel their cycles; they return in their appointed order. The uniformity of nature is reproduced in the uniform recurrence of the chances and changes of human life; for in this, as in that, God repeats Himself, recalling the past (ver. 15). The thing that is is that which hath been, and that which will be. Social laws are as constant and as inflexible as natural laws. The social generalisations of modern science--as given, for instance, in Buckle's History--are but a methodical elaboration of the conclusion at which the Preacher here arrives.

Of what use, then, was it for men to "kick against the goads," to attempt to modify immutable ordinances? "Whatever God hath ordained continueth for ever; nothing can be added to it, and nothing can be taken from it" (ver. 14). Nay, why should we care to alter or modify the social order? Everything is beautiful and appropriate in its season, from birth to death, from war to peace (ver. 11). If we cannot find the satisfying Good in the events and affairs of life, that is not because we could devise a happier order for them, but because "God hath put eternity into our hearts" as well as time, and did not intend that we should be satisfied till we attain an eternal good. If only we "understood" that, if only we recognised Gods design for us "from beginning to end," and suffered eternity no less than time to have its due of us, we should not fret ourselves in vain endeavours to change the unchangeable, or to find an enduring good in that which is fugitive and perishable. We should rejoice and do ourselves good all our brief life (Ver. 12); we should eat and drink and take pleasure in our labours (ver. 13); we should feel that this faculty for innocently enjoying simple pleasures and wholesome toils is "a gift of God;" we should conclude that God had ordained that regular cycle and order of events which so often forestalls the wish and endeavour of the moment, in order that we should fear Him in place of relying on

The Expositor's Bible: Ecclesiastes
ourselves (ver. 14), and trust our future to Him who so wisely and graciously recalls the past.

And by Human Injustice and Perversity. Ch. iii., v. 16.-Ch. iv., v. 3.

But not only are our endeavours to find the "good" of our labours thwarted by the gracious, inflexible laws of the just God; they are often baffled by the injustice of ungracious men. In the days of Coheleth, Iniquity sat in the seat of justice, wresting all rules of equity to its base private ends (ver. 16). Unjust judges and rapacious satraps put the fair rewards of labour and skill and integrity in jeopardy, insomuch that if a man by industry and thrift, by a wise observance of Divine laws and by taking occasions as they rose, had acquired affluence, he was too often, in the expressive Eastern phrase, but as a sponge which any petty despot might squeeze. The frightful oppressions of the time were a heavy burden to the Hebrew Preacher. He brooded over them, seeking for aids to faith and comfortable words wherewith to solace the oppressed. For a moment he thought he had lit on the true comfort, "Well, well," he said within himself, "God will judge the righteous and the wicked; for there is a time for everything and for every deed with Him" (ver. 17). Could he have rested in this thought, it would have been "a sovereign balm" to him, or indeed to any other Hebrew; although to us, who have learned to desire the redemption rather than the punishment of the wicked, their redemption through their inevitable punishments, the true comfort would still have been wanting. But he could not rest in it, could not hold it fast, and confesses that he could not. He lays his heart bare before us. We are permitted to trace the fluctuating thoughts and emotions which swept across it. No sooner has he whispered to his heart that God, who is at leisure from Himself and has endless time at his command, will visit the oppressors and avenge the oppressed, than his thoughts take a new turn, and he adds: "And yet God may have sifted the children of men only to shew them that they are no better than the beasts" (ver. 18): this may be his aim in all the wrongs by which they are tried. Repugnant as the thought is, it nevertheless fascinates him for the instant, and he yields to its wasting and degrading magic. He not only fears, suspects, thinks that man is no better than a beast; he is quite sure of it, and proceeds to argue it out. His argument is very sweeping, very sombre. "A mere chance is man, and the beast a mere chance." Both spring from a mere accident, no one can tell how, and have a blind hazard for a creator; and "both are subject to the same chance," or mischance, throughout their lives, all the decisions of their intelligence and will being overruled by the decrees of an inscrutable fate. Both perish under the same power of death, suffer the same pangs of dissolution, are taken at unawares by the same invisible yet resistless force. The bodies of both spring from the same dust, and moulder back into dust. Nay, "both have the same spirit;" and though vain man sometimes boasts that at death his spirit goeth upward, while that of the beast goeth downward, yet who can prove it? For himself, and in his present mood, Coheleth doubts, and even denies it. He is absolutely convinced that in origin and life and death, in body and spirit and final fate, man is as the beast is, and hath no advantage over the beast (vv. 19-21). And therefore he falls back on his old conclusion, though now with a sadder heart than ever, that man will do wisely, that, being so blind and having so dark a prospect, he cannot do more wisely than to take what pleasure and enjoy what good he can amid his labours. If he is a beast, as he is a beast, let him at least learn of the beasts that simple, tranquil enjoyment of the good of the passing moment, untroubled by any vexing presage of what is to come, in which it must be allowed that they are greater proficients than he (ver. 22).

Thus, after rising in the first fifteen verses of this Third Chapter, to an almost Christian height of patience, and resignation, and holy trust in the providence of God, Coheleth is smitten by the injustice and oppressions of man into the depths of a pessimistic materialism.

***

But now a new question arises. The Preacher's survey of human life has shaken his faith even in the conclusion which he has announced from the first, viz., that there is nothing better for a man than a quiet content, a busy cheerfulness, a tranquil enjoyment of the fruit of his toils. This at least he has supposed to be possible: but is it? All the activities, industries, tranquillities of life are jeopardised, now by the inflexible ordinances of Heaven, and again by the capricious tyranny of man. To this tyranny his fellow-countrymen are now exposed. They groan under its heaviest oppressions. As he turns and once more reflects (chap. iv., ver. 1) on their unalleviated and unfriended misery, he doubts whether content, or even resignation, can be expected of them. With a tender sympathy that lingers on the details of their unhappy lot, and deepens into a passionate and despairing melancholy, he witnesses their sufferings and "counts the tears" of the oppressed. With the emphasis of a Hebrew and an Oriental, he marks and emphasises the fact that "they had no comforter," that though "their oppressors were violent, yet they had no comforter." For throughout the East, and among the Jews to this day, the manifestation of sympathy with those who suffer is far more common and ceremonious than it is with us. Neighbours and acquaintances are expected to pay long visits of condolence; friends and kinsfolk will travel long distances to pay them. Their respective places and duties in the house of mourning, their dress, words, bearing, precedence, are regulated by an ancient and elaborate etiquette. And, strange as it may seem to us, these visits are regarded not only as gratifying tokens of respect to the dead, but as a singular relief and comfort to the living. To the Preacher and his fellow-captives, therefore, it would be a bitter aggravation of their grief that, while suffering under the most cruel oppressions of misfortune, they were compelled to forego the solace of these customary tokens of respect and sympathy. As he pondered their sad and unfriended condition, Coheleth--like Job, when his comforters failed him--is moved to curse his day. The dead, he affirms, are happier than the living, [33] --even the dead who died so long ago that the fate most dreaded in the East had befallen them, and the very memory of them had perished from the earth: while happier than either the dead, who have had to suffer in their time, or than the living, whose doom had still to be borne, were those who had never seen the light, never been born into a world all disordered and out of course (vv. 2, 3). [34]

It is rendered hopeless by the base origin of Human Industries. Ch. iv., vv. 4-8.

This stinging sense of the miserable estate of his race has, however, diverted the Preacher from the conduct of the main argument he had in hand: to that he now returns (ver. 4). And now he argues: You cannot hope get good fruit from a bad root. But the several industries in which you are tempted to seek "the chief good and market of your time" have a most base and evil origin; they "spring from man's jealous rivalry with his neighbour." Every man tries to outdo and to outsell his neighbours; to secure a larger business, to surround himself with a more profuse luxury, or to amass an ampler hoard of gold. This business life of yours is utterly selfish, and therefore utterly base. You are not content with a sufficient provision for simple wants. You do not seek your neighbour's good. You have no noble or patriotic aim. Your ruling intention is to enrich yourselves at the expense of neighbours who, in their turn, are your rivals rather than your neighbours, and who try to get the better of you just as you try to get the better of them. Can you hope to find the true Good in a life whose aims are so sordid, whose motives so selfish? The very sluggard who folds his hands in indolence so long as he has bread to eat is a wiser man than you; for he has at least his "handful of quiet," and knows some little enjoyment of life; while you, driven on by jealous competition and the eager cravings of insatiable desire, have neither leisure nor appetite for enjoyment; both your hands are full, indeed, but there is no quiet in them, only labour, labour, labour, with vexation of spirit (vv. 5, 6).

So intense and selfish was this rivalry, increase of appetite growing by what it fed upon, so keen grew the desire to amass, that the Preacher paints a portrait, for which no doubt many a Hebrew might have sat, of a man--nay, rather, of a miser--who, though solitary and kinless, with not even a son or a brother to inherit his wealth, nevertheless hoards up riches to the close of his life; there is no end to his labours; he never can be rich enough to allow himself any enjoyment of his gains (vv. 7, 8).

Yet these are capable of a nobler Motive and Mode. Ch. iv., vv. 9-16.

Now a jealous rivalry culminating in mere avarice,--that surely is not the wisest or noblest spirit of which those are capable who devote themselves to affairs. Even "the idols of the market" may have a purer cult. Business, like Wisdom or Mirth, may neither be, nor contain, the supreme Good: still, like them, it is not in itself and of necessity an evil. There must be a better mode of devotion to it than this selfish and greedy one; and such a mode Coheleth, before he pursues his argument to a close, pauses to point out. As if anticipating a modern theory which grows in favour with the wiser sort of mercantile men, he suggests that co-operation--of course I use the word in its etymological rather than in its technical sense--should be substituted for competition. "Two are better than one," he argues; "union is better than isolation; conjoint labour brings the larger reward" (ver. 9). To bring his suggestion home to the business bosom of men, he uses five illustrations, four of which have a strong Oriental colouring.

The first is that of two pedestrians (ver. 10); if one should fall--and such an accident, owing to the bad roads and long cumbrous robes common in the East, was by no means infrequent--the other is ready to set him on his feet; while, if he is alone, the least that can befall him is that his robe will be trampled and bemired before he can gather himself up again. In the second illustration (ver. 11), our two travellers, wearied by their journey, sleep together at its close. Now in Syria the nights are often keen and frosty, and the heat of the day makes men more susceptible to the cold. The sleeping-chambers, moreover, have only unglazed lattices which let in the frosty air as well as the welcome light; the bed is commonly a simple mat, the bedclothes only the garments worn through the day. And therefore the natives huddle together for the sake of warmth. To lie alone was to lie shivering in the chill night air. The third illustration (ver. 12) is also taken from the East. Our two travellers, lying snug and warm on their common mat, buried in slumber, that "dear repose for limbs with travel tired," were very likely to be disturbed by thieves who had dug a hole through the clay walls of the house, or crept under the tent, to carry off what they could. These thieves, always on the alert for travellers, are marvellously supple, rapid, and silent in their movements; but as the traveller, aware of his danger, commonly puts his "bag of needments" or valuables under his head, it does sometimes happen that the deftest thief will rouse him by withdrawing it. If one of our two wayfarers was thus aroused, he would call on his comrade for help, and between them the thief would stand a poor chance; but the solitary traveller, suddenly roused from sleep, with no helper at hand, might very easily stand a worse chance than the thief. The fourth illustration (ver. 12) is that of the threefold cord--three strands twisted into one, which, as we all know, English no less than Hebrew, is much more than three times as strong as any one of the separate strands.

But in the fifth and most elaborate illustration (vv. 13, 14), we are once more carried back to the East. The slightest acquaintance with Oriental history will teach us how uncertain is the tenure of royal power; how often it has happened that a prisoner has been led from a dungeon to a throne, and a prince suddenly deposed and reduced to impotence and penury. Coheleth supposes such a case. On the one hand, we have a king old, but not venerable, since, long as he has lived, he has not "even yet learned to accept admonition;" he has led a solitary, selfish, suspicious life, secluded himself in his harem, surrounded himself with a troop of flattering courtiers and slaves. On the other hand, we have the poor but wise young man, "the affable youth," who has lived with all sorts and conditions of men, acquainted himself with their habits and wants and desires, and conciliated their regard. His growing popularity alarms the old despot and his minions. He is cast into prison. His wrongs and sufferings endear him to the wronged and suffering people. By a sudden outbreak of popular wrath, by a revolution such as often sweeps through Eastern states, he is set free, and led from the prison to the throne, although he was once so poor that none would do him reverence. This is the picture in the mind's eye of the Preacher; and, as he contemplates it, he rises into a kind of prophetic rapture, and cries, "I see--I see all the living who walk under the sun flocking to the youth who stands up in the old king's stead; there is no end to the multitude of the people over whom he ruleth!" (ver. 15).

By these graphic illustrations Coheleth sets forth the superiority of the sociable over the solitary and selfish temper, of union over isolation, of the neighbourly goodwill which leads men to combine for common ends over the jealous rivalry which prompts them to take advantage of each other, and to labour each for himself alone.

But even as he urges this better, happier temper on men occupied with business and public affairs, even as he contemplates its brightest illustration in the youthful prisoner whose winning and sociable qualities have lifted him to a throne, the old mood of melancholy comes back on him; there is the familiar pathetic break in his voice as he concludes (ver. 16), that even this wise youth, who wins all hearts for a time, will soon be forgotten; that "even this," for all so hopeful as it looks, "is vanity and vexation of spirit."

***

A profound gloom rests on the second act of this Drama. It has already taught us that we are helpless in the grip of laws which we had no voice in making; that we often lie at the mercy of men whose mercy is but a caprice; that in our origin and end, in body and spirit, in faculty and prospect, in our lives and pleasures, we are no better than the beasts which perish: that the avocations into which we plunge, and amid which we seek to forget our sad estate, spring from our jealousy the one of the other, and tend to a lonely miserliness without use or charm. The Preacher's familiar conclusion--"Be tranquil, be content, enjoy as much as you can"--has grown doubtful to him. He has seen the brightest promise come to nought. In a new and profounder sense, "all is vanity and vexation of spirit."

But, though passing through a great darkness, he sees, and reflects, some little light. Even when facts seem to contradict it, he holds fast to the conclusion that wisdom is better than folly, and kindness better than selfishness, and to do good even though you lose by it better than to do evil and gain by it. His faith wavers only for a moment; it never wholly loosens its hold. And, in the fifth chapter, the light grows, though even here the darkness does not altogether disappear. We are sensible that the twilight in which we stand is not that of evening, which will deepen into night, but that of morning, which will shine more and more until the day dawn, and the daystar arise in the calm heaven of patient tranquil hearts.

So also a happier and more effective Method of Worship is open to Men; Ch. v., vv. 1-7.

The men of affairs are led from the vocations of the Market and the intrigues of the Divan into the House of God. Our first glance at the worshippers is not hopeful or inspiriting. For here are men who offer sacrifices in lieu of obedience; and here are men whose prayers are a voluble repetition of phrases which run far in advance of their limping thoughts and desires: and there are men quick to make vows in moments of peril, but slow to redeem them when the peril is past. At first the House of God looks very like a House of Merchandise, in which brokers and traders drive a traffic as dishonest as any that disgraces the Exchange. But while the merchants and politicians stand criticising the conduct of the worshippers, the Preacher turns upon them and shows them that they are the worshippers whom they criticise; that he has held up a glass in which they see themselves as others see them; that it is they who vow and do not pay, they who hurry on their mouths to utter words which their hearts do not prompt, they who take the roundabout course of sinning and sacrificing for sin instead of that plain road of

Samuel Cox, D.D.

obedience which leads straight to God.

But what comfort for them is there in that? How should it help them, to be beguiled into condemning themselves? Truly there would not be much comfort in it did not the compassionate Preacher forthwith disclose the secret of this dishonest worship, and give them counsels of amendment. He discloses the secret in two verses (vv. 3 and 7), which have much perplexed the readers of this Book. He there explains that just as a mind harassed by much occupation and the many cares it breeds cannot rest even at nights, but busies itself in framing wild disturbing dreams, so also is it with the foolish worshipper who, for want of thought and reverence, pours out before God a multitude of unsifted and unconsidered wishes in a multitude of words. In effect he says to them: "You men of affairs often get little help or comfort from the worship of God because you come to it with preoccupied hearts, just as a man gets little comfort from his bed because his brain, jaded and yet excited by many cares, will not suffer him to rest. Hence it is that you promise more than you perform, and utter prayers more devout than any honest expression of your desires would warrant, and offer sacrifices to avoid the charge and trouble of obedience to the Divine laws. And as I have shown you a more excellent way of transacting business than the selfish grasping mode to which you are addicted, so also I will show you a more excellent style of worship. Go to the House of God 'with a straight foot,' a foot trained to walk in the path of obedience. Keep your heart, set a watch over it, lest it should be diverted from the simple and devout homage it should pay. Do not urge and press it to a false emotion, to a strained and insincere mood. Let your words be few and reverent when you speak to the Great King. Do not vow except under the compulsion of stedfast resolves, and pay your vows even to your own hurt when once they are made. Do not anger God, or the angel of God who, as you believe, presides over the altar, with idle unreal talk and idle half-meant resolves, making vows of which you afterwards repent and do not keep, pleading that you made them in error or infirmity. But in all the exercises of your worship show a holy fear of the Almighty; and then, under the worst oppressions of fortune and the heaviest calamities of time, you shall find the House of God a Sanctuary, and his worship a strength, a consolation, and a delight." This, surely, was very wholesome counsel for men of business in hard times.

And a more helpful and consolatory Trust in the Divine Providence. Ch. v., vv. 8-17.

Not content with this, however, the Preacher goes on to show how, when they returned from the House of God to the common round of life, and were once more exposed to its miseries and distractions, there were certain comfortable and sustaining thoughts on which they might stay their spirits. To the worship of the Sanctuary he would have them add a strengthening trust in the Providence of God. That Providence was expressed, as in other ordinances, so also in these two:--

First; whatever oppressions and perversions of justice and equity there were in the land (ver. 8), still the judges and satraps who oppressed them were not supreme; there was an official hierarchy in which superior watched over superior, and if justice were not to be had of the one, it might be had of another who was above him; if it were not to be had of any, no, not even of the king himself, there was this reassuring conviction that, in the last resort, even the king was "the servant of the field" (ver. 9), i.e., was dependent on the wealth and produce of the land, and could not, therefore, be unjust with impunity, or push his oppressions too far lest he should decrease his revenue or depopulate his realm. This was "the advantage" the people had; and if it were in itself but a slight advantage to this man or that, clearly it was a great advantage to the body politic; while as an indication of the Providence of God, of the care with which He had arranged for the general well-being, it was full of consolation.

The second fact, or class of facts, in which they might recognise the gracious care of God was this,--That the unjust judges and wealthy rapacious "lords" who oppressed them had very much less satisfaction in their fraudulent gains than they might suppose. God had so made men that injustice and selfishness defeated their own ends, and those who lived for wealth, and would do evil to acquire it, made but a poor bargain after all. "He that loveth silver is never satisfied with silver, nor he that clings to wealth with what it yields" (ver. 10). "When riches increase, they increase that consume them"-- dependents, parasites, slaves, flock around the man who rises to wealth and place. He cannot eat and drink more, or enjoy more, than when he was a man simply well-to-do in the world; the only advantage he has is that he sees others consume what he has acquired at so great a cost (ver. 11). [35] He cannot know the sweet refreshing sleep of husbandmen weary with toil (ver. 12), for his heart is full of care and apprehension. Robbers may drive off his flocks, or "lift" his cattle; his investments may fail, or his secret hoard be plundered; he must trust much to servants, and they may be unfaithful to their trust; his official superiors may ruin him with the bribes they extort, or the prince himself may want a sponge to squeeze. If none of these evils befall him, he may apprehend, and have cause to apprehend, that his heir longs for his death, and will prove little better than a fool, wasting in wanton riot what he has amassed with much painful toil (vv. 13, 14). And, in any event, he cannot take his wealth with him on his last journey (vv. 15, 16). So that, naturally enough, he is much perturbed, and "hath great vexation and grief" (ver. 17), cannot sleep for his apprehensive care for his "abundance;" and at last must go out of the world as bare and unprovided as he came into it. [36] He "labours for the wind," and reaps what he has sown. Was such a life, mounting to such a close, a thing to long for and toil for? Was it worth while to hurl oneself against the adamantine laws of Heaven and risk the oppressions of earth, to injure one's neighbours, to sink into an insincere and distracted worship and a weakening distrust of the providence of God, in order to spend anxious toilsome days and sleepless nights, and at last to go out of the world naked of all but guilt, and rich in nothing but the memory of frauds and wrongs? Might not even a captive or a slave, whose sleep was sweetened by toil, and who, from his trust in God and the sacred delights of honest worship, gathered strength to endure all the oppressions of the time, and to enjoy whatever alleviations and innocent pleasures were vouchsafed him--might not even he be a wiser, happier man than the despot at whose caprice he stood?

The Conclusion. Ch. v., vv. 18-20.

For himself Coheleth has a very decided opinion on this point. He is quite sure that his first conclusion is sound, though for a moment he had questioned its soundness, and that a quiet, cheerful, and obedient heart is greater riches than the wealthiest estate. With all the emphasis of renewed and now immovable conviction he declares,

Behold, that which I have said holds good; it is well for a man to eat and to drink, and to enjoy the good of all his labours through the brief day of his life. And I have also said--and this too is true--that a man to whom God hath given riches and wealth--for even a rich man may be a good man and use his wealth wisely--if He hath also enabled him to eat thereof, and to take his portion, and to rejoice in his labour--this too is a most Divine gift. He does not fret over the brevity of his life; it is not much, or often, or sadly in his thoughts: for he knows that the joy his heart takes in the toils and pleasures of life is approved by God, or even, as the phrase seems to mean, corresponds in some measure with the joy of God Himself; that his tranquil enjoyment is a reflection of the Divine peace.

***

II. [37] There are not many Englishmen who devote themselves solely or mainly to the acquisition of Wisdom, and who, that they may teach the children of men that which is good, live laborious days, withdrawing from the general pursuit of wealth and scorning the lures of ease and self-indulgence; such men, indeed, are but a small minority in any age or land. Nor do those who give themselves exclusively to the pursuit of Pleasure constitute more than a small and miserable class, though most of us have wasted on it days that we could ill spare. But when the Hebrew Preacher, having followed his quest of the supreme Good in Pleasure and Wisdom, turns to the affairs of Business--and I use that term as including both commerce and politics--he enters a field of action and inquiry with which we are nearly all familiar, and can hardly fail to speak words which will touch us close home. For, whatever else we may or may not be, we are most of us among the worshippers of the great god Traffic--a god whose wholesome, benignant face too often lowers and darkens, or ever we are aware, into the sordid and malignant features of Mammon.

Now in dealing with this broad and momentous province of human life the Preacher exhibits the candour and the temperance which marked his treatment of Wisdom and Mirth. Just as he would not suffer us to think of Wisdom as in itself an evil, nor of Pleasure as an evil, so neither will he allow us to think of Business as essentially and of necessity an evil. This, like those, may be abused to our hurt; but none the less may all be used, and were meant to be used, for our own and our neighbours' good. Pursued in the right method, from the right motive, with the due moderation and reserve, Business, as he is careful to point out, besides bringing other great advantages, may be a new bond of union and brotherhood: it develops intercourse among men and races of men, and should develop sympathy, goodwill, and a mutual helpfulness. Nevertheless, thrift may degenerate into miserliness, and the honest industry of content into a dishonest eagerness for undue gains, and a wise attention to business into an excessive devotion to it. These degenerate tendencies had struck their roots deep into the Hebrew mind of his day, and brought forth many bitter fruits. The Preacher describes and denounces them; he lays an axe to the very roots of these evil growths: but it is only that he may clear a space for the fairer and more wholesome growths which sprang beside them, and of which they were the wild bastard offshoots.

Throughout this second section of the Book, his subject is excessive devotion to Business, and the correctives to it which his experience enables him to suggest.

1. His handling of the subject is very thorough and complete. Men of business might do worse than get the lessons he here teaches by heart. According to him, their excessive devotion to affairs springs from a "jealous rivalry"; it tends to form in them a grasping covetous temper which can never be satisfied, to produce a materialistic scepticism of all that is noble, spiritual, aspiring in thought and action, to render their worship formal and insincere, and, in general, to incapacitate them for any quiet happy enjoyment of their life. This is his diagnosis of their disease, or of that diseased tendency which, if it be for the most part latent in them, always threatens to become pronounced and to infect all healthy conditions of the soul.

Samuel Cox, D.D.

Devotion to Business springs from Jealous Competition: Ch. iv., v. 4. [38]

(a) Let us glance once more at the several symptoms we have already heard him discuss, and consider whether or not they accord with the results of our own observation and experience. Is it true, then--or, rather, is it not true--that our devotion to business is becoming excessive and exhausting, and that this devotion springs mainly from our jealous rivalry and competition with each other? If, some two or three and twenty centuries ago, the Jews were bent every man on outdoing and outselling his neighbour; if his main ambition was to amass greater wealth or to secure a larger business than his competitors, or to make a handsomer show before the world; if in the urgent pursuit of this ambition he held his neighbours not as neighbours, but as unscrupulous rivals, keen for gain at his expense and to rise by his fall; if, to reach his end, he was willing to get up early and go late to rest, to force all his energies into an injurious activity and strain them close to the snapping-point: if this were what a Jew of that time was like, might you not easily take it for a portrait of many an English merchant, manufacturer, lawyer, or politician? Is it not as accurate a delineation of our life as it could be of any ancient form of life? If it be, as I think it is, we have grave need to take the Preacher's warning. We gravely need to remember that the stream cannot rise above its source, nor the fruit be better than the root from which it grows; that the business ardour which has its origin in a base and selfish motive can only be a base and selfish ardour. When men gather grapes from thorns and figs from thistles, then, but not before, we may look to find a satisfying good in "all the toil and all the dexterity in toil" which spring from this "jealous rivalry of the one with the other."

It tends to form a Covetous Temper: Ch. iv., v. 8.

(b) Nor, in the face of facts patent to the most cursory observer, can we deny that this eager and excessive devotion to the successful conduct of business tends to produce a grasping, covetous temper which, however much it has gained, is for ever seeking more. It is not only true that the stream cannot rise above its source; it is also true that the stream will run downward, and must inevitably contract many pollutions from the lower levels on which it declines. The ardour which impels men to devote themselves with eager intensity to the labours of the Market may often have an origin as pure as that of the stream which bubbles up on the hills, amid grass and ferns, and runs tinkling along its clear rocky channels, setting its labour to a happy music, singing its low sweet song to the sweet listening air. But as it runs on, if it swell in volume and power, it also sinks and grows foul. Bent at first on acquiring the means to support a widowed mother, or to justify him in taking a wife, or to provide for his children, or to win an honourable place in his neighbours' eyes, or to achieve the chance of self-culture and self-development, or to serve some public and worthy end, the man of business and affairs too often suffers himself to become more and more absorbed in his pursuits. He conceives larger schemes, is drawn into more perilous enterprises, and advances through these to fresh openings and opportunities, until at last, long after his original ends are compassed and forgotten, he finds himself possessed by the mere craving to extend his labours, resources, influence, if not by the mere craving to amass--a craving which often "teareth" and "tormenteth" him, but which can only be exorcised by an exertion of spiritual force which would leave him half dead. "He has no one with him, not even a son or a brother;" the dear mother or wife is long since dead; his children, to use his own detestable phrase, are "off his hands"; the public good has slipped from his memory and aims: but still "there is no end to all his labours, neither are his eyes satisfied with riches." Coheleth speaks of one such man: alas, of how many such might we speak!

To produce a Materialistic Scepticism; Ch. iii., vv. 18-21.

(c) The "speculation" in the eye of business men is not commonly of a philosophic cast, and therefore we do not look to find them arguing themselves into the materialism which infected the Hebrew Preacher as he contemplated them and their blind devotion to their idol. They are far, perhaps very far, from thinking that in body and spirit, in origin and end, man is no better than the beast, a creature of the same accident and subject to "the same chance." But though they do not reason out a conclusion so sombre and depressing, do they not practically acquiesce in it? If it is far from their thoughts, do they not live in its close neighbourhood? Their mind, like the dyer's hand, is subdued to that it works in. Accustomed to think mainly of material interests, their character is materialised. They are disposed to weigh all things--truth, righteousness, the motives and aims of nobler men--in the scales of the market, and can very hardly believe that they should attach any grave value to ought which will not lend itself to their coarse handling. In their judgment, mental culture, or the graces of moral character, or single-hearted devotion to lofty ends, are not worthy to be compared with a full purse or large possessions. They regard as little better than a fool, of whom it is very kind of them to take a little care, the man who has thrown away what they call "his chances," in order that he may learn wisdom or do good. Giving, perhaps, a cheerful and unforced accord to the current moral maxims and popular creed, they permit neither to rule their conduct. If they do not say, "Man is no better than a beast," they carry themselves as if he were no better, as though he had no instincts or interests above those of the thrifty ant, or the cunning beaver, or the military locust, or insatiable leech--although they are both surprised and affronted when one is at the pains to translate their deeds into words. Judged by their deeds, they are sceptics and materialists, since they have no vital faith in that which is spiritual and unseen. They have found "the life of their hands," and they are content with it. Give them whatever furnishes the senses, whatever in them holds by sense, and they will cheerfully let all else go. But such a materialism as this is far more injurious, far more likely to be fatal, than that which reflects, and argues, and utters itself in words, and refutes itself by the very powers which it employs. With them the malady has struck inward, and is beyond the reach of cure save by the most searching and drastic remedies.

To make Worship Formal and Insincere; Ch. v., vv. 1-7.

(d) But now if, like Coheleth, we follow these men to the Temple, what is the scene that meets our eye? In the English Temple, I fear, that which would first strike an unaccustomed observer would be the fact that very few men of business are there. They are "conspicuous by their absence," or, at best, noted for an only occasional attendance. The Hebrew Temple was crowded with men; in the English Temple it is the other sex which predominates. But glance at the men who are there? Do you detect no signs of weariness and perfunctoriness? Do you hear no vows which will never be paid, and which they do not intend to pay even when they make them? no prayers which go beyond any honest and candid expression of their desires? Do you not feel and know that many of them are making an unwilling sacrifice to the decencies and the proprieties, instead of worshipping God the Spirit in spirit and nerving themselves for the difficulties of obedience to the Divine law? Listen: they are saying, "Almighty God, Father of all mercies, we bless Thee for our creation, preservation, and all the blessings of this life; but above all for Thine inestimable love in the redemption of the world by our Lord Jesus Christ, for the means of grace, and for the hope of glory." But are these ineffable spiritual benefits "above all" else to them? Do they care for "the means of grace" as much even as for the state of the market, or for "the hope of glory" as much as for success or promotion? Which is most in their thoughts, their lives, their aspirations, for which will they take most pains and make most sacrifices--for what they mean by the beautiful phrase "all the blessings of this life," or for that sacred and crowning act of the Divine Mercy, "the redemption," in which God has once for all revealed his fatherly forgiving love?

What is it that makes their worship formal and insincere? It is the very cause which, as the Preacher tells us, produced the like evil effect upon the Jews. They come into the Temple with pre-occupied hearts. Their thoughts are distracted by the cares of life even as they bend in worship. And hence even the most sacred words turn to "idle talk" on their lips, as remote from the true feeling of the moment as "the multitude of dreams" which haunt the night; they utter fervent prayers without any due sense of their meaning, or any hearty wish to have them granted.

And to take from Life its Quiet and Innocent Enjoyments. Ch. v., vv. 10-17.

(e) Now surely a life so thick with perils, so beset with temptations, should have a very large and certain reward to offer. But has it? For one, Coheleth thinks it has not. In his judgment, according to his experience, instead of making a man happier even in this present time, to which it limits his thoughts and aims, it robs him of all quiet and happy enjoyment of his life. And, mark, it is not the unsuccessful man of business, who might naturally feel sore and aggrieved, but the successful man, the man who has made a fortune and prospered in his schemes, whom the Preacher describes as having lost all faculty of enjoying his gains. Even the man who has wealth and abundance, so that his soul lacketh nothing of all that he desireth, is placed before us as the slave of unsatisfied desire and constant apprehension. Both his hands are so full of labour that he cannot lay hold on quiet. Though he loves silver so well, and has so much of it, he is not satisfied therewith; his riches yield him no certain and abiding delight. And how can he be in "happy plight" who is

> *"debarred the benefit of rest?*
> *When day's oppression is not eased by night,*
> *But day by night, and night by day, oppress'd?*
> *And each, though enemies to either's reign,*
> *Do in consent shake hands to torture him."*

The sound sleep of humble contented labour is denied him. He is haunted by perpetual apprehensions that "there is some ill a-brewing to his rest," that evil in some dreaded shape will befall him. He doubts "the filching age will steal his treasure." He knows that when he is called hence he can carry away nothing in his hand; all his gains must be left to his heir, who may either turn out a wanton fool or be crushed and degraded by the burden and temptations of a wealth for which he has not laboured. And hence, amid all his toils and gains, even the most prosperous and successful man suspects that he has been "labouring for the wind" and may reap the whirlwind: "he is much perturbed, and hath vexation and grief."

Is the picture overdrawn? Is not the description as true to modern experience as to that of "the

Samuel Cox, D.D.

antique world"? Shakespeare, who is our great English authority on the facts of human experience, thought it quite as true. His Merchant of Venice has argosies on every sea; and two of his friends, hearing him confess that sadness makes such a want-wit of him that he has much ado to know himself, tell him that his "mind is tossing on the ocean" with his ships. They proceed to discuss the natural effects of having so many enterprises on hand. One says--

"Believe me, Sir, had I such venture forth,
The better part of my affections would
Be with my hopes abroad. I should be still
Plucking the grass, to know where sits the wind;
Peering in maps for ports, and piers, and roads;
And every object that might make me fear
Misfortune to my ventures, out of doubt
Would make me sad."
And the other adds--
"My wind, cooling my broth,
Would blow me to an ague, when I thought
What harm a wind too great at sea might do.
I should not see the sandy hour-glass run,
But I should think of shallows and of flats,
And see my wealthy Andrew, dock'd in sand,
Vailing her high-top lower than her ribs
To kiss her burial. Should I go to church
And see the holy edifice of stone,
And not bethink me straight of dangerous rocks,
Which, touching but my gentle vessel's side,
Would scatter all her spices in the stream;
Enrobe the roaring waters with my silks:
And, in a word, but even now worth this,
And now worth nothing? Shall I have the thought
To think on this; and shall I lack the thought
That such a thing bechanced would make me sad?"

"Abundance suffereth not the rich to sleep;" the thought that his "riches may perish in some unlucky adventure" rings a perpetual alarum in his ears: "all his days he eateth in darkness, and is much perturbed, and hath vexation and grief." These are the words of the Hebrew Preacher: are not our own great poet's words an expressive commentary on them, an absolute confirmation of them, covering them point by point? And shall we envy the wealthy merchant whose two hands are thus "full of labour and vexation of spirit"? Is not "the husbandman whose sleep is sweet, whether he eat little or much," better off than he? Nay, has not even the sluggard who, so long as he hath meat, foldeth his hands in quiet, a truer enjoyment of his life?

Of course Coheleth does not mean to imply that every man of business degenerates into a miserly sceptic, whose worship is a formulated hypocrisy and whose life is haunted with saddening apprehensions of misfortune. No doubt there were then, as there are now, many men of business who were wise enough to "take pleasure in all their labours," to cast their burden of care on Him in whose care stand both to-morrow and to-day; men to whom worship was a calming and strengthening communion with the Father of their spirits, and who advanced, through toil, to worthy or even noble ends. He means simply that these are the perils to which all men of business are exposed, and into which they fall so soon as their devotion to its affairs grows excessive. "Make business, and success in business, your chief good, your ruling aim, and you will come to think of your neighbours as selfish rivals; you will begin to look askance on the lofty spiritual qualities which refuse to bow to the yoke of Mammon; your worship will sink into an insincere formalism; your life will be vexed and saddened with fears which will strangle the very faculty of tranquil enjoyment:" this is the warning of the Preacher; a warning of which our generation, in such urgent sinful haste to be rich, stands in very special need.

2. But what checks, what correctives, what remedies, would the Preacher have us apply to the diseased tendencies of the time? How shall men of business save themselves from being absorbed in its interests and affairs?

The Expositor's Bible: Ecclesiastes
The Correctives of this Devotion are a Sense of its Perils; Ch. v., vv. 10-17.

(a) Well, the very sense of the danger to which they are exposed--a danger so insidious, so profound, so fatal--should surely induce caution and a wary self-control. The symptoms of the disease are described that we may judge whether or not we are infected by it; its dreadful issues that, if infected, we may study a cure. The man who loves riches is placed before us that we may learn what he is really like--that he is not the careless happy being we often assume him to be. We see him decline on the low bare levels of covetousness and materialism, hypocrisy and fear; and, as we look, the Preacher turns upon us with, "There, that is the slave of Mammon in his habit as he lives. Do you care to be like that? Will you break your heart unless you are allowed to assume his heavy and degrading burden?"

And the Conviction that it is opposed to the Will of God as expressed in the Ordinances of his Providence, Ch. iii., vv. 1-8.

This is one help to a wise content with our lot; but he has many more at our service, and notably this,--that an undue devotion to the toils of business is contrary to the will, the design, the providence of God. God, he argues, has fixed a time for every undertaking under heaven, and has made each of them beautiful in its season, but only then. By his wise kindly ordinances He has sought to divert us from an injurious excess in toil. Our sowing and our reaping, our time of rest and our time for work, the time to save and the time to spend, the time to gain and the time to lose,--all these, with all the fluctuating feelings they excite in us: in short, our whole life, from the cradle to the grave, is under, or should be under, law to Him. It is only when we violate his gracious ordinances,--working when we should be at rest, waking when we should sleep, saving when we should spend, weeping over losses which are real gains, or laughing over gains which will prove to be losses--that we run into excess, and break up the peaceful order and tranquil flow of the life which He designed for us.

In the Wrongs which He permits Men to inflict upon us; Ch. iii., v. 16-Ch. iv., v. 3.

Because we will not be obsequious to the ordinances of his wisdom, He permits us to meet a new check in the caprice and injustice of man--making even these to praise Him by subserving our good. If we do not suffer the violent oppressions which drew tears from the Preacher's fellow-captives, we nevertheless stand very much at the mercy of our neighbours in so far as our outward haps are concerned. Unwise human laws or an unjust administration of them, or the selfish rapacity of individual men--brokers who rig the market; bankers whose long prayers are a pretence under cloak of which they rob widows and orphans, and sometimes make them; bankrupts for whose wounds the Gazette has a singular power of healing, since they come out of it "sounder" men than they went in: these are only some of the instruments by which the labours of the diligent are shorn of their due reward. And we are to take these checks as correctives, to find in the losses which men inflict the gifts of a gracious God. He permits us to suffer these and the like disasters lest our hearts should be overmuch set on getting gain. He graciously permits us to suffer them that, seeing how often the wicked thrive (in a way and for a time) on the decay of the upright, we may learn that there is something better than wealth, more enduring, more satisfying, and may seek that higher good.

But above all, in the immortal Cravings which He has quickened in the Soul. Ch. iii., v. 11.

Nay, going to the very root of the matter and expounding its whole philosophy, the Preacher teaches us that wealth, however great and greatly used, cannot satisfy men, since God has "put eternity into their hearts" as well as time: and how should all the kingdoms of a world that must soon pass content those who are to live for ever? [39] This saying, "God has put eternity into their hearts," is one of the most profound in the whole Book, and one of the most beautiful and suggestive. What it means is that, even if a man would confine his aims and desires within "the bounds and coasts of Time," he cannot do it. The very structure of his nature forbids it. For time, with all that it inherits, sweeps by him like a torrent, so that, if he would secure any lasting good, he must lay hold of that which is eternal. We may well call this world, for all so solid as it looks, "a perishing world;" for, like our own bodies, it is in a perpetual flux, perishing every moment that it may live a little longer, and must soon come to an end. But we, in our true selves, we who dwell inside the body and use its members as the workman uses his tools, how can we find a satisfying good whether in the body or in the world which is akin to it? We want a good as lasting as ourselves. Nothing short of that can be our chief good, or inspire us with a true content.

> "Like as the waves make towards the pebbled shore,
> So do our minutes hasten to their end;
> Each changing place with that which goes before,
> In sequent toil all forwards do contend:"

and we might as well think to build a stable habitation on the waves which break upon the pebbled shore as to find an enduring good in the sequent minutes which carry us down the stream of time. It is only because we do not understand this "work of God" in putting eternity into our hearts and therefore making it impossible for us to be content with anything less than an eternal good; it is because, plunged in the flesh and its cares and delights, we forget the grandeur of our nature, and are tempted to sell our immortal birthright for a mess of pottage which, however much we enjoy it to-day, will leave us hungry to-morrow: it is only, I say, because we fail to understand this work of God "from beginning to end," that we ever delude ourselves with the hope of finding in ought the earth yields a good in which we can rest.

Practical Maxims deduced from this View of the Business-life.

(b) A noble philosophy this, and pregnant with practical counsels of great value. For if, as we close our study of this Section of the Book, we ask, "What good advice does the Preacher offer that we can take and act upon?" we shall find that he gives us at least three serviceable maxims.

A Maxim on Co-operation. Ch. iv., vv. 9-16.

To all men of business conscious of their special dangers and anxious to avoid them, he says, first: Replace the competition which springs from your jealous and selfish rivalry, with the co-operation which is born of sympathy and breeds goodwill. "Two are better than one. Union is better than isolation. Conjoint labour has the greater reward." Instead of seeking to take advantage of your neighbours, try to help them. Instead of standing alone, associate with your fellows. Instead of aiming at purely selfish ends, pursue your ends in common. Indeed the wise Hebrew Preacher anticipates the golden rule to a remarkable extent, and, in effect, bids us love our neighbour as ourself, look on his things as well as our own, and do to all men as we would that they should do to us.

A Maxim on Worship. Ch. v., vv. 1-7.

His second maxim is: Replace the formality of your worship with a reverent and steadfast sincerity. Keep your foot when you go to the House of God. Put obedience before sacrifice. Do not hurry on your mouth to the utterance of words which transcend the desires of your heart. Be not of those who

> *"words for virtue take,*
> *As though mere wood a shrine would make."* [40]

Do not come into the Temple with a pre-occupied spirit, a spirit distracted with thoughts that travel different ways. Realise the presence of the Great King, and speak to Him with the reverence due to a King. Keep the vows you have made in his House after you have left it. Seek and serve Him with all your hearts, and ye shall find rest to your souls.

A Maxim on Trust in God. Ch. v., vv. 8-17.

And his last maxim is: Replace your grasping self-sufficiency with a constant trust in the fatherly providence of God. If you see oppression or suffer wrong, if your schemes are thwarted and your enterprises fail, you need not therefore lose the quiet repose and settled peace which spring from a sense of duty discharged and the undisturbed possession of the main good of life. God is over all, and rules all the undertakings of man, giving each its season and place, and causing all to work together for the good of the loving and trustful heart. Trust in Him, and you shall feel, even though you cannot prove,

> *"That every cloud that spreads above,*
> *And veileth love, itself is love."*
> Trust in Him, and you shall find that
> *"The slow sweet hours that bring us all things good,*
> *The slow sad hours that bring us all things ill*
> *And all good things from evil,"*

as they strike on the great horologe of Time, are set to a growing music by the hand of God; a music which rises and falls as we listen, but which nevertheless swells through all its saddest cadences and dying falls toward that harmonious close, that "undisturbed concent," in which all discords will be drowned.

Footnotes:

33. Xerxes, in his invasion of Greece, conceived the wish "to look upon all his host." A throne was erected for him on a hill near Abydos, sitting on which he looked down and saw the Hellespont covered with his ships, and the vast plain swarming with his troops. As he looked, he wept; and when his uncle Artabanus asked him the cause of his tears, he replied: "There came upon me a sudden pity when I thought of the shortness of man's life, and considered that of all this host, so numerous as it is, not one will be alive when a hundred years are gone by." This is one of the most striking and best known incidents in the life of the Persian despot; but the rejoinder of Artabanus, though in a far higher strain, is less generally known. I quote it here as an illustration of the Preacher's mood. Said Artabanus: "And yet there are sadder things in life than that. Short as our time is, there is no man, whether it be here among this multitude or elsewhere, who is so happy as not to have felt the wish--I will not say once, but full many a time--that he were dead rather than alive. Calamities fall on us, sicknesses vex and harass us, and make life, short though it be, to appear long. So death, through the wretchedness of our life, is a most sweet refuge to our race."--Herodotus, Book VII., c. 46.

34. So in Sophocles (Oed. Col., 1225) we read--I quote from Dean Plumptre's translation:

*"Never to be at all
Excels all fame;
Quickly, next best, to pass
From whence we came."*

35. Ginsburg quotes a capital illustration of this verse from the dialogue of Pheraulas and Sacian (Xenophon, Cyrop., viii. 3); "Do you think, Sacian, that I live with more pleasure the more I possess?... By having this abundance I gain merely this, that I have to guard more, to distribute to others, and have the trouble of taking care of more; for a great many attendants now demand of me their food, their drink, and their clothes. Whosoever, therefore, is greatly pleased with the possession of riches will, be assured, feel much annoyed at the expenditure of them."

36. Compare Psalm xlix., vv. 16, 17:

*Be not afraid though one be made rich,
Or if the glory of his house be increased;
For he shall carry away nothing with him when he dieth
Neither shall his pomp follow him.*

37. In commenting on Sections II. and III. of this Book I found that both the exposition of the sacred text and the application of its lessons to the details of modern life would gain in force by being handled separately. The second part of each of these chapters consists mainly, therefore, of an exhortation based on the previous exposition, the marginal notes indicating the passages of Holy Writ on which these exhortations are based.

38. Coheleth's description is so true and pertinent, it hits so many of our modern faults and sins, that I am obliged to cite my authority for every paragraph lest I should be suspected of putting a private and personal interpretation on these ancient words.

39. M. de Lamennais--the founder of the most religious school of thinkers in modern France, from whom such men as Count Montalembert, Père Lacordaire, and Maurice Guérin, drew their earliest inspiration--asks, "Do you know what it is that makes man the most suffering of all creatures?" and replies, "It is that he has one foot in the finite and the other in the infinite, and that he is torn asunder, not by four horses, as in the horrible old times, but between two worlds."

40. Horace, Ep. 6, Lib. I: "Virtutem verba putant, ut Lucum ligna."

Samuel Cox, D.D.

THIRD SECTION

THE QUEST OF THE CHIEF GOOD IN WEALTH, AND IN THE GOLDEN MEAN.

Chaps. VI., VII., and VIII., vv. 1-15.

In the foregoing Section Coheleth has shown that the Chief Good is not to be found in that Devotion to the affairs of Business which was, and still is, characteristic of the Hebrew race. This devotion is commonly inspired either by the desire to amass great wealth, for the sake of the status, influence, and means of lavish enjoyment it is assumed to confer; or by the more modest desire to secure a competence, to stand in that golden mean of comfort which is darkened by no harassing fears of future penury or need. By a logical sequence of thought, therefore, he advances from his discussion on Devotion to Business, to consider the leading motives by which it is inspired. The questions he now asks and answers are, in effect, (1) Will Wealth confer the good, the tranquil and enduring satisfaction which men seek? And if not, (2) Will that moderate provision for the present and for the future to which the more prudent restrict their aim?

The Quest in Wealth. Ch. vi.

His discussion of the first of these questions, although very matterful, is comparatively brief; in part, perhaps, because in the previous Section he has already dwelt on many of the drawbacks which accompany wealth; and still more, probably, because, while there are but few men in any age to whom great wealth is possible, there would be unusually few in the company of poor men for whose instruction he wrote. Brief and simple as the discussion is, however, we shall misapprehend it unless we bear in mind that Coheleth is arguing, not against wealth, but against mistaking wealth for the Chief Good.

The Man who makes Riches his Chief Good is haunted by Fears and Perplexities: Ch. vi., vv. 1-6.

Let us observe, then, that throughout this sixth Chapter the Preacher is dealing with the lover of riches, not with the rich man; that he is speaking, not against wealth, but against mistaking wealth for the Chief Good. The man who trusts in riches is placed before us; and, that we may see him at his best, he has the riches in which he trusts. God has given him "his good things," given him them to the full. He lacks nothing that he desireth--nothing at least that wealth can command. Yet, because he does not accept his abundance as the gift of God, and hold the Giver better than the gift, he cannot enjoy it. But how do we know that he has suffered his riches to take an undue place in his regard? We know it by this sure token--that he cannot leave God to take care of them, and of him. He frets about them, and about what will become of them when he is gone. He has no son, perchance, to inherit them, no child, only some "stranger" whom he has adopted (ver. 2)--and almost all childless Orientals adopt strangers to this day, as we have found, to our cost, in India. A profound horror at the thought of being dead to name and fame and use through lack of heirs was, and is, very prevalent in the East. Even faithful Abraham, when God had promised him the supreme good, broke out with the remonstrance, "What canst Thou give me when I am going off childless, and have no heir but my body-servant, Eliezer of Damascus?" Because this feeling lay close to the Oriental heart, the Preacher is at some pains to show what a "vanity" it is. He argues: "Even if you should beget a hundred children, instead of being childless; even though you should live a thousand years, and the grave did not wait for you instead of lying close before you: yet, so long as you were not content to leave your riches in the hands of God, you would fret and perplex yourself with fears. An abortion would be better off than you, although it cometh in nothingness and goeth in darkness; for it would know a rest denied to you, and sink without apprehension into the 'place' from which all your apprehensions cannot save you (vv. 3-6). Foolish man! it is not because you lack an heir that you are perturbed in spirit. If you had one, you would find some other cause for care; you would be none the less fretted and perturbed; for you would still be thinking of your riches rather than of the God who gave them, and still dread the moment in which you must part with them, in order to return to Him."

For God has put Eternity into his Heart; Ch. vi., vv. 7-10.

From this plain practical argument Coheleth passes to an argument of more philosophic reach. "All the labour of this man is for his mouth:" that is to say, his wealth, with all that it commands, appeals only to sense and appetite; it feeds "the lust of the eye, or the lust of the flesh, or the pride of life," and therefore "his soul cannot be satisfied therewith" (ver. 7). That craves a higher nutriment, a more enduring good. God has put eternity into it: and how can that which is immortal be contented with the lucky haps and comfortable conditions of time? Unless some immortal provision be made for the immortal spirit, it will pine, and protest, and crave, till all power of happily enjoying outward good be lost. Nay, if the spirit in man be craving and unfed, whatever his outward conditions, or his faculty for enjoying them, he cannot be at rest. The wise man may be able to extract from the gains of time a pleasure denied to the fool; and the poor man, his penury preventing him from indulging passion and appetite to satiety, may have a keener enjoyment of them than the magnate who has tried them to the full and has grown weary of them. In a certain sense, as compared the one with the other, the poor man may have an "advantage" over the rich, and the wise man over the fool; for "it is better to enjoy the good we have than to crave a good beyond our reach;" and this much the wise man, or even the poor man, may achieve. Yet, after all, what advantage have they? The thirst of the soul is still unslaked; no sensual or sensuous enjoyment can satisfy that. All human action and enjoyment is under law to God. No one is so wise, or so strong, as to contend successfully against Him or his ordinances. And it is He who has given men an immortal nature, with cravings that wander through eternity; it is He who has ordained that they shall know no rest until they rest in Him (vv. 8-10).

And much that he gains only feeds Vanity; Ch. vi., v. 11.

Look once more at your means and possessions. Multiply them as you will. Still there are many reasons why if you seek your chief good in them, they should prove vanity and breed vexation of spirit. One is, that beyond a certain point you can neither use nor enjoy them. They add to your pomp. They enable you to fill a larger place in the world's eye. They swell and magnify the vain show in which you walk. But, after all, they add to your discomfort rather than your comfort. You have so much the more to manage, and look after, and take care of: but you yourself, instead of being better off than you were, have only taken a heavier task on your hands. And what advantage is there in that?

Neither can he tell what it will be good for him to have, Ch. vi., v. 12.

Another reason is, that it is hard, so hard as to be impossible, for you to know "what it is good" for you to have. That on which you have set your heart may prove to be an evil rather than a good when at last you get it. The fair fruit, so pleasant and desirable to the eye that, to posses it, you were content to labour and deny yourself for years, may turn to an apple of Sodom in your mouth, and yield you, in place of sweet pulp and juice, only the bitter ashes of disappointment.

Nor foresee what will become of his Gains. Ch. vi., v. 12.

And a third reason is, that the more you acquire the more you must dispose of when you are called away from this life: and who can tell what shall be after him? How are you so to dispose of your gains as to be sure that they will do good and not harm, and carry comfort to the hearts of those whom you love, and not breed envy, alienation, and strife?

These are the Preacher's arguments against an undue love of riches, against making them so dear a good that we can neither enjoy them while we have them, nor trust them to the disposal of God when we must leave them behind us. Are they not sound arguments? Should we be saddened by them, or comforted? We can only be saddened by them if we love wealth, or long for it, with an inordinate desire. If we can trust in God to give us all that it will be really good for us to have in return for our honest toil, the arguments of the Preacher are full of comfort and hope for us, whether we be rich or whether we be poor.

The Quest in the Golden Mean. Ch. vii., viii., vv. 1-15.

There be many that say, "Who will show us any gold?" mistaking gold for their god or good. For though there can be few in any age to whom great wealth is possible, there are many who crave it and believe that to have it is to possess the supreme felicity. It is not only the rich who "trust in riches." As a rule, perhaps, they trust in them less than the poor, since they have tried them, and know pretty exactly both how much, and how little, they can do. It is those who have not tried them, and to whom poverty brings many undeniable hardships, who are most sorely tempted to trust in them as the sovereign remedy for the ills of life. So that the counsels of the sixth chapter may have a wider scope than we sometimes think they have. But, whether they apply to many or to few, there can be no doubt that the counsels of the seventh and eighth chapters are applicable to the vast majority of men. For here the Preacher discusses the Golden Mean in which most of us would like to stand. Many of us dare not ask for great wealth lest it should prove a burden we could very hardly bear; but we have no scruple in

Samuel Cox, D.D.

adopting Agur's prayer, "Give me neither poverty nor riches; Feed me with food proportioned to my need: Let me have a comfortable competence in which I shall be at an equal remove from the temptations whether of extreme wealth or of extreme penury."

Now the endeavour to secure a competence may be, not lawful only, but most laudable; since God means us to make the best of the capacities He has given us and the opportunities He sends us. Nevertheless, we may pursue this right end from a wrong motive, in a wrong spirit. Both spirit and motive are wrong if we pursue our competence as if it were a good so great that we can know no content unless we attain it. For what is it that animates such a pursuit save distrust in the providence of God? Left in his hands, we do not feel that we should be safe; whereas if we had our fortune in our own hands, and were secured against chances and changes by a few comfortable securities, we should feel safe enough. This feeling is, surely, very general: we are all of us in danger of slipping into this form of unquiet distrust in the fatherly providence of God.

The Method of the Man who seeks a Competence. Ch. vii., vv. 1-14.

Because the feeling is both general and strong, the Hebrew Preacher addresses himself to it at some length. His object now is to place before us a man who does not aim at great affluence, but, guided by prudence and common sense, makes it his ruling aim to stand well with his neighbours and to lay by a moderate provision for future wants. The Preacher opens the discussion by stating the maxims or rules of conduct by which such an one would be apt to guide himself. One of his first aims would be to secure "a good name," since that would prepossess men in his favour, and open before him many avenues which would otherwise be closed. [41] Just as one entering a crowded Oriental room with some choice fragrance exhaling from person and apparel would find bright faces turned toward him, and a ready way opened for his approach, so the bearer of a good name would find many willing to meet him, and traffic with him, and heed him. As the years passed, his good name, if he kept it, would diffuse itself over a wider area with a more pungent effect, so that the day of his death would be better than the his birth--to leave a good name being so much more honourable than to inherit one (chap. vii., ver. 1).

But how would he go about to acquire his good name? Again the answer carries us back to the East. Nothing is more striking to a Western traveller than the dignified gravity of the superior Oriental races. In public they rarely smile, almost never laugh, and hardly ever express surprise. Cool, courteous, self-possessed, they bear good news or bad, prosperous or adverse fortune, with a proud equanimity. This equal mind, expressing itself in a grave dignified bearing, is, with them, well-nigh indispensable to success in public life. And, therefore, our friend in quest of a good name betakes himself to the house of mourning rather than to the house of feasting; he holds that serious thought on the end of all men is better than the wanton foolish mirth which crackles like thorns under a kettle, making a great sputter, but soon going out; and would rather have his heart bettered by the reproof of the wise than listen to the song of fools over the wine-cup (vv. 2-6). Knowing that he cannot be much with fools without sharing their folly, fearing that they may lead him into those excesses in which the wisest mind is infatuated and the kindest heart hardened and corrupted (ver. 7), he elects rather to walk with a sad countenance, among the wise, to the house of mourning and meditation, than to hurry with fools to the banquet in which wine and song and laughter drown serious reflection, and leave the heart worse than they found it. What though the wise reprove him when he errs? What though, as he listens to their reproof, his heart at times grows hot within him? The end of their reproof is better than the beginning (ver. 8); as he reflects upon it, he learns from it, profits by it, and by patient endurance of it wins a good from it which haughty resentment would have cast away. Unlike the fools, therefore, whose wanton mirth turns into bitter anger at the mere sound of reproof, he will not suffer his spirit to be hurried into a hot resentment, but will compel that which injures them to do him good (ver. 9). Nor will he rail even at the fools who fleet the passing hour, or account that, because they are so many and so bold, "the time is out of joint." He will show himself not only wiser than the foolish, but wiser than many of the wise; for while they--and here surely the Preacher hits a very common habit of the studious life--are disposed to look fondly back on some past age as greater or happier than that in which they live, and ask, "How is it that former days were better than these?" he will conclude that the question springs rather from their querulousness than from their wisdom, and make the best of the time, and of the conditions of the time, in which it has pleased God to place him (ver. 10).

But if any ask, "Why has he renounced the pursuit of that wealth on which many are bent who are less capable of using it than he?" the answer comes that he has discovered Wisdom to be as good as Wealth, and even better. Not only is Wisdom as secure a defence against the ills of life as Wealth, but it has this great advantage--that "it fortifies or vivifies the heart," while wealth often burdens and enfeebles it. Wisdom quickens and braces the spirit for any fortune, gives it new life or new strength, inspires an inward serenity which does not lie at the mercy of outward accidents (vv. 11, 12). It teaches a man to regard all the conditions of life as ordained and shaped by God, and weans him from the vain endeavour, on which many exhaust their strength, to straighten that which God has made crooked, that which crosses and thwarts his inclinations (ver. 13); once let him see that the thing is crooked, and was

The Expositor's Bible: Ecclesiastes
meant to be crooked, and he will accept and adapt himself to it, instead of wearying himself in futile attempts to make, or to think, it straight.

And there is one very good reason why God should permit many crooks in our lot, very good reason therefore why a wise man should look on them with an equal mind. For God sends the crooked as well as the straight, adversity as well as prosperity, in order that we should know that He has "made this as well as that," and accept both from his benign hand. He interlaces his providences, and veils his providences, in order that, unable to foresee the future, we may learn to put our trust in Him rather than in any earthly good (ver. 14). It therefore behoves a man whose heart has been bettered by much meditation, and by the reproofs of the wise, to take both crooked and straight, both evil and good, from the hand of God, and to trust in Him whatever may befall. [42]

The Perils to which it exposes him. Ch. vii., v. 15-Ch. viii., v. 13.
So far, I think, we shall follow and assent to this theory of human life; our sympathies will go with the man who seeks to acquire a good name, to grow wise, to stand in the Golden Mean. But when he proceeds to apply his theory, to deduce practical rules from it, we can only give him a qualified assent, nay, must often altogether withhold our assent. The main conclusion he draws is, indeed, quite unobjectionable: it is, that in action, as well as in opinion, we should avoid excess, that we should keep the happy mean between intemperance and indifference.

He is likely to compromise Conscience: Ch. vii., vv. 15-20.
But the very first moral he infers from this conclusion is open to the most serious objection. He has seen both the righteous die in his righteousness without receiving any reward from it, and the wicked live long in his wickedness to enjoy his ill-gotten gains. And from these two mysterious facts, which much exercised many of the Prophets and Psalmists of Israel, he infers that a prudent man will neither be very righteous, since he will gain nothing by it, and may lose the friendship of those who are content with the current morality; nor very wicked, since, though he may lose little by this so long as he lives, he will very surely hasten his death (vv. 16, 17). It is the part of prudence to lay hold on both; to permit a temperate indulgence both in virtue and in vice, carrying neither to excess (ver. 18)--a doctrine still very dear to the mere man of the world. In this temperance there lies a strength greater than that of an army in a beleaguered city; for no righteous man is wholly righteous (vv. 19, 20): to aim at so lofty and ideal will be to attempt "to wind ourselves too high for mortal man below the sky;" we shall only fail if we make the attempt; we shall be grievously disappointed if we expect other men to succeed where we have failed; we shall lose faith in them, and in ourselves; we shall suffer many pangs of shame, remorse, and defeated hope; and, therefore, it is well at once to make up our minds that we are, and need be, no better than our neighbours, that we are not to blame ourselves for customary and occasional slips; that, if we are but moderate, we may lay one hand on righteousness and another on wickedness without taking much harm. A most immoral moral, though it is as popular to-day as it ever was.

To be indifferent to Censure: Ch. vii., vv. 21, 22.
The second rule which this temperate Monitor infers from his general theory is, That we are not to be overmuch troubled by what people say about us. Servants are adduced as an illustration, partly, no doubt, because they are commonly acquainted with their masters' faults, and partly because they do sometimes speak about them, and even exaggerate them. "Let them speak," is his counsel, "and don't be too curious to know what they say; you may be sure that they will say pretty much what you often say of your neighbours or superiors; if they depreciate you, you depreciate others, and you can hardly expect a more generous treatment than you accord." Now if this moral stood alone, it would be both shrewd and wholesome. But it does not stand alone; and in its connection it means, I fear, that if we take the moderate course prescribed by worldly prudence; if we are righteous without being too righteous, and wicked without being too wicked, and our neighbours should begin to say, "He is hardly so good as he seems," or "I could tell a tale of him an if I would," we are not to be greatly moved by "any such ambiguous givings out;" we are not to be overmuch concerned that our neighbours have discovered our secret slips, since we have often discovered the like slips in them, and know very well that "there is not on earth a righteous man who doeth good and sinneth not." In short, as we are not to be too hard on ourselves for an occasional and decorous indulgence in vice, so neither are we to be very much vexed by the censures which neighbours as guilty as ourselves pass on our conduct. Taken in this its connected sense, the moral is as immoral as that which preceded it.

Here, indeed, our prudent Monitor drops a hint that he himself is not content with a theory which leads to such results. He has tried this "wisdom," but he is not satisfied with it. He desired a higher wisdom, suspecting that there must be a nobler theory of life than this; but it was too far away for him to reach, too deep for him to fathom. After all his researches that which was far off remained far off, deep remained deep: he could not attain the higher wisdom he sought (vv. 23, 24). And so he falls back on

Samuel Cox, D.D.

the wisdom he had tried, and draws a third moral from it which is somewhat difficult to handle.

To despise Women: Ch. vii., vv. 25-29.

It is said of an English satirist that when any friend confessed himself in trouble and asked his advice, his first question was, "Who is she?"--taking it for granted that a woman must be at the bottom of the mischief. And the Hebrew cynic appears to have been of his mind. He cannot but see that the best of men sin sometimes, that even the most temperate are hurried into excesses which their prudence condemns. And when he turns to discover what it is that bewitches them, he finds no other solution of the mystery than--Woman. Sweet and pleasant as she seems, she is "more bitter than death," her heart is a snare, her hands are chains. He whom God loves will escape from her net after brief captivity; only the fool and the sinner are held fast in it (vv. 25, 26). Nor is this a hasty conclusion. Our Hebrew cynic has deliberately gone out, with the lantern of his wisdom in his hand, to search for an honest man and an honest woman. He has been scrupulously careful in his search, "taking things," i.e. indications of character, "one by one;" but though he has found one honest man in a thousand, he has never lit on an honest and good woman (vv. 27, 28). Was not the fault in the eyes of the seeker rather than in the faces into which he peered? Perhaps it was. It would be to-day and here; but was it there and on that far-distant yesterday? The Orientals would still say "No." All through the East, from the hour in which Adam cast the blame of his disobedience on Eve to the present hour, men have followed the example of their first father. Even St. Chrysostom, who should have known better, affirms that when the devil took from Job all he had, he did not take his wife, "because he thought she would greatly help him to conquer that saint of God." Mohammed sings in the same key with the Christian Father: he affirms that since the creation of the world there have been only four perfect women, though it a little redeems the cynicism of his speech to learn that, of these four perfect women, one was his wife and another his daughter; for the good man may have meant a compliment to them rather than an insult to the sex. But if there be any truth in this estimate, if in the East the women were, and are, worse than the men, it is the men who have made them what they are. [43] Robbed of their natural dignity and use as helpmeets, condemned to be mere toys, trained only to minister to sense, what wonder if they have fallen below their due place and honour? Of all cowardly cynicisms that surely is the meanest which, denying women any chance of being good, condemns them for being bad. Our Hebrew cynic seems to have had some faint sense of his unfairness; for he concludes his tirade against the sex with the admission that "God made man upright"--the word "man" here, as in Genesis, standing for the whole race, male and female--and that if all women, and nine hundred and ninety-nine men out of every thousand, have become bad, it is because they have degraded themselves and one another by the evil "devices" they have sought out (ver. 29).

And to be indifferent to Public Wrongs. Ch. viii., vv. 1-13.

The fourth and last rule inferred from this prudent moderate view of life is, That we are to submit with hopeful resignation to the wrongs which spring from human tyranny and injustice. Unclouded by gusts of passion, the wise temperate Oriental carries a "bright countenance" to the king's divan. Though the king should rate him with "evil words," he will remember his "oath of fealty," and not rise up in resentment, still less rush out in open revolt. He knows that the word of a king is potent; that it will be of no use to show a hot mutinous temper; that by a meek endurance of wrath he may allay or avert it. He knows, too, that obedience and submission are not likely to provoke insult and contumely; and that if now and then he is exposed to an undeserved insult, any defence, and especially an angry defence, will but damage his cause (chap. viii., vv. 1-5). Moreover, a man who keeps himself cool and will not permit anger to blind him may, in the worst event, foresee that a time of retribution will surely come on the king, or the satrap, who is habitually unjust; that the people will revolt from him and exact heavy penalties for the wrongs they have endured; that death, "that fell arrest without all bail," will carry him away. He can see that time of retribution drawing nigh, although the tyrant, fooled by impunity, is not aware of its approach; he can also see that when it comes it will be as a war in which no furlough is granted, and whose disastrous close no craft can evade. All this execution of long-delayed justice he has seen again and again; and therefore he will not suffer his resentment to hurry him into dangerous courses, but will calmly await the action of those social laws which compel every man to reap the due reward of his deeds (vv. 5-9).

Nevertheless he has also seen times in which retribution did not overtake oppressors; times even when, in the person of children as wicked and tyrannical as themselves, they "came again" to renew their injustice, and to blot out the memory of the righteous from the earth (ver. 10). And such times have no more disastrous result than this, that they undermine faith and subvert morality. Men see that no immediate sentence is pronounced against the wicked, that they live long in their wickedness and beget children to perpetuate it; and the faith of the good in the overruling providence of God is shaken and strained, while the vast majority of men set themselves to do the evil which flaunts its triumphs before their eyes (ver. 11). None the less the Preacher is quite sure that it is the part of wisdom to trust in the laws and look for the judgments of God: he is quite sure that the triumph of the wicked will soon pass,

The Expositor's Bible: Ecclesiastes

while that of the good will endure (vv. 12, 13); and therefore, as a man of prudent and forecasting spirit, he will submit to injustice, but not inflict it, or at least not carry it to any dangerous excess.

The Preacher condemns this Theory of Human Life, and declares the Quest to be still unattained. Ch. viii., vv. 14, 15.

This is by no means a noble or lofty view of human life; the line of conduct it prescribes is often as immoral as it is ignoble; and we may feel some natural surprise at hearing counsels so base from the lips of the inspired Hebrew Preacher. But we ought to know him, and his method of instruction, well enough by this time to be sure that he is at least as sensible of their baseness as we can be; that he is here speaking to us, not in his own person, but dramatically, and from the lips of the man who, that he may secure a good name and an easy position in the world, is disposed to accommodate himself to the current maxims of his time and company. If we ever had any doubt on this point, it is set at rest by the closing verses of the Section before us. For in these verses the Preacher lowers his mask, and tells us plainly that we cannot and must not attempt to rest in the theory he has just put before us, that to follow out its practical corollaries will lead us away from the Chief Good, not toward it. More than once he has already hinted to us that this "wisdom" is not the highest wisdom; and now he frankly avows that he is as unsatisfied as ever, as far as ever from ending his Quest; that his last key will not unlock those mysteries of life which have baffled him from the first. He still holds, indeed, that it is better to be righteous than to be wicked, though he now sees that even the prudently righteous often have a wage like that of the wicked, and that the prudently wicked often have a wage like that of the righteous (ver. 14). This new theory of life, therefore, he confesses to be "a vanity" as great and deceptive as any of those he has hitherto tried. And as even yet it does not suit him to give us his true theory and announce his final conclusion, he falls back on the conclusion we have so often heard, that the best thing a man can do is to eat and to drink, and to carry a clear enjoying temper through all the days, and all the tasks, which God giveth him under the sun (ver. 15). How this familiar conclusion fits into his final conclusion, and is part of it, though not the whole, we shall see in our study of the next and last section of the Book.

II.--If, as Milton sings,

> "To know
> That which before us lies in daily life
> Is the prime wisdom,"

we are surely much indebted to the Hebrew Preacher. He does not "sit on a hill apart" discussing fate, freewill, foreknowledge absolute, or any lofty abstruse theme. He walks with us, in the common round, to the daily task, and talks to us of that which lies before and around us in our daily life. Nor does he speak as one raised high above the folly and weakness by which we are constantly betrayed. He has trodden the very paths we tread. He shares our craving and has pursued our quest after "that which is good." He has been misled by the illusions by which we are beguiled. And his aim is to save us from fruitless researches and defeated hopes by placing his experience at our command. He speaks, therefore, to our real need, and speaks with a cordial sympathy which renders his counsel very welcome.

We are so made that we can find no rest until we find a supreme Good, a Good which will satisfy all our faculties, passions, aspirations. For this we search with ardour; but our ardour is not always under law to wisdom. We often assume that we have reached our chief Good while it is still far off, or that we are at least looking for it in the right direction when in truth we have turned our back upon it. Sometimes we seek for it in the pursuit of knowledge, sometimes in pleasure and self-indulgence, sometimes in fervent devotion to secular affairs; sometimes in love, sometimes in wealth, and sometimes in a modest yet competent provision for our future wants. And if, when we have acquired the special good we seek, we find that our hearts are still craving and restless, still hungering for a larger good, we are apt to think that if we had a little more of that which so far has disappointed us; if we were somewhat wiser, or if our pleasures were more varied; if we had a little more love or a larger estate, all would be well with us, and we should be at peace. Perhaps in time we get our "little more," but still our hearts do not cry, "Hold, enough!"--enough being always a little more than we have; till at last, weary and disappointed in our quest, we begin to despair of ourselves and to distrust the goodness of God. "If God be good," we ask, "why has He made us thus--always seeking yet never finding, urged on by imperious appetites which are never satisfied, impelled by hopes which for ever elude our grasp?" And because we cannot answer the question, we cry out, "Vanity of vanities! all is vanity and vexation of spirit!"

"Ah, no," replies the kindly Preacher who has himself known this despairing mood and surmounted it; "no, all is not vanity. There is a chief Good, a satisfying Good, although you have not found it yet; and you have not found it because you have not looked for it where alone it can be found.

Samuel Cox, D.D.

Once take the right path, follow the right clue, and you will find a Good which will make all else good to you, a Good which will lend a new sweetness to your wisdom and your mirth, your labour and your gain." But men are very slow to believe that they have wasted their time and strength, that they have wholly mistaken their path; they are reluctant to believe that a little more of that of which they have already acquired so much, and which they have always held to be best, will not yield them the satisfaction they seek. And therefore the wise Preacher, instead of telling us at once where the true Good is to be found, takes much pains to convince us that it is not to be found where we have been wont to seek it. He places before us a man of the largest wisdom, whose pleasures were exquisitely varied and combined, a man whose devotion to affairs was the most perfect and successful, a man of imperial nature and wealth, and whose heart had glowed with all the fervours of love: and this man--himself under a thin disguise--so rarely gifted and of such ample conditions, confesses that he could not find the Chief Good in any one of the directions in which we commonly seek it, although he had travelled farther in every direction than we can hope to go. If we are of a rational temper, if we are open to argument and persuasion, if we are not resolved to buy our own experience at a heavy, perhaps a ruinous, cost, how can we but accept the wise Hebrew's counsel, and cease to look for the satisfying Good in quarters in which he assures us it is not to be found?

We have already considered his argument as it bore on the men of his own time; we have now to make its application to our own age. As his custom is, the Preacher does not develop his argument in open logical sequence; he does not write a moral essay, but paints us a dramatic picture.

The Quest in Wealth. Ch. vi.

He depicts a man who trusts in riches, who honestly believes that wealth is the chief Good, or, at lowest, the way to it. This man has laboured diligently and dexterously to acquire affluence, and he has acquired it. Like the rich man of the Parable, he has much goods, and barns that grow fuller as they grow bigger. "God has given him riches and wealth and abundance, so that his soul"--not having learned how to look for anything higher--"lacks nothing of all that it desireth."

The Man who makes Riches his Chief Good is haunted by Fears and Perplexities. Ch. vi., vv. 1-6.

He has reached his aim, then, acquired what he holds to be good. Can he not be content with it? No; for though he bids his soul make merry and be glad, it obstinately refuses to obey. It is darkened with perplexities, haunted by vague longings, fretted and stung with perpetual care. Now that he has his riches, he goes in dread lest he should lose them; he is unable to decide how he may best employ them, or how to dispose of them when he must leave them behind him. God has given them to him; but he is not at all sure that God will show an equal wisdom in giving them to some one else when he is gone. And so the poor rich man sits steeped in wealth up to his chin--up to his chin, but not up to his lips, for he has no "power to enjoy" it. Burdened with jealous care, he grudges that others should share what he cannot enjoy, grudges above all that, when he is dead, another should possess what has been of so little comfort to him. "If thou art rich," says Shakespeare,

"thou art poor;
For like an ass whose back with ingots bows,
Thou bearest thy heavy riches but a journey,
And Death unloads thee."

But our rich man is not only like an ass; he is even more stupid: for the ass would not have his back bent even with golden ingots if he could help it, and is only too thankful when the burden is lifted from his back; while the rich man not only will plod on beneath his heavy load, but, in his dread of being unladen at his journey's end, imposes on himself a burden heavier than all his ingots, and will bear that as well as his gold. He creeps along beneath his double load, and brays quite pitifully if you so much as put out a hand to ease him.

Much that he gains only feeds Vanity. Chap. vi., v. 11.
He cannot tell what it will be good for him to have; Chap. vi., v. 12.
Nor foresee what will become of his Gains: Chap. vi., v. 12.

It is not of much use, perhaps, to argue with one so besotted; but lest we should slip into his degraded estate, the Preacher points out for our instruction the source of his disquiet, and shows why it is impossible in the very nature of things that he should know content. Among other sources of disquiet he notes these three. (1) That "there are many things which increase vanity:" that is to say, many of the acquisitions of the rich man only augment his outward pomp and state. Beyond a certain point he cannot possibly enjoy the good things he possesses; he cannot, for instance, live in all his costly mansions at once, nor eat and drink all the sumptuous fare set on his table, nor carry his whole wardrobe on his back. He is hampered with superfluities which breed care, but yield him no comfort. And, as he grudges that others should enjoy them, all this abundance, all that goes beyond his personal gratification, so far from

The Expositor's Bible: Ecclesiastes

being an "advantage" to him, is only a burden and a torment. (2) Another source of disquiet is, that no man, not even he, "can tell what is good for man in life," what will be really helpful and pleasant to him. Many things which attract desire pall upon the taste. And as "the day of our vain life is brief," gone "like a shadow," he may flit away before he has had a chance of using much that he has laboriously acquired. (3) And a third source of disquiet is, that the more a man has the more he must leave: and this is a fact which cuts him two ways, with a keen double edge. For the more he has the less he likes leaving it; and the more he has the more is he puzzled how to leave it. He cannot tell "what shall be after him," and so he makes one will to-day and another to-morrow, and very likely dies intestate after all.

Is not that a true picture, a picture true to life? Bulwer Lytton tells us how one of our wealthiest peers once complained to him that he was never so happy and well-served as when he was a bachelor in chambers; that his splendid mansion was a dreary solitude to him, and the long train of domestics his masters rather than his servants. And more than once he depicts, as in The Caxtons, a man of immense fortune and estate as so occupied in learning and discharging the heavy duties of property, so tied and hampered by the thought of what was expected of him, as to fret under a constant weight of care and to lose all the sweet uses of life. And have not we ourselves known men who have grown more penurious as they have grown richer, men unable to decide what it would be really good or even pleasant for them to do, more and more anxious as to how they should devise their abundance? "I am a poor rich man, burdened with money; but I have nothing else," was the saying of a notorious millionaire, who died while he was signing a cheque for £10,000, some twenty years ago.

And because God has put Eternity into his Heart, He cannot be content with Temporal Good. Ch. vi., vv. 7-10.

But the Hebrew Preacher is not content to paint a picture of the Rich Man and his perplexities--a picture as true to the life now as it was then. He also points out how it is that the lover of riches came to be the man he is, and why he can never lay hold on the supreme Good. "All the labour of this man is for his mouth," for the senses and whatever gratifies sense; and therefore, however prosperous he may be, "yet his soul cannot be satisfied." For the soul is not fed by that which feeds the senses. God has "put eternity" into it. It craves an eternal sustenance. It cannot rest till it gains access to "the living water," and "the meat which endureth," and the good "wine of the kingdom." A beast--if indeed beasts have no souls, which I neither deny nor admit--may be content if only he be placed in comfortable outward conditions; but a man, simply because he is a man, must have a wholesome and happy inward life before he can be content. His hunger and thirst after righteousness must be satisfied. He must know that, when flesh and heart fail him, he will be received into an eternal habitation. He must have a treasure which the moth cannot corrupt, nor the thief filch from him. We cannot escape our nature any more than we can jump off our shadow; and our very nature cries out for an immortal good. Hence it is that the rich man who trusts in his riches, and not in the God who gave them to him, carries within him a hungry craving soul. Hence it is that all who trust in riches, and hold them to be the Chief Good, are restless and unsatisfied. For, as the Preacher reminds us, it is very true both that the rich man may not be a fool, and that the poor man may trust in the riches he has not won. By virtue of his wisdom, the wise rich man may so vary and combine the good things of this life as to win from them a gratification denied to the sot whose sordid heart is set on gold; and the poor man, because he has so few of the enjoyments which wealth can buy, may snatch at the few that come his way with the violent delight which has violent ends. Both may "enjoy the good they have" rather than "crave a good beyond their (present) reach:" but if they mistake that good for the Supreme Good, neither their poverty nor their wisdom will save them from the misery of a fatal mistake. For they too have souls, are souls; and the soul is not to be satisfied with that which goes in at the mouth. Wise or foolish, rich or poor, whosoever trusts in riches is either like the ass whose back is bent with a weight of gold, or he is worse than the ass, and longs to take a burden on his back of which only Death can unlade him.

The Quest in the Golden Mean. Ch. vii., v. 1-Ch. viii., v. 15.

2. But now, to come closer home, to draw nearer to that prime wisdom which consists in knowing that which lies before us in our daily life, let us glance at the Man who aims to stand in the Golden Mean; the man who does not aspire to heap up a great fortune, but is anxious to secure a modest competence. He is more on our own level; for our trust in riches is, for the most part, qualified by other trusts. If we believe in Gold, we also believe in Wisdom and in Mirth; if we labour to provide for the future, we also wish to use and enjoy the present. We think it well that we should know something of the world about us, and take some pleasure in our life. We think that to put money in our purse should not be our only aim, though it should be a leading aim. We admit that "the love of money is a root of all evil"--one of the roots from which all forms and kinds of evil may spring; and, to save ourselves from falling into that base lust, we limit our desires. We shall be content if we can put by a moderate sum, and we flatter ourselves that we desire even so much as that, not for its own sake, but for the means of knowledge, or of usefulness, or of innocent enjoyment with which it will furnish us. "Nothing I should

like better," says many a man, "than to retire from business as soon as I have enough to live upon, and to devote myself to this branch of study or that province of art, or to take my share of public duties, or to give myself to a cheerful domestic life." It speaks well for our time, I think, that while in a few large cities there are still many in haste to be rich and very rich, in the country and in hundreds of provincial towns there are thousands of men who know that wealth is not the Chief Good, and who do not care to don the livery of Mammon. Nevertheless, though their aim be "most sweet and commendable," it has perils of its own, imminent and deadly perils, which few of us altogether escape. And these perils are clearly set before us in the sketch of the Hebrew Preacher. As I reproduce that sketch, suffer me, for the sake of brevity, while carefully retaining the antique outlines, to fill in with modern details.

The Method of the Man who seeks a Competence. Ch. viii., vv. 1-14.

Suppose a young man to start in life with this theory, this plan, this aim, distinctly before him:--he is to be ruled by prudence and plain common sense: he will try to stand well with the world, and to make a moderate provision for future wants. This aim will beget a certain temperance of thought and action. He will permit himself no extravagances--no wandering out of bounds, and perhaps no enthusiasms, for he wants to establish "a good name," a good reputation, which shall go before him like "a sweet perfume" and dispose men's hearts toward him. And, therefore, he carries a sober face, frequents the company of older, wiser men, is grateful for any hints their experience may furnish, and takes even their "reproof" with a good grace. He walks in the beaten paths, knowing the world to be impatient of novelties. The wanton mirth and crackling laughter of fools in the house of feasting are not for him. He is not to be seduced from the plain prudent course which he has marked out for himself whether by inward provocation or outward allurements. If he is a young lawyer, he will write no poetry, attorneys holding literary men in suspicion. If he is a young doctor, homoeopathy, hydropathy, and all new-fangled schemes of medicine will disclose their charms to him in vain. If he is a young clergyman, he will be conspicuous for his orthodoxy, and for his emphatic assent to all that the leaders of opinion in the Church think or may think. If he is a young manufacturer or merchant, he will be no breeder of costly patents and inventions, but will be among the first to profit by them whenever they are found to pay. Whatever he may be, he will not be of those who try to make crooked things straight and rough places plain. He wants to get on; and the best way to get on is to keep the beaten path and push forward in that. And he will be patient--not throwing up the game because for a time the chances go against him, but waiting till the times mend and his chances improve, so far as he can, he will keep the middle of the stream that, when the tide which leads on to fortune sets in, he may be of the best to take it at the flood and sail easily on to his desired haven.

In all this there may be no conscious insincerity, and not much perhaps that calls for censure. For all young men are not wise with the highest wisdom, nor original, nor brave with the courage which follows Truth in scorn of consequence. And our young man may not be dowered with the love of loves, the hate of hates, the scorn of scorns. He may be of a nature essentially prudent and commonplace, or training and habit may have superinduced a second nature. To him a primrose may be a primrose and nothing more; his instinctive thought, as he looks at it, may be how he can reproduce its colour in some of his textures or extract a saleable perfume from its nectared cup. He may even think that primroses are a mistake, and that 'tis pity they were not pot-herbs; or he may assume that he shall have plenty of time to gather primroses by-and-bye, but that for the present he must be content to pick pot-herbs for the market. In his way, he may even be a religious man; he may admit that both prosperity and adversity are of God, that we must take patiently whatever He may send; and he may heartily desire to be on good terms with Him who alone "can order all things as He please."

The Perils to which it exposes him. Ch. vii., v. 15-Ch. viii., v. 13.
He is likely to compromise Conscience; Ch. vii., vv. 15-20.

But here we light on his first grave peril; for he will carry his temperance into his religion, and he may subordinate even that to his desire to get on. Looking on men in their religious aspect, he sees that they are divided into two classes, the righteous and the wicked. As he considers them, he concludes that on the whole the righteous have the best of it, that godliness is real gain. But he soon discovers that this first rough conclusion needs to be carefully qualified. For, as he studies men more closely, he perceives that at times the righteous die in their righteousness without being the better for it, and the wicked live on in their wickedness without being the worse for it. He perceives that while the very wicked die before their time, the very righteous, those who are always reaching forth to that which is before them and rising to new heights of insight and obedience, are "forsaken," that they are left alone in the thinly-peopled solitude to which they have climbed, losing the sympathy even of those who once walked with them. Now, these are facts; and a prudent sensible man tries to accept facts, and to adjust himself to them, even when they are adverse to his wishes and conclusions. He does not want to be left alone, nor to die before his time. And therefore, taking these new facts into account, he infers that it will be best to be good without being too good, and to indulge himself with an occasional lapse into some general and customary wickedness without being too wicked. Nay, he is disposed to believe that "whoso feareth God," studying the facts of his providence and drawing logical inferences from them, "will lay hold of both" wickedness and righteousness, and will blend them in that proportion which the facts seem to favour. But here Conscience protests, urging that to do evil can never be good. To pacify it, he adduces the notorious fact that "there is not a righteous man on earth who doeth good, and sinneth not." "Conscience," he says, "you are really too strict and straitlaced, too hard on one who wants to do as well as he can. You go quite too far. How can you expect me to be better than great saints and men after God's own heart?" And so, with a wronged and pious air, he turns to lay one hand on wickedness and another on righteousness, quite content to be no better than his neighbours and to let Conscience sulk herself into a sweeter mood.

To be indifferent to Censure; Ch. vii., vv. 21, 22.
Conscience being silenced, Prudence steps in. And Prudence says, "People will talk. They will take note of your slips, and tattle about them. Unless you are very very careful, you will damage your reputation; and if you do that, how can you hope to get on?" Now as the man is specially devoted to Prudence, and has found her kind mistress and useful monitress in one, he is at first a little staggered to find her taking part against him. But he soon recovers himself, and replies: "Dear Prudence, you know as well as I do that people don't like a man to be better than themselves. Of course they will talk if they catch me tripping; but I don't mean to do more than trip, and a man who trips gains ground in recovering himself, and goes all the faster for a while. Besides we all trip; some fall even. And I talk of my neighbours just as they talk of me; and we all like each other the better for being birds of one feather."

To despise Women; Ch. vii., vv. 25-29.
At this Prudence smiles and stops her mouth. But being very willing to assist so quick-witted a disciple, she presently returns and says: "Are you not rather a long while in securing your little Competence? Is there no short cut to it? Why not take a wife with a small fortune of her own, or with connexions who could help you on?" Now the man, not being a bad man, but one who would fain be good so far as he knows goodness, is somewhat taken aback by such a suggestion as this. He thinks Prudence must be growing very worldly and mercenary. He says within himself, "Surely love should be sacred! A man should not prostitute that in order to get on! If I marry a woman simply or mainly for her money, what worse degradation can I inflict on her or on myself? how shall I be better than those old Hebrews and Orientals who held women to be only a toy or a convenience? To do that, would be to make a snare and a net of her indeed, to degrade her from her true place and function, and possibly would lead me to think of her as even worse than I had made her." Nevertheless, his heart being very much set on securing a Competence, and an accident of the sort which he calls "providences" putting a foolish woman with a pocketful of money in his way, he takes both the counsel of Prudence and a wife to match.

And to be indifferent to Public Wrongs. Ch. viii., vv. 1-13.
The world, we may be sure, thinks none the worse of him for that. Once more he has proved himself a man whose eye is stedfastly bent on "the main chance," and who knows how to seize occasions as they rise. But he, who has thus profaned the inner sanctuary of his own soul, is not likely to be sensitive to the large claims of public duty. If he sees oppression, if the tyranny of a man or a class mounts to a height which calls for rebuke and opposition, he is not likely to sacrifice comfort and risk either property or popularity that he may assail iniquity in her strong places. It is not such men as he who, when the times are out of joint, feel that they are born to set them right. Prudence is still his guide, and Prudence says, "Let things alone; they will right themselves in time. The social laws will avenge themselves on the head of the oppressor, and deliver the oppressed. You can do little to hasten their action. Why, to gain so little, should you risk so much?" And the man is content to sit still with folded hands when every hand that can strike a blow for right is wanted in the strife, and can even quote texts of Scripture to prove that in "quietness, and confidence" in the action of Divine Laws, is the true strength.

The Preacher condemns this Theory, and declares the Quest to be still unattained. Ch. vii., vv. 14, 15.
Now I make my appeal to those who daily enter the world of business--is not this the tone of that world? are not these the very perils to which you lie open? How often have you heard men recount the slips of the righteous in order to justify themselves for not assuming to be righteous overmuch! How often have you heard them vindicate their own occasional errors by citing the errors of those who give greater heed to religion than they do, or make a louder profession of it! How often have you heard them congratulate a neighbour on his good luck in carrying off an heiress, or speak of wedded love itself as a mere help to worldly advancement! How often have you heard them sneer at the nonsensical enthusiasm which has led certain men to "throw away their chances in life" in order to devote themselves to the

service of truth, or to forfeit popularity that they might lead a forlorn hope against customary wrongs, and thank God that no such maggot ever bit their brains! If during the years which have lapsed since I too "went on 'Change," the general tone has not risen a whole heaven--and I have heard of no such miracle--I know that you must daily hear such things as these, and worse than these; and that not only from irreligious men of bad character, but from men who take a fair place in our Christian congregations. From the time of the wise Preacher to the present hour, this sort of talk has been going on, and the scheme of life from which it springs has been stoutly held. There is the more need, therefore, for you to listen to and weigh the Preacher's conclusion. For his conclusion is, that this scheme of life is wholly and irredeemably wrong, that it tends to make a man a coward and a slave, that it cannot satisfy the large desires of the soul, and that it cheats him of the Chief Good. His conclusion is, that the man who so sets his heart on acquiring even a Competence that he cannot be content without it, has no genuine trust in God, since he is willing to give in to immoral maxims and customs in order to secure that which, as he thinks, will make him largely independent of the Divine Providence.

The Preacher speaks as to wise men, to men of some experience of the world. Judge you what he says.

Footnotes:

41. "There are three crowns; of the law, the priesthood, and the kingship: but the crown of a good name is greater than them all."--Talmud.

42. So in the hymn of Cleanthes to Zeus, as rendered by the Dean of Wells:

"Thou alone knowest how to change the odd
To even, and to make the crooked straight;
And things discordant find accord in Thee.
Thus in one whole Thou blendest ill with good,
So that one law works on for evermore."

43. Not, however, that the sentiment was confined to the East. The Greek poets have many such sayings as, "A woman is a burden full of ills;" and, "Where women are, all evils there are found."

FOURTH SECTION

THE QUEST ACHIEVED. THE CHIEF GOOD IS TO BE FOUND, NOT IN WISDOM, NOR IN PLEASURE, NOR IN DEVOTION TO AFFAIRS AND ITS REWARDS; BUT IN A WISE USE AND A WISE ENJOYMENT OF THE PRESENT LIFE, COMBINED WITH A STEDFAST FAITH IN THE LIFE TO COME.

Chap. VIII., Ver. 16, to Chap. XII., Ver. 7.

At last we approach the end of our Quest. The Preacher has found the Chief Good, and will show us where to find it. But are we even yet prepared to welcome it and to lay hold of it? Apparently he thinks we are not. For, though he has already warned us that it is not to be found in Wealth or Industry, in Pleasure or Wisdom, he repeats his warning in this last Section of his Book, as if he still suspected us of hankering after our old errors. Not till he has again assured us that we shall miss our mark if we seek the supreme Good in any of the directions in which it is commonly sought, does he direct us to the sole path in which we shall not seek in vain. Once more, therefore, we must gird up the loins of our mind to follow him along his several lines of thought, encouraged by the assurance that the end of our journey is not now far off.

The Chief Good not to be found in Wisdom: Ch. viii., v. 16-Ch. ix., v. 6.

1. The Preacher commences this Section by carefully defining his position and equipment as he starts on his final course. As yet he carries no lamp of Revelation in his hand, although he will not venture beyond a certain point without it. For the present he will trust to Reason and Experience, and mark the conclusions to which these conduct when unaided by any direct light from Heaven. His first conclusion is that Wisdom, which of all temporal goods still stands foremost with him, is incapable of yielding a true content. Much as it can do for man, it cannot solve the moral problems which task and afflict his heart, the problems which he must solve before he can be at peace. He may be so bent on solving these by Wisdom as to see "no sleep with his eyes by day or night;" he may rely on Wisdom with a confidence so genuine as to suppose at times that by its help he has "found out all the work of God"--really solved all the mysteries of the Divine Providence; but nevertheless "he has not found it out;" the illusion will soon pass, and the unsolved mysteries reappear dark and sombre as of old (chap. viii., vv. 16, 17). And the proof that he has failed is, first, that he is as incompetent to foresee the future as those who are not so wise as he. With all his sagacity, he cannot tell whether he shall meet "the love or the hatred" of his fellows. His lot is as closely hidden in "the hand of God" as theirs, although he may be as much better as he is wiser than they (chap. ix., ver. 1). A second proof is that "the same fate" overtakes both the wise and the foolish, the righteous and the wicked, and he is as unable to escape it as any of his neighbours. All die; and to men ignorant of the heavenly hope of the Gospel the indiscrimination of Death seems the most cruel and hopeless of wrongs. The Preacher, indeed, is not ignorant of that bright hope; but as yet he has not taken the lamp of Revelation into his hand: he is simply speaking the thought of those who have no higher guide than Reason, no brighter light than Reflection. And to these, their wisdom having taught them that to do right is infinitely better than to do wrong, no fact was so monstrous and inscrutable as that their lives should run to the same disastrous close with the lives of evil and violent men, that all alike should fall into the hands of "that churl, Death." As they revolved this fact, their hearts grew hot with a fierce resentment as natural as it was impotent, a resentment all the hotter because they knew how impotent it was. Therefore the Preacher dwells on this fact, lingers over his description of it, adding touch to touch. "One fate comes to all," he says, "to the righteous and to the wicked, to the pure and to the impure, to the religious and to the irreligious, to the profane and to the reverent." If death be a good, the maddest fool and the vilest reprobate share it with the sage and the saint. If death be an evil, it is inflicted on the good as well as on the bad. None is exempt. Of all wrongs this is the greatest; of all problems this is the most insoluble. Nor is there any doubt as to the nature of death. To him for whom there shines no light of hope behind the darkness of the grave, death is the supreme evil. For to the living, however deject and wretched, there is still some hope that times may mend: even though in outward condition despicable as that unclean outcast, a dog--the homeless and masterless scavenger of Eastern cities--he has some advantage

over the royal lion who, once couched on a throne, now lies in the dust rotting to dust. The living know at least that they must die; but the dead know not anything. The living can recall the past, and their memory harps fondly on notes which were once most sweet; but the very memory of the dead has perished, no music of the happy past can revive on their dulled sense, nor will any recall their names. The heavens are fair; the earth is beautiful and generous; the works of men are many and diverse and great; but they have "no more any portion for ever in ought that is done under the sun" (vv. 2-6).

This is the Preacher's description of the hapless estate of the dead. His words would go straight home to the hearts of the men for whom he wrote, with a force even beyond that which they would have for heathen races. In their Captivity, they had renounced the worship of idols. They had renewed their covenant with Jehovah. Many of them were devoutly attached to the ordinances and commandments which they and their fathers had neglected in happier and more prosperous years. Yet their lives were made bitter to them with cruel bondage, and they had as little hope in their death as the Persians who embittered their lives, and probably even less. It was in this sore strait, and under the strong compulsions of this dreadful extremity, that the more studious and pious of their rabbis, like the Preacher himself, drew into an expressive context the passages scattered through their Sacred Books which hinted at a retributive life beyond the tomb, and settled into that firm persuasion of the immortality of the soul which, as a rule, they never henceforth altogether let go. But when the Preacher wrote, this settled and general conviction had not been reached. There were many among them who, as their thoughts circled round the mystery of death, could only cry, "Is this the end? is this the end?" To the great majority of them it seemed the end. And even the few, who sought an answer to the question by blending the Greek and Oriental with the Hebrew Wisdom, attained no clear answer to it. To mere human wisdom, Life remained a mystery, and Death a mystery still more cruel and impenetrable. Only those who listened to the Preachers and Prophets taught of God beheld the dawn which already began to glimmer on the darkness in which men sat.

Nor in Pleasure: Ch. ix., vv. 7-12.

Imagine, then, a Jew brought to the bitter pass which Coheleth has described. He has acquainted himself with Wisdom, native and foreign; and wisdom has led him to conclusions of virtue. Nor is he of those who love virtue as they love music--without practising it. Believing that a righteous and religious carriage of himself will ensure happiness and equip him to encounter the problems of life, he has striven to be good and pure, to offer his sacrifices and pay his vows. But he has found that, despite his best endeavours, his life is not tranquil, that the very calamities which overtake the wicked overtake him, that that wise carriage of himself by which he thought to win love has provoked hatred, that death remains a frowning and inhospitable mystery. He hates death, and has no great love for the life which has brought him only labour and disappointment. Where is he likely to turn next? Wisdom having failed him, to what will he apply? At what conclusion will he arrive? Will not his conclusion be that standing conclusion of the baffled and the hapless, "Let us eat and drink for to-morrow we die"? Will he not say, "Why should I weary myself any more with studies which yield no certain science, and self-denials which meet with no reward? If a wise and pure conduct cannot secure me from the evils I dread, let me at least try to forget them and to grasp such poor delights as are still within my reach?" This, at all events, is the conclusion in which the Preacher lands him; and hence he takes occasion to review the pretensions of Pleasure or Mirth. To the baffled and hopeless devotee of Wisdom he says, "Go, then, eat thy bread with gladness, and drink thy wine with a merry heart. Cease to trouble yourself about God and His judgments. He, as you have seen, does not mete out rewards and punishments according to our merit or demerit; and as He does not punish the wicked after their deserts, you may be sure that He has long since accepted your wise virtuous endeavours, and will keep no score against you. Deck yourself in white festive garments; let no perfume be lacking to your head; add to your harem any woman who charms your eye: and, as the day of your life is brief at the best, let no hour of it slip by unenjoyed. As you have chosen Mirth for your portion, be as merry as you may. Whatever you can get, get; whatever you can do, do. You are on the road to the dark dismal grave where there is no work nor device; there is, therefore, the more reason why your journey should be a merry one" (vv. 7-10).

Thus the Preacher describes the Man of Pleasure, and the maxims by which he rules his life. How true the description is I need not tarry to prove; 'tis a point every man can judge for himself. Judge also whether the warning which the Preacher subjoins be not equally true to experience (vv. 11, 12). For, after having depicted, or personated, the Man who trusts in Wisdom, and the Man who devotes himself to Pleasure, he proceeds to show that even the Man who blends mirth with study, whose wisdom preserves him from the disgusts of satiety and vulgar lust, is nevertheless--to say nothing of the Chief Good--very far from having reached a certain good. Then, at least, "the race was not (always) to the swift, nor the battle to the strong; neither was bread to the wise, nor riches to the intelligent, nor favour to the learned." Those who had the fairest chances had not always the happiest success; nor did those who bent themselves most strongly to their ends always reach their ends. Those who were wanton as birds, or heedless as fish, were often taken in the snare of calamity or swept up by the net of misfortune.

The Expositor's Bible: Ecclesiastes
At any moment a killing frost might blight all the growths of Wisdom and destroy all the sweet fruits of Pleasure: and if they had only these, what could they do but starve when they were gone? The good which was at the mercy of accident, which might vanish before the instant touch of disease or loss or pain, was not worthy to be, or to be compared with, the Chief Good, which is a good for all times, in all accidents and conditions, and renders him who has it equal to all events.

Nor in Devotion to Affairs and its Rewards. Ch. ix., v. 13-Ch. x., v. 20.

So far, then, Coheleth has been occupied in retracing the argument of the first Section of the Book. Now he returns upon the second and third Sections: he deals with the man who plunges into public affairs, who turns his wisdom to practical account, and seeks to attain a competence, if not a fortune. He lingers over this stage of his argument, probably because the Jews, then as always, even in exile and under the most cruel oppression, were a remarkably energetic, practical, money-getting race, with a singular faculty of dealing with political issues or handling the market; and, as he slowly pursues it, he drops many hints of the social and political conditions of the time. Two features of it he takes much to heart: first, that wisdom, even of the most practical and sagacious sort, did not win its fair recognition and reward--a very natural complaint in so wise a man; and, secondly, that his people were under tyrants so gross, self-indulgent, indolent, and unstatesman-like as the Persians of his day--also a natural complaint in a man of so wise and patriotic a spirit.

He opens with an anecdote in proof of the slight regard in which the most valuable and remunerative sagacity was held. He tells us of a poor man--and I have sometimes thought that this poor man may have been the Author himself; for the military leaders of the Jews, though among the most expert strategists of that era, were often very learned and studious men--who lived in a little city, with only a few inhabitants. A great king came up against the city, besieged it, threw up the lofty military causeway, as high as the walls, from which it was the fashion of the time to deliver the assault. By his Archimedian wit the poor man hit on a stratagem which saved the city; but though his service was so signal, and the city so little that the "few men in it" must have seen him every day, "yet no one remembered that same poor man," or lent a hand to lift him from his poverty. Wise as he was, his wisdom did not bring him bread, nor riches, nor favour (vv. 13-15). Therefore, concludes the Preacher, wisdom, great gift though it is, and better, as in this instance, than "an army to a beleaguered city" (chap. vii., ver. 19), is not of itself sufficient to secure success. A poor man's wisdom--as many an inventor has found--is despised even by those who profit by it. Although his counsel, in the day of extremity, is infinitely more valuable than the loud bluster of fools, or of a ruler among fools, nevertheless the ruler, because he is foolish, may be affronted to find one of the poorest men in the place wiser than himself; he may easily cast his "merit in the eye of scorn," and so rob him both of the honour and the reward of his achievement (vv. 16, 17)--an ancient saw not without modern instances. For the fool is a greater power in the world, especially the fool who is wise in his own conceit. Insignificant in himself, he may nevertheless do great harm and "destroy much good." Just as a tiny fly, when it is dead, may make the sweetest ointment offensive by infusing its own evil savour, so a man, when his wit is gone, may with his little folly cause many sensible men to distrust the wisdom they should honour (chap. x., ver. 1):--who has not met such a hot-headed want-wit in, for example, the lobbies of the House of Commons? To a wise man, such as Coheleth, the fool, the presumptuous conceited fool, is "rank and smells to heaven," infesting sweeter natures than his own with a most pestilent corruption. He paints us a picture of him--paints it with a keen graphic scorn which, if the eyes of the fool were in his head (chap. ii., ver. 14), and "what he is pleased to call his mind" could for a moment shift from his left hand to his right (ver. 2), might make him nearly as contemptible to himself as he is to others. As we read ver. 3 the unhappy wretch stands before us. We see him coming out of his house; he goes dawdling down the street, for ever wandering from the path, attracted by the merest trifle, staring at familiar objects with eyes that have no recognition in them, knowing neither himself nor others; and, with pointed finger, chuckles after every sober citizen he meets, "There goes a fool!"

Yet a fool quite as foolish and malignant as this, quite as indecent even in outward behaviour, may be lifted to high place, and has ere now sat on an imperial throne. [44] The Preacher had seen many of them suddenly raised to power, while nobles were depraved, and high functionaries of State reduced to an abject servitude. Now if the poor wise man have to attend the durbar, or sit in the divan, of a foolish capricious despot, how should he bear himself? The Preacher counsels meekness and submission. He is to sit unruffled even though the ruler should rate him, lest by resentment he should provoke some graver outrage (vv. 4-7; comp. chap. viii., ver. 3). To strengthen him in his submission, the Preacher hints at cautions and consolations which, because free and open speech was very dangerous under the Persian despotism, he wraps up in obscure maxims capable of a double sense--nay, as the commentators have shown, capable of a good many more senses than two--to the true sense of which "a foolish ruler" was by no means likely to penetrate, even if they fell into his hands.

The first of these maxims is, "He who diggeth a pit shall fall into it" (ver. 8). And the allusion is, of course, to an Eastern mode of trapping wild beasts and game. The huntsman dug a pit, covered it with twigs and sods, and strewed the surface with bait; but as he dug many such pits, and some of them were long without a tenant, he might at any inadvertent moment fall into one of them himself. The proverb is capable of at least two interpretations. It may mean that the foolish despot, plotting the ruin of his wise servant, might in his anger go too far; and, betraying his intention, provoke a retaliative anger before which he himself would fall. Or it may mean that, should the wise servant seek to undermine the throne of the despot, he might be taken in his treachery and bring on himself the whole weight of the tyrant's wrath.

The second maxim is, "Whoso breaketh down a wall, a serpent shall bite him" (ver. 8); and here, of course, the allusion is to the fact that snakes infect the crannies of old walls (comp. Amos v. 19). To set about dethroning a tyrant was like pulling down such a wall; you would break up the nest of many a reptile, many a venomous hanger-on, and might only get bit or stung for your pains. Or, again, in pulling out the stones of an old wall, you might let one of them fall on your foot; and in hacking out its timbers, you might cut yourself: that is to say, even if your conspiracy did not involve you in absolute ruin, it would be only too likely to do you serious and lasting injury (ver. 9).

The next adage runs (ver. 10), "If the axe be blunt, and he do not whet the edge, he must put on more strength, but wisdom should teach him to sharpen it," and is, perhaps, the most difficult passage in the Book. The Hebrew is read in a different way by almost every translator. As I read it, it means, in general, that it is not well to work with blunt tools when by a little labour and delay you may whet them to a keener edge. Read thus, the political rule implied in it is, "Do not attempt any great enterprise, any revolution or reform, till you have a well-considered scheme to go upon, and suitable instruments to carry it out with." But the special political import of it may be, "Your strength is nothing to that of the tyrant; do not therefore lift a blunt axe against the trunk of despotism: wait till you have put a sharp edge upon it." Or, the tyrant himself may be the blunt axe, and then the warning is, "Sharpen him up, repair him, use him and his caprices to serve your end; get your way by giving way to him, and by skilfully availing yourself of his varying moods." Which of these may be the true meaning of this obscure disputed passage, I do not undertake to say; but the latter of the two seems to be sustained by the adage which follows: "If the serpent bite because it is not charmed, there is no advantage to the charmer." For here, I think, there can be little doubt that the foolish angry ruler is the serpent, and the wise functionary the charmer who is to extract the venom of his anger. Let the foolish ruler be never so furious, the poor wise man, who is able "to cull the plots of best advantages," and to save a city, can surely devise a charm of soft submissive words which will turn away his wrath; just as the serpent-charmer of the East, by song and incantation, is at least reputed to draw serpents from their lurk, that he may pluck the venom from their teeth (ver. 11). For, as we are told in the very next verse, "the words of the wise man's mouth win him grace, while the lips of the fool destroy him."

And on this hint, on this casual mention of his name, the Preacher--who all this while, remember, is personating the sagacious man of the world, bent on rising to wealth, power, distinction--once more "comes down" on the fool. He speaks of him with a burning heat and contempt, as men versed in public affairs are wont to do, since they best know how much harm a voluble, impudent, self-conceited fool may do, how much good he may prevent. Here, then, is the fool of public life. He is a man always prating and predicting, although his words, only foolish at the first, swell and fret into a malignant madness before he has done, and although he of all men is least able to give good counsel, to seize occasions as they rise, or to foresee what is about to come to pass. Puffed up by the conceit of wisdom or of his own importance, he is for ever intermeddling with great affairs, though he has no notion how to handle them, and is incapable of even finding his way along the beaten road which leads to the capital city, of taking and keeping the plain and obvious path which the exigencies of the time require; while (ver. 3) he is forward to cry, "There goes a fool," of every man who is wiser than himself (vv. 12-15). If he would only hold his tongue, he might pass muster; beguiled by his gravity and silence, men might give him credit for sagacity, and fit his foolish deeds with profound motives; but he will speak, and his words betray and "swallow him up." Of course we have no such fools, "full of words," to rise in their high place and wag their tongues to their own hurt; they are peculiar to Antiquity or to the East.

But then there were so many of them, and their influence in the State was so disastrous that, as the Preacher thinks of them, he breaks into an almost dithyrambic fervour, and cries, "Woe to thee, O land, when thy king is a child, [45] and thy princes feast in the morning! Happy art thou, O land, when thy king is noble, and thy princes eat at due hours, for strength and not for revelry!" Through the sloth and riot of these foolish rulers, the whole fabric of the State was fast fading into decay--the roof rotting and the rain leaking in. To support their inopportune and profligate revelry, they imposed crushing taxes on the people, which inspired in some a revolutionary discontent, and in some the apathy of despair. The Wise Exile foresaw that the end of a despotism so unjust and luxurious could not be far off; that when the storm rose and the wind blew, the ancient House, unrepaired in its decay, would topple on the heads of those who sat in its halls, revelling in a wicked mirth (vv. 16-19). Meantime, the sagacious servant of the State, perchance too of foreign extraction, unable to arrest the progress of decay, or not caring how soon it was consummated, would make his "market of the time;" he would carry himself warily: and, because the whole land was infested with the spies bred by despotism, he would give them no hold on him, nor so much as speak the simple truth of his foolish debauched rulers in the privacy of his own bed-chamber, or mutter his thoughts on the roof, lest some "bird of the air should carry the report" (ver. 20).

But if this were the condition of the time, if to rise in public life involved so many mean crafts and submissions, so many deadly imminent risks from spies and from fools clad in a little brief authority, how could any man hope to find the Chief Good in it? Wisdom did not always win promotion; virtue was inimical to success. The anger of an incapable idiot, or the whisper of an envious rival, or the caprice of a merciless despot, might at any moment undo the work of years, and expose the most upright and sagacious of men to the worst extremities of misfortune. There was no tranquillity, no freedom, no security, no dignity in such a life as this. Till this were resigned and some nobler, loftier aim found, there was no chance of reaching that great satisfying Good which lifts man above all accidents, and fixes him in a happy security from which no blow of Circumstance can dislodge him.

But in a wise Use and a wise Enjoyment of the Present Life, Ch. xi., vv. 1-8.

What that Good is, and where it may be found, the Preacher now proceeds to show. But, as his manner is, he does not say in so many words, "This is the Chief Good of man," or "You will find it yonder;" but he places before us the man who is walking in the right path and drawing closer and closer to it. Even of him the preacher does not give us any formal description; but, following what we have seen to be his favourite method, he gives us a string of maxims and counsels from which we are to infer what manner of man he is who happily achieves this great Quest.

And, at the very outset, we learn that this happy person is of a noble, unselfish, generous temper. Unlike the man who simply wants to get on and make a fortune, he grudges no man his gains; he looks on his neighbours' interests as well as his own, and does good even to the evil and the unthankful. [46] He is one who "casts his bread upon the waters" (ch. xi., ver. 1), and who "gives a portion thereof to seven, and even to eight" (ver. 2). The familiar proverb of the first verse has long been read as an allusion to the sowing of rice and other grain from a boat, during the periodical inundation of certain Eastern rivers, especially the Nile. We have been taught to regard the husbandman pushing from the embanked village in his frail bark, to cast the grain he would gladly eat on the surface of the flood, as a type of Christian labour and charity. He denies himself; so also must we if we would do good. He has faith in the Divine laws, and trusts to receive his own again with usury, to reap a larger crop the longer he waits for it; and, in like manner, we are to trust in the Divine laws which bring us a hundredfold for every act of self-denying service, and bless our "long patience" with the ampler harvest. But it is doubtful whether the Hebrew usus loquendi admits of this interpretation. It probably suggests another which, if unfamiliar to us, has a beauty of its own. In the East bread is commonly made in thin flat cakes, something like Passover cakes; and one of these cakes flung on the stream, though it would float with the current for a time, would soon sink; and once sunk would, unlike the grain cast from the boat, yield no return. And our charity should be like that. We should do good, "hoping for nothing again." We should show kindnesses which will soon be forgotten, never be returned, and be undismayed by the thanklessness of the task. It is not so thankless as it seems. For, first, we shall "find the good of it" in the loftier, more generous temper which the habit of doing good breeds and confirms. If no one else be the better for our kindness, we shall be the better, because the more kindly, for it. The quality of charity, like that of mercy, is twice blessed;

"It blesseth him that gives and him that takes."

And, again, the task is not so thankless as it sometimes seems; for though many of our kind deeds may quicken no kindness in "him that takes," yet some of them will; and the more we help and succour the more likely are we to light upon at least a few who, when our need comes, will succour and console us. Even the most hardened have a certain tenderness for those who help them, if only the help meet a real need, and be given with grace. And, therefore, we may be very sure that if we give a portion of our bread to seven and even to eight, especially if they know that we ourselves have stomach for it all, at least one or two of them will share with us when we need bread.

But is not this, after all, only a refined selfishness? If we give because we do not know how soon we may need a gift, and in order that we may by-and-bye "find the good of it," do not even the heathen and the publicans the same? Well, not many of them, I think. I have not observed that it is their habit to cast their bread on thankless waters. If they forbode calamity and loss, they provide against them, not by giving, but by hoarding; and even they themselves would hardly accept as a model of charity a man who buttoned up his pocket against every appeal, lest he should be yielding to a selfish motive, or be suspected of it. The refined selfishness of showing kindness and doing good even to the evil and the unthankful because we hope to find the good of it is by no means too common yet; we need not go in dread of it. Nor is it an altogether unworthy motive. St. Paul urges us to help a fallen brother on the express ground that we may need similar help some day (Gal. vi. 1); and he was not in the habit of appealing to base motives. Nay, the very Golden Rule itself, which all men admire even if they do not walk by it, touches this spring of action; for among other meanings it surely has this, that we are to do to others as we would that they should do to us, in the hope that they will do to us as we have done to them. There are other higher meanings in the Rule of course, as there are other and purer motives for Charity; but I do not know that we are any of us of so lofty a virtue that we need fear to show kindness in order to win kindness, or to give help that we may get help when we need it. Possibly, to act on this motive may be the best and nearest way of rising to such higher motives as we can reach.

The first characteristic, then, of the man who is likely to achieve the Quest of the Chief Good is the Charity which prompts him to be gracious, and to show kindness, and to do good, even to the thankless and ungracious. And his second characteristic is the stedfast Industry which turns all seasons to account. The man of affairs, who wants to rise, waits on occasion; he is on the watch to avail himself of the moods and caprices of men and bend them to his interest. But he who has learned to value things at their true worth, and whose heart is fixed on the acquisition of the highest good, does not want to get on so much as to do his duty under all the variable conditions of life. Just as he will not withhold his hand from giving, lest some of the recipients of his charity should prove unworthy, so also he will not withdraw his hand from the labour appointed him, because this or that endeavour may be unproductive, or lest it should be thwarted by the ordinances of Heaven. He knows that the laws of Nature will hold on their way, often causing individual loss to promote the general good. He knows, for instance, that when the clouds are full of rain they will empty themselves upon the earth, even though they put his harvest in peril; and that when the wind is fierce it will blow down trees, even though it should also scatter the seed which he is sowing. But he does not therefore wait upon the wind till it is too late to sow, nor upon the clouds till his ungathered crops rot in the fields. He is conscious that, though he knows much, he knows little of these as of other works of God: he cannot tell whether this or that tree will be blown down; almost all he can be certain of is that, when the tree is down, it will lie where it has fallen, lifting its bleeding roots in dumb protest against the wind which has brought it low. But this too he knows, that it is "God who worketh all;" that he is not responsible for events beyond his control: that what he is responsible for is that he do the duty of the moment whatever wind may blow, and calmly leave the issue in the hand of God. And so he is not "over exquisite to cast the fashion of uncertain evils;" diligent and undismayed, he goes on his way, giving himself heartily to the present duty, "sowing his seed morning and evening, although he cannot tell which shall prosper, this or that, or whether both shall prove good" (vv. 3-6). Windy March cannot blow him from his constant purpose, though it may blow the seed out of his hand; nor a rainy August melt him to despairing tears, though it may damage his harvest. He has done his duty, discharged his responsibility: let God see to the rest; whatever pleases God will content him.

This man, then, has learned one or two of the profoundest secrets of Wisdom, plain as they look. He has learned that, giving, we gain; and, spending, thrive. He has also learned that a man's true care is himself; that all that pertains to the body, to the issues of labour, to the chances of fortune, is external to himself; that whatever form these may take, he may learn from them, and profit by them, and be content in them: that his true business in the world is to cultivate a strong and dutiful character which shall prepare him for any world or any fate; and that so long as he can do this, his main duty will be done, his ruling object attained. Totum in co est, ut tibi imperes. [47]

Is not this true wisdom? is it not an abiding good? Pleasures may bloom and fade. Speculations may shift and change. Riches may come and go--what else have they wings for? The body may sicken or strengthen. The favour of men may be conferred and withdrawn. There is no stability in these; and if we are dependent on them, we shall be variable and inconstant as they are. But if we make it our chief aim to do our duty whatever it may be, and to love and serve our neighbour whatever the attitude he may assume to us, we have an aim always within our reach, a duty we may always be doing, a good as enduring as ourselves, and therefore a good we may enjoy for ever. Standing on this rock, from which no wave of change can sweep us, "the light will be sweet to us, and it shall be pleasant to our eyes to behold the sun," whatever the day, or the world, on which he may rise (ver. 7).

But is all our life to be taken up in meeting the claims of Duty and of Charity? Are we never to relax into mirth, never to look forward to a time in which reward will be more exactly adjusted to service? Yes, we are to do both this and that. It is very true that he who makes it his ruling aim to do the present duty, and to leave the future with God, will have a happy because a useful life. He that walks this path of duty

The Expositor's Bible: Ecclesiastes
>   "only thirsting
>   For the right, and learns to deaden
>   Love of self, before his journey closes,
>   He shall find the stubborn thistle bursting
>   Into glossy purples, which outredden
>   All voluptuous garden roses."

The path may often be steep and difficult; it may be overhung with threatening rocks and strewn with "stones of offence;" but he who pursues it, still pressing on "through the long gorge" and winning his way upward,

>   "Shall find the toppling crags of Duty scaled,
>   Are close upon the shining table-lands
>   To which our God Himself is sun and moon."

Nevertheless, if his life is to be full and complete, he must be able to pluck whatever bright flowers of joy spring beside his path, to find "laughing waters" in the crags he climbs, and to rejoice not only in "the glossy purples" of the armed and stubborn thistle, but in the delicate beauty of the ferns, the pure grace of the cyclamens, and the sweet breath of the fragrant grasses and flowers which haunt those severe heights. If he is to be a Man, rather than a Stoic or an Anchorite, he must add to his sense of duty a keen delight in all beauty, all grace, all innocent and noble pleasure. For the sake of others, too, as well as for his own sake, he must carry with him "the merry heart which doeth good like a medicine," since, lacking that, he will neither do all the good he might, nor himself become perfect and complete. And it is proof, I think, of the good divinity, no less than of the broad humanity, of the Preacher that he lays much stress on this point. He not only bids us enjoy life, but gives us cogent reasons for enjoying it. "Even," he says, "if a man should live many years, he ought to enjoy them all." But why? "Because there will be many dark days," days of old age and growing infirmity in which pleasures will lose their charm; days of death through which he will sleep quietly in the dark stillness of the grave, beyond the touch of any happy excitement (ver. 8). Therefore the man who attains the Chief Good will not only do the duty of the moment; he will also enjoy the pleasure of the moment. He will not toil through the long day of life till, spent and weary, he has no power to enjoy his "much goods," or no time for his soul to "make merry the glad." While he is "a young man," he will "rejoice in his youth, and let his heart cheer him," and go after the pleasures which attract youth (ver. 9). While his heart is still fresh, when pleasures are most innocent and healthful, easiest of attainment and unalloyed by anxiety and care, he will cultivate that cheerful temper which is a prime safeguard against vice, discontent, and the morose fretfulness of a selfish old age.

Combined with a stedfast Faith in the Life to come. Ch. x., v. 9-Ch. xii, v. 7.
But, soft; is not our man of men becoming a mere man of pleasure? No; for he recognises the claims of Duty and of Charity. These keep his pleasures sweet and wholesome, prevent them from usurping the whole man, and landing him in the satiety and weariness of dissipation. But lest even these safeguards should prove insufficient, he has also this: he knows that "God will bring him into judgment;" that all his works, whether of charity or duty or recreation, will be weighed in the pure and even balance of Divine Justice (ver. 9). This is the secret of the pure heart--the heart that is kept pure amid all labours and cares and joys. But the intention of the Preacher in thus adverting to the Divine Judgment has been gravely misconstrued, wrested even to its very opposite. We too much forget what that Judgment must have seemed to the enslaved Jews;--how weighty a consolation, how bright a hope! They were captive exiles, oppressed by profligate despotic lords. Cleaving to the Divine Law with a passionate loyalty such as they had never felt in happier days, they were nevertheless exposed to the most dire and constant misfortunes. All the blessings which the Law pronounced on the obedient seemed withheld from them, all its promises of good and peace to be falsified; the wicked triumphed over them, and prospered in their wickedness. Now to a people whose convictions and hopes had suffered this miserable defeat, what truth would be more welcome than that of a life to come, in which all wrongs should be both righted and avenged, and all the promises in which they had hoped should receive a large fulfilment that would beggar hope? what prospect could be more cheerful and consolatory than that of a day of retribution on which their oppressors would be put to shame, and they would be recompensed for their fidelity to the law of God? This hope would be sweeter to them than any pleasure; it would lend a new zest to every pleasure, and make them more zealous in good works.

Nay, we know, from the Psalms composed during the Captivity, that the judgment of God was an incentive to hope and joy; that, instead of fearing it, the pious Jews looked forward to it with rapture and exultation. What, for example, can be more riant and joyful than the concluding strophe of Psalm xcvi.?

Samuel Cox, D.D.

Let the heavens rejoice, and let the earth be glad;
Let the sea roar, and the fulness thereof;
Let the field exult and all that therein is;
And let all the trees of the wood sing for joy
Before Jehovah: for He cometh,
For He cometh to judge the earth,
To judge the world with righteousness,
And the peoples with his truth;
or than the third strophe of Psalm xcviii.?
Let the sea roar, and the fulness thereof;
The world, and they that dwell therein;
Let the floods clap their hands,
And let the hills sing for joy together
Before Jehovah: for He cometh to judge the earth;
With righteousness shall He judge the world,
And the peoples with equity.

It is impossible to read these verses, and such verses as these, without feeling that the Jews of the Captivity anticipated the Divine Judgment, not with fear and dread, but with a hope and joy so deep and keen as that they summoned the whole round of Nature to share in it and reflect it.

If we remembered this, we should not so readily agree with the Preachers and Commentators who assume Coheleth to be speaking ironically in this verse, and as though he would defy his readers to enjoy their pleasures with the thought of God and his judgment of them in their minds. We should rather understand that he was making life more cheerful to them; that he was removing the blight of despair which had fallen on it; that he was kindling in their dreary prospect a light which would shine even into their darkened present with gracious and healing rays. All wrongs would be easier to bear, all duties would be faced with better heart, all alleviating pleasures would grow more welcome, if once they were fully persuaded that there was a life beyond death, a life in which the good would be "comforted" and the evil "tormented." It is on the express ground that there is a Judgment that the Preacher, in the last verse of this chapter, bids them banish "care" and "sadness," or, as the words perhaps mean, "moroseness" and "trouble;" though he also adds another reason which no longer afflicts him much, viz., that "youth and manhood are vanity," soon gone, never to be recalled, and never enjoyed if the brief occasion is suffered to pass.

Mark how quickly the force of this great hope has reversed his position. Only in ver. 8, the very instant before he discloses his hope, he urges men to enjoy the present "because all that is coming is vanity," because there were so many dark days, days of infirm querulous age and silent dreary death before them. But here, in ver. 10, the very moment he has disclosed his hope, he urges them to enjoy the present, not because the future is vanity, but because the present is vanity, because youth and manhood soon pass and the pleasures proper to them will be out of reach. Why should they any longer be fretted with care and anxiety when the lamp of Revelation shone so brightly on the future? Why should they not be cheerful when so happy a prospect lay before them? Why should they sit brooding over their wrongs when their wrongs were so soon to be righted, and they were to enter on so ample a recompense of reward? Why should they not travel toward a future so welcome and inviting with hearts attuned to mirth and responsive to every touch of pleasure?

But is the thought of Judgment to be no check on our pleasures? Well, it is certainly used here as an incentive to pleasure, to cheerfulness. We are to be happy because we are to stand at the bar of God, because in the Judgment He will adjust and compensate all the wrongs and afflictions of time. But it is not every one who can take to himself the full comfort of this argument. Only he can do that who makes it his ruling aim to do his duty and help his neighbour. And no doubt even he will find the hope of judgment--for with him it is a hope rather than a fear--a valuable check, not on his pleasures, but on those base counterfeits which often pass for pleasures, and which betray men, through voluptuousness, into satiety, disgust, remorse. Because he hopes to meet God, and has to give account of himself to God, he will resist the evil lusts which pollute and degrade the soul: and thus the prospect of Judgment will become a safeguard and a defence.

But he has a safeguard of even a more sovereign potency than this. For he not only looks forward to a future judgment, he is conscious of a present and constant judgment. God is with him wherever he goes. From "the days of his youth" he has "remembered his Creator" (chap. xii., ver. 1). He has remembered Him, and given to the poor and needy. He has remembered Him and, doing all things as to Him, duty has grown light. He has remembered Him, and his pleasures have grown the sweeter because they were gifts from Heaven, and because he has taken them, in a thankful spirit, for a temperate enjoyment. Of all safeguards to a life of virtue, this is the noblest and the best. We can afford, indeed, to part with none of them, for we are strangely weak, often where we least suspect it, and need all the helps

73

we can get: but least of all can we afford to part with this. We need to remember that every sin is punished here and now, inwardly if not outwardly, and that these inward punishments are the most severe. We need to remember that we must all appear before the judgment-seat of God, to render an account of the deeds done in the body. But above all--if love, and not fear, is to be the animating motive of our life--we need to remember that God is always with us, observing what we do; and that, not that He may spy upon us and accumulate heavy charges against us, but that He may help us to do well; not to frown upon our pleasures, but to hallow, deepen, and prolong them, and to be Himself our Chief Good and our Supreme Delight.

> "'Live while you live,' the Epicure would say,
> 'And seize the pleasure of the present day.'
> 'Live while you live,' the Sacred Preacher cries,
> 'And give to God each moment as it flies.'
> Lord, in my view let both united be:
> I live in pleasure while I live in Thee." [48]

Finally, the Preacher enforces this early and habitual reference of the soul to the Divine Presence and Will by a brief allusion to the impotence and weariness of a godless old age, and by a very striking description of the terrors of the death in which it culminates.

While "the dew of youth" is still fresh upon us we are to "remember our Creator" and his constant judgment of us lest, forgetting Him, we should waste our powers in sensual excess; lest temperate mirth should degenerate into an extravagant and wanton devotion to pleasure; lest the lust of mere physical enjoyment should outlive the power to enjoy, and, groaning under the penalties our unbridled indulgence has provoked, we should find "days of evil" rise on us in long succession, and draw out into "years" of fruitless desire, self-disgust, and despair (ver. 1). "Before the evil days come," and that they may not come; before "the years arrive of which we shall say, I have no pleasure in them," and that they may not arrive, we are to bethink us of the Pure and Awful Presence in which we daily stand. God is with us that we may not sin; with us in youth, that "the angel of his Presence" may save us from the sins to which youth is prone; with us, to save us from "the noted slips of youth and liberty," that our closing years may have the cheerful serenity of a happy old age.

To this admonition drawn from the miseries of godless age, the Preacher appends a description of the terrors of approaching death (vv. 2-5),--a description which has suffered many strange torments at the hands of critics and commentators. It has commonly been read as an allegorical, but singularly accurate, diagnosis of "the disease men call death," as setting forth in graphic figures the gradual decay of sense after sense, faculty after faculty. [49] Learned physicians have written treatises upon it, and have been lost in admiration of the force and beauty of the metaphors in which it conveys the results of their special science, although they differ in their interpretation of almost every sentence, and are driven at times to the most gross and absurd conjectures in order to sustain their several theories. I need not give any detailed account of these speculations, for the simple reason that they are based, as I believe, on an entire misconception of the Sacred Text. Instead of being, as has been assumed, a figurative description of the dissolution of the body, it sets forth the threatening approach of death under the image of a tempest which, gathering over an Eastern city during the day, breaks upon it toward evening: so, at least, I, with many more, take it. And I do not know how we can better arrive at it than by considering what would be the incidents which would strike us if we were to stroll through the narrow tortuous streets of such a city as the day was closing in.

As we passed along we should find small rows of houses and shops, broken here and there by a wide stretch of blank wall, behind which were the mansions, harems, courtyards of its wealthier inhabitants. Round and within the low narrow gates which gave access to these mansions, we should see armed men lounging whose duty it is to guard the premises against robbers and intruders; these are "the keepers of the house," over whom, as over the whole household, are placed superior officials--members of the family often--or "men of power." Going through the gates and glancing up at the latticed windows, we might catch glimpses of the veiled faces of the ladies of the house who, not being permitted to stir abroad except on rare occasions and under jealous guardianship, are accustomed to amuse their dreary leisure, and to learn a little of what is going on around them, by "looking out of the windows." Within the house, the gentlemen of the family would be enjoying the chief meal of the day, provoking appetite with delicacies such as "the locust," [50] or condiments such as "the caper-berry," [51] or with choice fruit such as "the almond." [52] Above all the shrill cries and noises of the city you would hear a loud humming sound rising on every side, for which you would be sorely puzzled to account if you were a stranger to Eastern habits. It is the sound of the cornmills which, towards evening, are at work in every house. A cornmill was indispensable to every Eastern family, since there were no public mills or bakers except the King's. The heat of the climate makes it necessary that corn should be ground and bread baked every day. And as the task of grinding at the mill was very irksome, only the most menial class of women, often slaves or captives, were employed upon it. Of course the noise caused by the revolution of the upper upon the nether millstone was very great when the mills were simultaneously at work in every house in the city. No sound is more familiar in the East; and, if it were suddenly stopped, the effect would be as striking as the sudden stoppage of all the wheels of traffic in an English town. So familiar was the sound, indeed, and of such good omen, that in Holy Writ it is used as a symbol of a happy, active, well-provided people; while the cessation of it is employed to denote want, and desolation, and despair. To an Oriental ear no threat would be more doleful and pathetic than that in Jeremiah (xxv. 10), "I will take from them the voice of mirth and the voice of gladness, the voice of the bridegroom and the voice of the bride, the sound of the millstones, and the light of the candle."

Now suppose the day on which we rambled through the city had been boisterous and lowering; that heavy rain had fallen, obscuring all the lights of heaven; and as the evening drew on, the thick clouds, instead of dispersing, had "returned after the rain," so that setting sun and rising moon, and the growing light of stars, were all blotted from view (ver. 2). The tempest, long in gathering, breaks on the city; the lightnings flash through the darkness, making it more hideous; the thunder crashes and rolls above the roofs; the tearing rain beats at all lattices and floods all roads. If we cared to abide the pelting of the storm, we should have before us the very scene which the Preacher depicts. "The keepers of the house," the guards and porters, would quake. "The men of power," the lords or owners of the house, or the officials who most closely attended on them, would crouch and tremble with apprehension. The maids at the mill would "stop" because one or other of the two women--two at least--whom it took to work the heavy millstone had been frightened from her task by the gleaming lightning and the pealing thunder. The ladies, looking out of their lattices, would be driven back into the darkest corners of the inner rooms of the harem. Every door would be closed and barred lest robbers, availing themselves of the darkness and its terrors, should creep in (ver. 3). "The noise of the mills" would grow faint or utterly cease, because the threatening tumult had terrified many, if not all, the grinding-maids from their work. The strong-winged "swallow," lover of wind and tempest, would flit to and fro with shrieks of joy; while the delicate "song-birds" would drop, silent and alarmed, into their nests. The gentlemen of the house would soon lose all gust for their delicate cates [53] and fruits; "the almond" would be pushed aside, "the locust loathed," and even the stimulating "caper-berry provoke no appetite," fear being a singularly unwelcome and disappetising guest at a feast. In short, the whole people, stunned and confused by the awful and stupendous majesty of a tropical storm, would be affrighted at the terrors which come flaming from "the height" of heaven, to confront them on every highway (vv. 4, 5).

Such and so terrible is the tempest that at times sweeps over an Eastern city. [54] Such and so terrible, adds the Preacher, is death to the godless and sensual. They are carried away as by a storm; the wind riseth and snatcheth them out of their place. For if we ask, "Why, O Preacher, has your pencil laboured to depict the terrors of a tempest?" he replies, "Because man goeth to his long home, and the mourners pace up and down the street" (ver. 5). He leaves us in no doubt as to the moral of the fable, the theme and motive of his picture. While painting it, while adding touch to touch, he has been thinking of "the long home"--or, as the Hebrew has it, "the house of eternity;" a phrase still used by the Jews as a synonym for "the grave"--which is appointed for all living, and of the mercenary professional mourners who loiter under the windows of the dying man in the hope that they may be hired to lament him. To the expiring sinner death is simply dreadful. It puts an end to all his activities and enjoyments, just as the tempest brings all the labours and recreations of the city to a pause. He has nothing before him but the grave, and none to mourn him but the harpies who already pace the street, longing for the moment when he will be gone, and who value their fee far above his life. If we would have death shorn of its terrors for us, we must "remember our Creator" before death comes; we must seek by charity, by a faithful discharge of duty, by a wise use and a wise enjoyment of the life that now is, to prepare ourselves for the life which is to come.

Death itself, as Coheleth proceeds to remind us (ver. 6), cannot be escaped. Some day the cord will break and the lamp fall; some day the jar or pitcher must be broken, and the wheel, shattered, fall into the well. Death is the common event. It befalls not only the sinful and injurious, but also the useful and the good. Our life may have been like a "golden" lamp suspended by a silver chain, fit for the palace of a king, and may have shed a welcome and cheerful light on every side and held out every promise of endurance but, none the less, the costly durable chain will be snapped at last, and the fair costly bowl be broken. Or our life may have been like the "pitcher" dipped, by village maidens, into the village fountain; or, again, like "the wheel" by which water is drawn, by a thousand hands, from the city well; it may have conveyed a vital refreshment to the few or to the many around us: but, none the less, the day must come when the pitcher will be shattered on the edge of the fountain, and the time-worn wheel fall from its rotten supports. There is no escape from death. And, therefore, as we must all die, let us all live as cheerfully and helpfully as we can; let us all prepare for the better life beyond the grave, by serving our Creator before "the body is cast into the earth from which it came, and the spirit returns to God who gave it" (ver. 7).

This, then, according to the Hebrew Preacher, is the ideal man, the man who achieves the Quest of the Chief Good:--Charitable, dutiful, cheerful, he prepares for death by a useful and happy life, for future judgment by a constant reference to the present judgment, for meeting God hereafter by walking with Him here.

Has he not achieved the Quest? Can we hope to find a more solid and enduring Good? What to him are the shocks of Change, the blows of Circumstance, the mutations of Time, the fluctuations of Fortune? These cannot touch the Good which he holds to be Chief. If they bring trouble, he can bear trouble and profit by it: if they bring prosperity, success, mirth, he can bear even these, and neither value them beyond their worth nor abuse them to his hurt; for his Good, and therefore his peace and blessedness, are founded on a Rock over which the changeful waves may wash, but against which they cannot prevail. Let the sun shine never so hotly, let the storm beat never so furiously, the Rock stands firm, and the house which he has built for himself upon the Rock. Whatever may befall, he can be doing his main work, enjoying his supreme satisfaction, since he can meet all changes with a dutiful and loving heart; since, through all, he may be forming a noble character and helping his neighbours to form a character as noble as his own. Because he has a gracious God always with him, and because a bright future stretches before him in endless and widening vistas of hope, he can carry to all the wrongs and afflictions of time a cheerful spirit which shines through them with transfiguring rays,--a spirit before which even the thick darkness of death will grow light, and the solemnities of the Judgment be turned into holiday festivity and a triumph. Ah, foolish and miserable that we are who, with so noble a life, and so bright a prospect, and a Good so enduring open to us--and with such helps to them in the Gospel of Christ as Coheleth could not know--nevertheless creep about the earth the slaves of every accident, the very fools of Time!

Footnotes:

44. To cite only one instance out of many--other instances may be found in the Introduction--let the reader recall the Emperor Caligula, and refer, for example, to his reception of the Alexandrian Jews, as recorded by Philo, Legat ad Caium, cc. 44, 45; or by Merivale, in his History of the Romans, chap. xlvii., pp. 47-50; or by Milman, in his History of the Jews, Book xii., pp. 141-45. He will then know, to quote the phrase of Apollonius of Tyana, what "the kind of beast called a tyrant" is or may be.

45. What Coheleth means by the king being "a child" is best explained by Isa. iii. 12: "As for my people, their ruler is a wilful child, and women rule over him."

46. One of the most elaborate proverbs in the Talmud is on Charity:--"Iron breaks the stone, fire melts iron, water extinguishes fire, the clouds drink up the water, a storm drives away the clouds, man withstands the storm, fear unmans man, wine dispels fear, sleep drives away wine, and death sweeps all away--even sleep. But Solomon the Wise says, Charity saves from death." And there is hardly a finer passage in Shakespeare's Sonnets than that (CXVI.) in which he sings the disinterestedness of Love, and its superiority to all change:

"Love is not love
Which alters when it alteration finds,
Or bends with the remover to remove.
* * * * * *
Love's not Time's fool, though rosy lips and cheeks
Within his bending sickle's compass come;
Love alters not with his brief hours and weeks,
But bears it out even to the edge of doom."

47. Cicero, Tusc., lib. II., cap. 22.
48. Dum vivimus vivamus.--Doddridge.
49. It may be worth while to specify some of the gross and absurd conjectures, some also of the strange differences, into which what may be called the medical reading of this passage has betrayed its advocates. Ginsburg has a marvellous collection of them in his "notes" to these verses. I select and combine only a few of them. The darkening of the light, the sun, the moon, and the stars (ver. 2) is taken by one great authority (the Talmud) to mean the darkening of the forehead, the nose, the soul, and the teeth; by another (the Chaldee Paraphrast), the obscuring of the face, the eyes, the cheeks, and the apples of the eyes; by a third (Dr. Smith, in his "Portraiture of Old Age"), for the decay of all the mental faculties. That "the clouds return after the rain" signifies, according to Ibn Ezra, the constant dimness of the eyes; according to Le Clerc, a bad influenza, accompanied with unceasing snuffling. "The keepers of the house" (ver. 3) are the ribs and the loins (Talmud), the knees (Chaldee), and the hands and arms (Ibn

Ezra). "The men of power" are the thighs (Talmud) and the arms (Chaldee). "The grinding maids" are the teeth, and "the ladies who look out of the lattices" are the eyes, by general consent. "The door closed on the street" is the pores of the skin (Dr. Smith), the lips (Ibn Ezra), and the eyes (Henstenberg). That "the noise of the mills ceases" or "grows faint" (ver. 4) means that the mastication of food becomes imperfect (Dr. Smith), that the appetite fails (Chaldee), that the voice grows feeble (Grotius). That "the songbirds descend to their nests" signifies that music and songs are a bore to the aged man (Talmud), that he is no longer able to sing (Chaldee), that his ears are heavy (Grotius). The allusion to "the almond" (ver. 5) denotes that the haunch-bone shall come out from leanness (Talmud), or (Reynolds) it denotes the hoary hair which comes quickly on a man just as the almond-tree thrusts out her blossoms before any other tree; while at least half-a-dozen scholars and physicians take it as pointing to membrum genitale or glans virilis. That "the locust becomes a burden" means that the ankles swell (Chaldee), gout in the feet (Jerome), a projecting stomach (Le Clerc), the dry shrivelled frame of an old man (Dr. Smith). Almost all modern commentators take the reference to "the caper-berry" as marking the fact that condiments lose their power to provoke appetite with the aged, while many of the ancients took it as marking the failure of sexual desire. The "silver cord" and "golden bowl" of ver. 6 are the tongue and the skull (Chaldee), backbone and brain (Dr. Smith), urine and bladder (Gasper Sanctius); while the "bucket" is either the gall or the right ventricle of the heart, and "the wheel" that draws the water stands for the air-inspiring lungs. Now of course it would not be just to condemn any interpretation simply because it is weighted with absurdities and contradictions such as these, though it surely requires a very strong reading to carry them. But when an interpretation is so obviously forced and fanciful, when it is so remarkably ingenious and leaves to ingenuity so wide and lawless a scope, we shall do well to hesitate before accepting it. And if another interpretation be offered us, as in the text, which gives a literal rendering to every phrase instead of a figurative one, which bases itself on the common household facts of Eastern experience instead of on the technicalities of Western science, which instead of being so indeterminate and fanciful as at times to be self-contradictory and grotesque, is coherent and impressive, we really have no alternative before us. We cannot but choose the one and reject the other.

    50. This locust (châgâb) is one of the four kinds which the Law of Moses marked out as fit for human food. To this day several kinds of locust are held to be an agreeable and nutritious diet. There are many ways of preparing them for the table. They may be pounded with flour and water, and made into cakes. They may be smoked, boiled, roasted, stewed, and fried in butter. They may be salted with salt; and thus treated are eaten by the Arabs as a great delicacy. Or they may be dried in the sun, and then steeped in wine: baskets of them, prepared in this way, are to be commonly seen in Eastern markets. Dr. Kitto, who often ate them, says that they taste like shrimps; Dr. Shaw says that they are quite as good as our freshwater crayfish.

    51. The caper-plant grows abundantly in Asia, as it does also in Africa and Southern Europe. It commonly springs in the crevices of walls, on heaps of ruins, or on barren wastes, and forms a diffuse many-branched shrub. Its flowers are large and showy: the four petals are white, but the long numerous stamens have their filaments tinged with purple, and terminate in yellow anthers. As the ovary ripens it droops and forms a pear-shaped berry, which holds in its pulp many small seeds. Almost every part of the shrub has been used as a condiment by the ancients. The stalk and seed were salted, or preserved in vinegar or wine. Its buds are still held to be an agreeable sauce--we eat them with boiled mutton. And the berries possess irritant properties which win them high esteem among the Orientals as a provocative to appetite.

    52. The fruit of the almond-tree is still reckoned one of the most delicate and delicious fruits in the East. We may fancy that we are acquainted with it, that we know "almonds" at least as well as we know "raisins." But, I believe, that the almond we eat is only the kernel of the stone in the true almond; the fruit itself is of the same order with apricots, peaches, plums.

    53. Sir Henry Rawlinson says: "At the present day, among the bons vivants of Persia, it is usual to sit down for hours before dinner, drinking wine, and eating dried fruits, such as filberts, almonds, pistachio-nuts, melon-seeds, etc. A party, indeed, often sits down at seven o'clock, and the dinner is not brought in till eleven. The dessert dishes, intermingled as they are with highly seasoned delicacies, are supposed to have the effect of stimulating the appetite."--Notes to Rawlinson's Herodotus, vol. i., p. 274.

    54. It should be borne in mind that the comparative rarity of thunderstorms in Syria and the adjacent lands makes them much more dreadful to the inhabitants of those countries. Throughout the Old Testament, and especially in the Psalms, we find many traces of the dread which such storms inspired--a dread almost unaccountable to our accustomed nerves.

THE EPILOGUE

IN WHICH THE PROBLEM OF THE BOOK IS CONCLUSIVELY SOLVED.

Chap. XII., Vers. 8-14.

"Students," says the Talmud, "are of four kinds; they are like a sponge, a funnel, a strainer, and a sieve: like a sponge that sucketh all up; like a funnel which receiveth at one end and dischargeth at the other; like a strainer which letteth the wine pass but retaineth the lees; and like a sieve which dischargeth the bran but retaineth the corn." Coheleth is like the sieve. He is the good student who has sifted all the schemes and ways and aims of men, separating the wheat from the bran, teaching us to know the bran as bran, the wheat as wheat. It is a true "corn of heaven" which he offers us, and not any of the husks to obtain which reckless and prodigal man has often wasted his whole living--husks which, though they have the form and hue of wheat, have not its nutriment, and cannot therefore satisfy the keen hunger of the soul.

We have now followed the sifting process to its close; much bran lies about our feet, but a little corn is in our hands, and from this little there may grow "a harvest unto life." Starting in quest of that Chief Good in which, when once it is attained, we can rest with an unbroken and measureless content, we have learned that it is not to be found in Wisdom, in Pleasure, in Devotion to Business or Public Affairs, in a modest Competence or in boundless Wealth. We have learned that only he achieves this supreme Quest who is "charitable, dutiful, cheerful;" only he who "by a wise use and a wise enjoyment of the present life prepares himself for the life which is to come." We have learned that the best incentive to this life of virtue, and its best safeguards, are a constant remembrance of our Creator and of his perpetual presence with us, and a constant hope of that future judgment in which all the wrongs of time are to be redressed. And here we might think our task was ended. We might suppose that the Preacher would dismiss us from the School in which he has so long held us by his sage maxims, his vivid illustrations, his gracious warnings and encouragements. But even yet he will not suffer us to depart. He has still "words to utter for God," words which it will be well for us to ponder. As in the Prologue he had stated the problem he was about to take in hand, so now he subjoins an Epilogue in which he re-states the solution of it at which he has arrived. His last words are, as we should expect them to be, heavily weighted with thought. So closely packed are his thoughts and allusions, indeed, as to give a disconnected and illogical tone to his words. Every saying seems to stand alone, complete in itself; and hence our main difficulty in dealing with this Epilogue is to trace the links of sequence which bind saying to saying and thought to thought, and so to get "the best part" of his work. Every verse supplies a text for patient meditation, or a theme which needs to be illustrated by historic facts that lie beyond the general reach; and the danger is lest, while dwelling on these separate themes and texts, we should fail to collect their connected meaning, and to grasp the large conclusion to which they all conduct. [55]

Coheleth commences (ver. 8) by once more striking the keynote to which all his work is set: "Vanity of vanities, saith the Preacher, all is vanity!" We are not, however, to take these words as announcing his deliberate verdict on the sum of human endeavours and affairs; for he has now discovered the true abiding Good which underlies all the vanities of earth and time. His repetition of this familiar phrase is simply a touch of art by which the Poet reminds us of what the main theme of his Poem has been, of the pain and weariness and disappointment which have attended his long Quest. As it falls once more, and for the last time, on our ear, we cannot but remember how often, and in what connections, we have heard it before. Memory and imagination are set to work. The whole course of the sacred drama passes swiftly before us, with its mournful pauses of defeated hope, as we listen to this echo of the despair with which the baffled Preacher has so often returned from seeking the true Good in this or that province of human life in which it was not to be found.

Having thus reminded us of the several stages of his Quest, and of the verdict which he had been compelled to pronounce at the close of each but the last, Coheleth proceeds (ver. 9) to set forth his qualifications for undertaking this sore task: "Not only was the Preacher a wise man, he also taught the people wisdom, and composed, collected, and arranged many proverbs" or parables, the proverb being a condensed parable and the parable an expanded proverb. His claims are that he is a sage, and a public teacher, who has both made many proverbs of his own, collected the wise sayings of other sages, and has so arranged them as to convey a connected and definite teaching to his disciples; and his motive in setting forth these claims is, no doubt, that he may the more deeply impress upon us the conclusion to which he has come, and which it has cost him so much to reach.

Now during the Captivity there was a singular outbreak of literary activity in the Hebrew race. Even yet this crisis in their history is little studied and understood; but we shall only follow the Preacher's meaning through vv. 9-12 as we read them in the light of this striking event. That a change of the most radical and extraordinary kind passed upon the Hebrews of this period, that they were by some means drawn to a study of their Sacred Writings much more thorough and intense than any which went before it, we know; but of the causes of this change we are not so well informed. [56] A great, and perhaps the greatest, authority [57] on this subject writes: "One of the most mysterious and momentous periods in the history of humanity is that brief space of the Exile. What were the influences brought to bear on the captives during that time, we know not. But this we know, that from a reckless, lawless, godless populace, they returned transformed into a band of Puritans. The religion of Zerdusht (Zoroaster), though it has left its traces in Judaism, fails to account for that change.... Yet the change is there, palpable, unmistakable--a change which we may regard as almost miraculous. Scarcely aware before of their glorious national literature, the people now began to press round these brands plucked from the fire--the scanty records of their faith and history--with a fierce and passionate love, a love stronger even than that of wife and child. These same documents, as they were gradually formed into a canon, became the immediate centre of their lives, their actions, their thoughts, their very dreams. From that time forth, with scarcely any intermission, the keenest as well as the most poetical minds of the nation remained fixed upon them."

The more we think of this change, the more the wonder grows. Good kings and inspired prophets had desired to see the nation devoted to the Word of the Lord, had spent their lives in vain endeavours to recall the thought and affection of their race to the Sacred Records in which the will of God was revealed. But what they failed to do was done when the inspiration of the Almighty was withdrawn and the voice of Prophecy had grown mute. In their Captivity, under the strange wrongs and miseries of their exile, the Jews remembered God their Maker, Giver of songs in the night. They betook themselves to the study of the Sacred Oracles. They began to acquaint themselves with all wisdom that they might define and illustrate whatever was obscure in the Scriptures of their fathers. They commenced that elaborate systematic commentary of which many noble fragments are still extant. They drew new truths from the old letter, or from the collocation of scattered passages,--as, for instance, the truths of the immortality of the soul and of the resurrection of the body. They laid the hidden foundations of the Synagogues and Schools which afterwards covered the land. Ezra and Nehemiah, who, by grace of the Persian conquerors, led them back from Babylonia to Jerusalem, are still claimed as the founders of the Great Synagogue, i.e. as the leaders of that great race of jurists, sages, authors, whose utterances are still a law in Israel, and of whom the lawyers and the scribes of the New Testament were the modern successors. Before the Captivity there was not a term for "school" in their language; there were at least a dozen in common use within two or three centuries after the accession of Cyrus. Education had become compulsory. Its immense value in the popular estimation is marked in innumerable sayings such as these: "Jerusalem was destroyed because the education of the young was neglected;" "Even for the rebuilding of the Temple the schools must not be interrupted;" "Study is more meritorious than sacrifice;" "A scholar is greater than a prophet;" "You should revere the teacher even more than your father; the latter only brought you into this world, the former shews you the way into the next." To meet the national craving indicated in these and similar proverbs, innumerable copies of the Sacred Books, of commentaries, traditions, and the gnomic utterances of the Wise, were written and circulated, of which, in the Canon, in some of the Apocryphal Scriptures, in the works of Philo, and in the legal and legendary sections of the Talmud, many specimens have come down to us. In fine, whatever was the cause of this marvellous outburst, there can be no doubt that the whole Rabbinical period was characterised by devotion to learning, a mental and literary activity, much more general and vital than it is easy for us to conceive.

In such an age the words of a professed and acknowledged Sage would carry great weight. If, besides being "a wise man," he was a recognised "teacher," a man whose wisdom was stamped by public and official approval, whatever fell from his lips would command public attention: for these teachers, or rabbis, were the real rulers of the time, and not the pharisees or the priests, or even the politicians. They might be, they often were, "tent-makers, sandal-makers, weavers, carpenters, tanners, bakers, cooks"; for it is among their highest claims to our respect that these learned rabbis reverenced labour, however menial or toilsome, that they held mere scholarship and piety of little worth unless conjoined with regular and healthy physical exertion. But, however toilsome their lives or humble their circumstances, these wise men were "masters of the law." It was their special function to interpret the Law of Moses--which, remember, was the law of the land--to explain its bearing on this case or that, if not, as many modern critics maintain, to add to its precepts and codes; and, as members of the local courts or the metropolitan Sanhedrin, to administer the law they expounded. An immense power, therefore, was in their hands. To obey the Law was to be at once loyal and religious, happy here and hereafter. Hence the rabbis, whose business it was to apply the law to all the details of life, and whose decisions were authoritative and final, could not fail to command universal deference and respect. They were lawyers, judges, schoolmasters, heads of colleges, public orators and lecturers, statesmen and preachers, all in one or all in turn, and therefore concentrated in themselves the esteem which we distribute on many offices and many men.

Such a rabbi was Coheleth. He was of "the Wise"; he was a "master of the law." And, in addition to these claims, he was also a teacher and an author who, besides "composing," had "collected and arranged many proverbs." Than this latter he could hardly have any higher claim to the regard, and even to the affection, of the Hebrew public. The passionate fondness of Oriental races for proverbs, fables, stories of any kind, is well known. And the Jews for whom Coheleth wrote took, as was natural at such a time, an extraordinary delight, extraordinary even for the East, in listening to and repeating the wise or witty sayings, the parables and poems, of their national authors. Some of these are still in our hands: as we read them, we cease to wonder at the intense enjoyment with which they were welcomed by a generation not cloyed, as we are, with books. They are not only charming as works of art: they have also this charm, that they convey lofty ethical instruction. Take a few of these pictorial proverbs, not included in the Canonical Scriptures. "The house that does not open to the poor will open to the physician." "Commit a sin twice, and you will begin to think it quite allowable." "The reward of good works is like dates--sweet, but ripening late." "Even when the gates of prayer are shut in heaven, the gate of tears is open." "When the righteous dies, it is the earth that loses; the lost jewel is still a jewel, but he who has lost it--well may he weep." "Who is wise? He who is willing to learn from all men. Who is strong? He who subdues his passions. Who is rich? He that is satisfied with his lot." These are surely happy expressions of profound moral truths. But the rabbis are capable of putting a keener edge on their words; they can utter witty epigrams as incisive as those of any of our modern satirists, and yet use their wit in the service of good sense and morality. It would not be easy to match, it would be very hard to beat, such sayings as these:--"The sun will go down without your help." "When the ox is down, many are the butchers." "The soldiers fight, and kings are the heroes." "The camel wanted horns, and they took away his ears." "The cock and the owl both wait for morning: the light brings joy to me, says the cock, but what are you waiting for?" "When the pitcher falls on the stone, woe to the pitcher; when the stone falls on the pitcher, woe to the pitcher: whatever happens, woe to the pitcher." "Look not at the flask, but at that which is in it: for there are new flasks full of old wine, and old flasks which have not even new wine in them:" ah, of how many of those "old flasks" have some of us had to drink, or seem to drink! When the rabbis draw out their moral at greater length, when they tell a story, their skill does not desert them. Here is one of the briefest, which can hardly fail to remind us of more than one of the parables uttered by the Great Teacher Himself. "There was once a king who bade all his servants to a great repast, but did not name the hour. Some went home, and put on their best garments, and came and stood at the door of the palace. Others said, 'There is time enough, the king will let us know beforehand.' But the king summoned them of a sudden; and those that came in their best garments were well received, but the foolish ones, who came in their slovenliness, were turned away in disgrace. Repent ye to-day, lest ye be summoned to-morrow."

Is it any wonder that the Jews, even in the sorrows of their Captivity, liked to hear such proverbs and parables as these? that they had an immense and grateful admiration for the men who spent much thought and care on the composition and arrangement of these wise, beautiful sayings? Should not we ourselves be thankful to hear them when the day's work was done, or even while it was doing? If, then, such an one as Coheleth--a sage, a rabbi, a composer and collector of proverbs and parables--came to them and said, "My children, I have sought what you are all seeking; I have been in quest of that Chief Good which you still pursue; and I will tell you the story of the Quest in the parables and proverbs which you are so fond of hearing:"--we can surely understand that they would be charmed to listen, that they would hang upon his words, that they would be predisposed to accept his conclusions. As they listened, and found that he was telling them their own story no less than his, that he was trying to lead them away from the vanities which they themselves felt to be vanities, toward an abiding Good in which he had found rest; as they heard him enforce the duties of charity, industry, hilarity--duties which all their rabbis urged upon them, and invite them to that wise use and wise enjoyment of the present life which their own consciences approved: above all, as he unfolded before them the bright hope of a future judgment in which all wrongs would be redressed and all acts of duty receive a great recompense of reward,--would they not hail him as the wisest of their teachers, as the great rabbi who had achieved the supreme Quest? Assuredly few books were, or are, more popular than the book Ecclesiastes. Its presence and influence may be traced on every subsequent age and department of Hebrew literature; it has entered into our English literature hardly less deeply. Many of its verses are familiar to us as household words, are household words. Brief as the Book is, I am disposed to think it is better known among us than any other of the Old Testament Books except Genesis, the Psalter, and the prophecies of Isaiah. Job is an incomparably finer, as it is a much longer poem; but I doubt whether most of us could not quote at least two verses from the shorter for every one that we could repeat from the longer

Samuel Cox, D.D.

Scripture. We can very easily understand, therefore, that the Wise Preacher, as he himself assures us (ver. 10), bestowed on this work much care and thought; that he had made diligent search for "words of comfort" by which he might solace and strengthen the hearts of his oppressed brethren; and that, having found words of comfort and of truth, he wrote them down with a frank sincerity and uprightness.

From this description of the motives which had impelled him to publish the results of his thought and experience, and of the spirit in which he had composed his work, Coheleth passes, in ver. 11, to a description of the twofold function of the Teacher which is really a marvellous little poem in itself, a pastoral cut on a gem. That function is, on the one hand, progressive, and, on the other hand, conservative. At times the Teacher's words are like "goads" with which the herdsmen prick on their cattle to new pastures, correcting them when they loiter or stray; at other times they are like the "spikes" which the shepherds drive into the ground when they pitch their tents on pastures where they intend to linger: "The words of the Wise are like goads," he says; and "the Wise" was a technical term for the sages who interpreted and administered the law; while "those of the Masters of the Assemblies are like spikes driven home," "Masters of Assemblies" being a technical name for the heads of the colleges and schools which, during the Rabbinical period, were to be found in every town, and almost in every hamlet, of Judea. The same man might, and commonly did, wear both titles; and, probably, Coheleth was himself both a Wise Man and a Master. So much as this, indeed, seems implied in the very name by which he introduces himself in the Prologue. For Coheleth means, as we have seen, "one who calls an assembly together and addresses them," i.e. precisely such a wise man as was reckoned the "master of an assembly" among the Jews.

What did these Masters teach? Everything almost--at least everything then known. It is true that their main function was to interpret and enforce the law of Moses; but this function demanded all science for its adequate fulfilment. Take a simple illustration. The Law said, "Thou shalt not kill." Here, if ever, is a plain and simple statute, with no ambiguities, no qualifications, capable neither of misconstruction nor evasion. Anybody may remember it, and know what it means. May they? I am not so sure of that. The Law says I am not to kill. What, not in self-defence! not to save honour from outrage! not in a patriotic war! not to save my homestead from the freebooter or my house from the midnight thief! not when my kinsman is slain before my eyes and in my defence! Many similar cases might be mooted, and were mooted, by the Jews. The Master had to consider such cases as these, to study the recorded and traditional verdicts of previous judges, the glosses and comments of other Masters; he had to lay down rules and to apply rules to particular and exceptional cases, just as our English Judges have to define the Common Law or to interpret a Parliamentary Statute. The growing wants of the Commonwealth, the increasing complexity of the relations of life as the people of Israel came into contact with foreign races, or were carried into captivity in strange lands, necessitated new laws, new rules of conduct. And as there was no recognised authority to issue a decree, no Parliament to pass an Act, the wise Masters, learned in the law of God, were compelled to lay down these rules, to extend and qualify the ancient statutes till they covered modern cases and wants. Thus in this very Book, Coheleth gives the rules which should govern a wise and pious Jew in the new relations of Traffic (ch. iv., vv. 4-16), and in the service of foreign despots (ch. x., vv. 1-20). For such contingencies as these the Law made no provision; and hence the rabbis, who sat in Moses' chair, made provision for them by legislating in the spirit of the Law.

Even in the application of known and definite laws there was need for care, and science, and thought. "The Mosaic code," says Deutsch, "has injunctions about the Sabbatical journey; the distance had to be measured and calculated, and mathematics were called into play. Seeds, plants, and animals had to be studied in connection with many precepts regarding them, and natural history had to be appealed to. Then there were the purely hygienic paragraphs, which necessitated for their precision a knowledge of all the medical science of the time. The seasons and the feast-days were regulated by the phases of the moon; and astronomy, if only in its elements, had to be studied." As the Hebrews came successively into contact with Babylonians, Persians, Greeks, Romans, the political and religious systems of these foreign races could not fail to leave some impressions on their minds, and that these impressions might not be erroneous and misleading, it became the Master to acquaint himself with the results of foreign thought. Nay, "not only was science, in its widest sense, required of him, but even an acquaintance with its fantastic shadows, such as astrology, magic, and the rest, in order that, both as lawgiver and judge, he might be able to enter into the popular feeling about these 'arts,'" and wisely control it.

The proofs that this varied knowledge was acquired and patiently applied to the study of the Law by these "masters in Israel" are still with us in many learned sayings and essays of that period; and in all these the conservative element or temper is sufficiently prominent. Their leading aim was, obviously, to honour the law of Moses; to preserve its spirit even in the new rules or codes which the changed circumstances of the time imperatively required; to fix their stakes and pitch their tents in the old fields of thought. So obvious is this aim, even in the familiar pages of the New Testament, that I need not illustrate it.

But, on the other hand, the signs of progress are no less decisive, though we may be less familiar with them. Through all this mass of learned and deferential comment on the Mosaic Code, there perpetually crop up sayings which savour of the Gospel rather than of the Law--sayings that denote a great advance in thought. "Study is better than sacrifice," for example, must have been a very surprising proverb to the backward-looking Jew. It is only one of many Rabbinical sayings conceived in the same spirit: but would not the whole Levitical family listen to it with the wry, clouded face of grave suspicion? So, when Rabbi Hillel, anticipating the golden rule, said, "Do not unto another what thou wouldest not have another do unto thee; this is the whole law, the rest is mere commentary," the lawyers, with all who had trusted in ordinances and observances, could hardly fail to be shocked and alarmed. So, too, when Rabbi Antigonous said, "Be not as men who serve their master for the sake of reward, but be like men who serve not looking for reward;" or when Rabbi Gamaliel said, "Do God's will as if it were thy will, that He may accomplish thy will as if it were his," there would be many, no doubt, who would feel that these venerable rabbis were bringing in very novel, and possibly very dangerous, doctrine. Nor could they fail to see what new fields of thought were being thrown open to them when Coheleth affirmed the future judgment and the future life of men. Such "words" as these were in very deed "goads," correcting the errors of previous thought, and urging men on to new pastures of truth and godliness.

Sometimes, as I have said, the progressive Sage and the conservative Master would be united in the same person; for there are those, though there are not too many of them, who can "stand on the old ways" and yet "look for the new." But, often, no doubt, the two would be divided and opposed, then as now. For in thought, as in politics, there are always two great parties; the one, looking back with affectionate reverence and regret on the past, and set to "keep invention in a noted weed;" the other, looking forward with eager hope and desire to the future, and attached to "new-found methods and to compounds strange;" the one, bent on conserving as much as possible of the large heritage which our fathers have bequeathed us; the other, bent on leaving a larger and less encumbered inheritance to those that shall be after them. The danger of the conservative thinker is that he may hold the debts on the estate as part of the estate, that he may set himself against all liquidations, all better methods of management, against improvement in every form. The danger of the progressive thinker is that, in his generous ambition to improve and enlarge the estate, he may break violently from the past, and cast away many heirlooms and hoarded treasures that would add largely to our wealth. The one is too apt to pitch his tents in familiar fields long after they are barren; the other is too apt to drive men on from old pastures to new before the old are exhausted or the new ripe. And, surely, there never was a larger or a more tolerant heart than that of the Preacher who has taught us that both these classes of men and teachers, both the conservative thinker and the progressive thinker, are of God and have each a useful function to discharge; that both the shepherd who loves his tent and the herdsman who wields the goad, both the sage who urges us forward and the sage who holds us back, are servants of the one Great Pastor, and owe whether goad or tent-spike to Him. Simply to entertain the conception widens and raises our minds; to have conceived it and thrown it into this perfect form proves the Sacred Preacher to have been all he claims and more--not only Sage, Teacher, Master, Author, but also a true Poet and a true man of God.

It is to be observed, however, that our accomplished Sage limits the field of mental activity on either hand (ver. 12). His children, his disciples--"my son" was the rabbi's customary term for his pupils, as "rabbi," i.e. "my father," was the title by which the pupil addressed his master--are to beware both of the "many books" of the making of which there was even then "no end," and of that over-addiction to study which was a "weariness to the flesh." The latter caution, the warning against "much study," was a logical result of that sense of the sanitary value of physical labour by which, as we have seen, the masters in Israel were profoundly impressed. They held bodily exercise to be good for the soul as well as for the body, a safeguard against the dreamy abstract moods and the vague fruitless reveries which relax rather than brace the intellectual fibre, and which tend to a moral languor all the more perilous because its approaches are masked under the semblance of mental occupation. They knew that those who attempt or affect to be "creatures too bright and good for human nature's daily food" are apt to sink below the common level rather than to rise above it. They did not want their disciples to resemble many of the young men who lounged through the philosophical schools of Greece and Rome, and who, though always ready to discuss the "first true, first perfect, first fair," did nothing to raise the tone of common life whether by their example or their words; young men, as Epictetus bitterly remarked of some of his disciples, whose philosophy lay in their cloaks and their beards rather than in any wise conduct of their daily lives or any endeavour to better the world. It was their aim to develop the whole man--body, soul, and spirit; to train up useful citizens as well as accomplished scholars, to spread the love and pursuit of wisdom through the whole nation rather than to produce a separate and learned class. And, in the prosecution of this aim, they enjoined neither the exercises of the ancient palæstra, nor athletic sports like those in vogue at our English seats of learning, which are often a mere waste of good muscle, but useful and productive toils. With Ruskin, they believed, not in "the gospel of the cricket-bat" or of the gymnasium, but in the gospel of the plough and the spade, the saw and the axe, the hammer and the trowel; and saved their disciples from the weariness of overtaxed brains by requiring them to become skilled artisans, and to labour heartily in their vocations.

Nor is the caution against "many books," at which some critics have taken grave offence, the illiberal sentiment it has often been pronounced. For, no doubt, Coheleth, like other wise Hebrews, was fully prepared to study whatever science would throw light on the Divine Law, or teach men how to live. Mathematics, astronomy, natural history, medicine, casuistry, the ethical and religious systems of the East and the West,--some knowledge of all these various branches of learning was necessary, as has been shown, to those who had to interpret and administer the statutes of the Mosaic code, and to supplement them with rules appropriate to the new conditions of the time. In these and kindred studies the rabbis were "masters"; and what they knew they taught. That which distinguished them from other men of equal learning was that they did not "love knowledge for its own sake" merely, but for its bearing on practice, on conduct. Like Socrates, they were not content with a purely intellectual culture, but sought a wisdom that would mingle with the blood of men and mend their ways, a wisdom that would hold their baser passions in check, infuse new energy into the higher moods and aptitudes of the soul, and make duty their supreme aim and delight. To secure this great end, they knew no method so likely to prove effectual as an earnest, or even an exclusive, study of the Sacred Scriptures in which they thought they had "eternal life," i.e. the true life of man, the life which is independent of the chances and changes of time. Whatever studies would illuminate and illustrate these Scriptures they pursued and encouraged; whatever might divert attention from them, they discouraged and condemned. Many of them, as we learn from the Talmud, refused to write down the discourses they delivered in School or Synagogue lest, by making books of their own, they should withdraw attention from the Inspired Writings. It was better they thought to read the Scriptures than any commentary on the Scriptures, and hence they confined themselves to oral instruction: even their profoundest and most characteristic sayings would have perished if "fond tradition" had not "babbled" of them for many an age to come.

If the sentiment which dictated this course was in part a mistaken sentiment, it sprang from a noble motive. For no ordinance could be more self-denying to a learned and literary class than one which forbade them to put on record the results of their researches, the conclusions of their wisdom, and thus to win name and fame and use in after generations. But was their course, after all, one which calls for censure? Has the world ever produced a literature so noble, so pure, so lofty and heroic in its animating spirit, as that of the Hebrew historians and poets? "The world is forwarded by having its attention fixed on the best things," says Matthew Arnold in his Preface to his selection of Wordsworth's poems, and proceeds to define the best things as those works of the great masters of song which have won the approval "of the whole group of civilised nations." But even those whom the civilised world has acclaimed as its highest and best have confessed that in the Bible, viewed simply as literature, their noblest work is far excelled: and what sane man will deny that "Faust," for example, would cut a sorry figure if compared with "Job," which our own greatest living poet has pronounced "the finest poem whether of ancient or of modern times," or Wordsworth himself if placed side by side with Isaiah? Who can doubt, then, that the world would have been "forwarded" if its attention had been fixed on this "best"? Who can doubt that it would be infinitely sweeter and better than it is if these ancient Scriptures had been studied before and above all other writings, if they had been brooded over and wrought into the minds of men till "the life" in them had been assimilated and reproduced? The man who has had a classical or scientific education, and profited by it, must be an ingrate indeed, unless he be the slave of some dominant crotchet, if he do not hold in grateful reverence the great masters at whose feet he has sat; but the man who has really found "life" in the Scriptures must be worse than an ingrate if he does not feel that a merely mental culture is a small good when compared with the treasures of an eternal life, if he does not admit that the main object of all education should be to conduct men through a course of intellectual training which shall culminate in a moral and spiritual discipline. To be wise is much; but how much more is it to be good! Better be a child in the kingdom of heaven than a philosopher or a poet hanging vaguely about its outskirts.

If any of us still suspect the Preacher's words of illiberality, and say, "There was no need to oppose the one Book to the many, and to depreciate these in order to magnify that," we have only to consider the historical circumstances in which he wrote in order to acquit him of the charge. For generations the Holy Scriptures had been neglected by the Jews; copies had grown scarce, and were hidden away in obscure nooks in which they were hard to find; some of the inspired writings had been lost, and have not been recovered to this day. The people were ignorant of their own history, and law, and hope. Suddenly they were awaked from the slumber of indifference, to find themselves in a night of ignorance. During the miseries of the Captivity a longing for the Divine Word was quickened within them. They were eager to acquaint themselves with the Revelation which they had neglected and forgotten. And their teachers, the few men who knew and loved the Word, set themselves to deepen and to satisfy the craving. They multiplied copies of the Scriptures, circulated them, explained them in the Schools, exhorted from them in the Synagogues. And, till the people were familiar with the Scriptures, the wiser rabbis would not write books of their own, and looked with a jealous eye on the "many books" bred by the literary activity of the time. It was the very feeling which preceded and accompanied the English Reformation. Then the newly-discovered Bible threw all other books into the shade. The people thirsted for the pure Word of God; and the leaders of the Reformation were very well content that they should read nothing else till they had read that; that they should leave all other fountains to drink of "the river of life." The translation and circulation of the Scriptures was the one work, almost the exclusive work, to which they bent their energies. Like the Jewish rabbis, Tyndale and his fellow-labourers did not care to write books themselves, nor wish the people to read the books they were compelled to write in self-defence. There is a remarkable passage in Fryth's Scripture Doctrine of the Sacrament, in which, replying to Sir Thomas More, the Reformer says: "This hath been offered you, is offered, and shall be offered. Grant that the Word of God, I mean the text of Scripture, may go abroad in our English tongue ... and my brother Tyndale and I have done, and will promise you to write no more. If you will not grant this condition, then will we be doing while we have breath, and show in few words that the Scripture doth in many, and so at the least save some." The Hebrew Reformers of the school of Coheleth were animated by precisely the same lofty and generous spirit. They were content to be nothing, that the Word of God might be all in all. "The Bible, and the Bible only," they conceived to be the want of their age and race; and hence they were content to forego the honours of authorship, and the study of many branches of learning which under other conditions they would have been glad to pursue, and besought their disciples to concentrate all their thoughts on the one Book which was able to make them wise unto salvation. Learned themselves, and often profoundly learned, it was no contempt for learning which actuated them, but a devout godliness and the fervours of a most self-denying piety.

So far the Epilogue may seem a mere digression, not without interest and value indeed, but having no vital connection with the main theme of the Poem. It tells us that the Preacher was a sage, a recognised official teacher, the master of an assembly, a doctor of laws, an author who had expended much labour on many proverbs, a conservative shepherd pitching his tent on familiar fields of thought, a progressive herdsman goading men on to new pastures--not Solomon therefore, by the way, for who would have described him in such terms as these? If we are glad to know so much of him, we cannot but ask, What has all this to do with the quest of the Chief Good? It has this to do with it. Coheleth has achieved the quest; he has solved his problem, and has given us his solution of it. He is about to repeat that solution. To give emphasis and force to the repetition, that he may carry his readers more fully with him, he dwells on his claims to their respect, their confidence, their affection. He is all that they most admire; he carries the very authority to which they most willingly defer. If they know this--and, scattered as they were through many cities and provinces, how should they know it unless he told them?--they cannot refuse him a hearing; they will be predisposed to accept his conclusion; they will be sure not to reject it without consideration. It is out of any personal conceit, therefore, nor any pride of learning, nor even that he may grant himself the relief of lifting his mask from his face for a moment, that he recounts his titles to their regard. He is simply gathering force from the willing respect and deference of his readers in order that he may plant his final conclusion more strongly and more deeply in their hearts.

And what is the conclusion which he is at such pains to enforce? "The conclusion of the matter is this; that God taketh cognizance of all things: fear Him, therefore, and keep his commandments, for this it behoveth every man to do; since God will bring every deed to the judgment appointed for every secret thing, whether it be good or whether it be bad" (vv. 13, 14).

Now that this "conclusion" is simply a repetition, in part expanded and in part condensed, of that with which the Preacher closes the previous Section, is obvious. There he incites men to a life of virtue with two leading motives: first, by the fact of the present constant judgment of God; and, secondly, by the prospect of a future, a more searching and decisive, judgment. Here he appeals to precisely the same motives, though now, instead of implying a present judgment under the injunction "Remember thy Creator," he broadly affirms that "God takes note of all things;" and, instead of simply reminding the young that God will bring "the ways of their heart" into judgment, he defines that future judgment at once more largely and more exactly as "appointed for every secret thing" and extending to "every deed," both good and bad. In dealing with the motives of a virtuous life, therefore, he goes a little beyond his former lines of thought, gives them a wider scope, makes them more sharp and definite. On the other hand, in speaking of the forms which the virtuous or ideal life assumes, he is very curt and brief. All he has to say on that point now is, "Fear God and keep his commandments;" whereas, in his previous treatment of it, he had much to say, bidding us for instance, "cast our bread upon the waters," and "give a portion to seven, and even to eight;" bidding us "sow our seed morning and evening," though "the clouds" should be "full of rain," and whatever "the course of the wind;" bidding us "rejoice" in all our labours, and carry to all our self-denials the merry heart that physics pain. As we studied the meaning of the beautiful metaphors of chapter xi., sought to gather up their several meanings into an orderly connection, and to express them in a more literal logical form--to translate them, in short, from the Eastern to the Western mode--we found that the main virtues enjoined by the Preacher were charity, industry, cheerfulness; the charity which does good hoping for nothing again, the industry which bends itself to the present duty in scorn of omen or consequence; and the cheerfulness which springs from a consciousness of the Divine presence, from the conviction that, however men may misjudge us, God knows us altogether and will do us justice. This was our summary of the Preacher's argument, of his solution of the supreme moral problem of human life. Here, in the Epilogue, he gives us his own summary in the words, "Fear God, and keep his commandments."

If we compare these two summaries, there seems at first rather difference than resemblance between them: the one appears, if more indefinite, much more comprehensive, than the other. Yet there is one point of resemblance which soon strikes us. For we know by this time that on the Preacher's lips "Fear God" does not mean "Be afraid of God;" that it indicates and demands just that reverent sense of the Divine Presence, that strong inward conviction of the constant judgment He passes on all our ways and motives and thoughts, which Coheleth has already affirmed to be a prime safeguard of virtue. It is the phrase "and keep his commandments" that sounds so much larger than anything we have heard from him before, so much more comprehensive. For the commandments of God are many and very broad. He reveals his will in the natural universe and the laws which govern it; laws which, as we are part of the universe, we need to know and to obey. He reveals his will in the social and political forces which govern the history and development of the various races of mankind, which therefore meet and affect us at every turn. He reveals his will in the ethical intuitions and codes which govern the formation of character, which enter into and give shape to all in us that is most spiritual, profound, and enduring. To keep all the commandments revealed in these immense fields of Divine activity with an intelligent and invariable obedience is simply impossible to us; it is the perfection which flows round our imperfection, and towards which it is our one great task to be ever reaching forth. Is it as inciting us to this impossible perfection that the Preacher bids us "fear God and keep his commandments"?

Yes and No. It is not as having this large perfect ideal distinctly before his mind that he utters the injunction, although in the course of this Book he has glanced at every element of it; nor even as having so much of it in his mind as is expressed in the law that came by Moses, although that too includes precepts for the physical and the political as well as for the moral and religious provinces of human life. What he meant by bidding us "keep the commandments" was, I apprehend, that we should take the counsels he has already given us, and follow after charity, industry, cheerfulness. Every other phrase in this final "conclusion" is, as we have seen, a repetition of the truths announced at the close of the previous Section, and therefore we may fairly assume this phrase to contain a truth--the truth of Duty--which he there illustrates. Throughout the whole Book there is not a single technical allusion, no allusion to the Temple, to the feasts, to the sacrifices, rites, ceremonies of the Law; and therefore we can hardly take this reference to the "commandments" as an allusion to the Mosaic table. By the rules of fair interpretation we are bound to take these commandments as previously defined by the Preacher himself, to understand him as once more enforcing the virtues which, for him, comprised the whole duty of man.

Do we thus limit and degrade the moral ideal, or represent him as degrading and limiting it? By no means: for to love our neighbour, to discharge the present duty whatever rain may fall and whatever storm may blow, to carry a bright hopeful spirit through all our toils and charities; to do this in the fear of God, as in his Presence, because He is judging and will judge us--this, surely, includes all that is essential even in the loftiest ideal of moral duty and perfection. For how are we to be cheerful and dutiful and kind except as we obey the commandments of God in whatever form they may have been revealed? The diseases which result from a violation of sanitary laws, as also the ignorance or the wilfulness or the impotence which lead us to violate social or ethical laws, of necessity and by natural consequence impair our cheerfulness, our strength for laborious duties, our neighbourly serviceableness and good-will. To live the life which the Preacher enjoins, on the inspiration of the motives which he supplies, is therefore, in the largest and broadest sense, to keep the commandments of God.

What advantage, then, is there in saying, "Be kind, be dutiful, be cheerful," over saying, "Obey the laws of God"? There is this great practical advantage that, while in the last resort the one rule of life is as comprehensive as the other, and just as difficult, it is more definite, more portable, and does not sound so difficult. It is the very advantage which our Lord's memorable summary, "Thou shalt love the Lord thy God with all thy heart, and thy neighbour as thyself," has over the Law and the Prophets. Bid a man keep the whole Mosaic code as interpreted by the prophets of a thousand years, and you set him a task so heavy, so hopeless, that he may well decline it; only to understand the bearing and harmony of the Mosaic statutes, and to gather the sense in which the prophets--to say nothing of the rabbis--interpreted them, is the labour of a lifetime, a labour for which even the whole life of a trained scholar is insufficient. But bid him "love God and man," and you give him a principle which his own conscience at once accepts and confirms, a golden rule or principle which if he be of a good heart and a willing mind, he will be able to apply to the details and problems of life as they arise. In like manner if you say: "The true ideal of life is to be reached only by the man who comprehends and obeys all the laws of God revealed in the physical universe, in the history of humanity, in the moral intuitions and discoveries of the race," you set men a task so stupendous as that no man ever has or will be able to accomplish it. Say, on the other hand, "Do the duty of every hour as it passes, without fretting about future issues; help your neighbour to do his duty or to bear his burden, even though he may never have helped you; be blithe and cheerful even when your work is hard and your neighbour is ungrateful or unkind," and you speak straight to a man's heart, to his sense of what is right and good; you summon every noble and generous instinct of his nature to his aid. He can begin to practise this rule of life without preliminary and exhausting study of its meaning; and if he finds it work, as assuredly he will, he will be encouraged to make it his rule. He will soon discover, indeed, that it means more than he thought, that it is not so easy to apply to the complexities of human affairs, that it is very much harder to keep than he supposed: but its depth and difficulty will open on him gradually, as he is able to bear them. If his heart now and then faint, if hand and foot falter, still God is with him, with him to help and reward as well as to judge; and that conviction once in his mind is there for ever, a constant spur to thought, to obedience, to patience.

In nothing, indeed, does the wisdom of the Hebrew sages show its superiority over that of the other sages of antiquity more decisively than in its adaptation to the practical needs of men busied in the common affairs of life, and with no learning and no leisure for the study of large intricate problems. It comes straight down into the beaten ways of men. If you read Confucius, for example, and still more if you read Plato, you cannot fail to be struck with their immense grasp of thought, or their profound learning, or even their moral enthusiasm; as you read, you will often meet with wise rules of life expressed in beautiful forms. And yet your main feeling will be that they give you, and men like you, if at least you be of the common build, as most of us are, little help; that unless you had their rare endowments, or could give yourself largely and long to the study of their works, you could hardly hope to learn what they have to teach, or order your life by their plan. And that this feeling is just is proved by the histories of China and Greece, different as they are. In China only students, only literati, are so much as supposed to understand the Confucian system of thought and ethics; the great bulk of the people have to be content with a few rules and forms and rites which are imposed on them by authority. In ancient Greece, the wisdom to which her great masters attained was only taught in the Schools to men addicted to philosophical studies; even the natural and moral truths on which the popular mythology was based were hidden in "mysteries" open only to the initiated few; while the great mass of the people were amused with fables which they misapprehended, and with rites which they soon degraded into licentious orgies. No man cared for their souls; their errors were not corrected, their license was not rebuked. Their wise men made no effort to lift them to a height from which they might see that the whole of morality lay in the love of God and man, in charity, diligent devotion to duty, cheerfulness. But it was far otherwise with the Hebrews and their sages. Men such as the Preacher confined themselves to no school or class, but carried their wisdom to the synagogue, to the market-place, to the popular assemblies. They invented no "mysteries," but brought down the mysteries of Heaven to the understanding of the simple. Instead of engaging in lofty abstract speculations in which only the learned could follow them, they compressed the loftiest wisdom into plain moral rules which the unlettered could apprehend, and urged them to obedience by motives and promises which went home to the popular heart. And they had their reward. The truths they taught became familiar to all sorts and conditions of Hebrew men; they became a factor, and the most influential factor, in the national life. Fishermen, carpenters, tent-makers, sandal-makers, shepherds, husbandmen, grew studious of the Divine Will and learned the secrets of righteousness and peace. During the wonderful revival of literary and religious activity which followed the exile in Babylon--a revival mainly owing to these Sages-- every child was compelled to attend a common school in which the sacred Scriptures were taught by the ablest and most learned rabbis; in which, as we learn from the Talmud, the duty of leading a religious life in all outward conditions, even to the poorest, was impressed upon them, and the virtues of charity, industry, and cheerfulness were enforced as the very soul of religion. Here, for example, is a legend from the Talmud, and it is only one of many, which illustrates and confirms all that has just been said.-- "A sage, while walking in a crowded market-place suddenly encountered the prophet Elijah, and asked him who, out of that vast multitude, would be saved. Whereupon the Prophet first pointed out a weird-looking creature, a turnkey, 'because he was merciful to his prisoners,' and next two common-looking tradesmen who were walking through the crowd, pleasantly chatting together. The sage instantly rushed after them, and asked them what were their saving works. But they, much puzzled, replied: 'We are but poor working-men who live by our trade. All that can be said for us is that we are always cheerful and good-natured. When we meet anybody who seems sad, we join him, and we talk to him and cheer him up, that he may forget his grief. And if we know of two people who have quarrelled, we talk to them, and persuade them till we have made them friends again. This is our whole life.'" It is impossible that such a legend should have sprung up on any but Hebrew soil. Had Confucius been asked to point out the man whom Heaven most approved, he would probably have replied, "The superior man is catholic, not sectarian; he is observant of the rules of propriety and decorum; and he does not do to others what he would not have done to himself:" [58] and he would certainly have looked for him in some state official distinguished by his wise administration. Had any of the Greek sages been asked the same question, they would have found their perfect man in the philosopher who, raised above the common passions and aims of men, gave himself to the pursuit of an abstract and speculative wisdom. Only a Hebrew would have looked for him in that low estate in which the one truly Perfect Man dwelt among us. And yet how that Hebrew legend charms and touches and satisfies us! What a hope for humanity there is in the thought that the poor weird-looking jailer who was merciful to his prisoners, and the kindly, industrious, cheerful working-men, living by their craft, and incapable of regarding their diligence and good-nature as "saving works," stood higher than priest or rabbi, ruler or philosopher! How welcome and ennobling is the conviction that there are last who yet are first--last with men, first with God; that turnkeys and artisans, publicans and sinners even, may draw nearer to Heaven than sophist or flamen, sage or prince! Who so poor but that he has a little "bread" to cast on the thankless unreturning waters? who so faint of heart but that he may sow a little "seed" even when the winds rave and the sky is full of clouds? who so solitary and forlorn but that he may say a word of comfort to a weeping neighbour, or seek to make "two people who have quarrelled friends again"? And this is all that the Preacher, all that God through the Preacher, asks of us.

All--yet even this is much; even for this we shall need the pressure of constant and weighty motives: for it is not only occasional acts which are required of us, but settled tempers and habits of goodwill, industry, and cheerfulness; and to love all men, to rejoice alway, to do our duty in all weathers and all moods, is very hard work to our feeble, selfish, and easily-dejected natures. Does the Preacher supply us with such motives as we need? He offers us two motives; one in the present judgment, another in the future judgment of God. "God is with you," he says, "taking cognizance of all you do; and you will soon be with God, to give Him an account of every secret and every deed." But that is an appeal to fear--is it not? It is, rather, an appeal to love and hope. He has no thought of frightening us into obedience--for the obedience of fear is not worth having, is not obedience in the true sense; but he is trying to win and allure us to obedience. For whatever terrors God's judgment or the future world may have for us, it is very certain that these terrors were in large measure unknown to the Jews. The Talmud knows nothing of "hell," nothing of an everlasting torture. Even the "Sheol" of the Old Testament is simply the "under-world" in which the Jews believed the spirits of both good men and bad to be gathered after death. And, to the Jews for whom Coheleth wrote, the judgment of God, whether here or hereafter, would have singular and powerful attractions. They were in captivity to merciless and capricious despots who took no pains to understand their character or to deal with them according to their works, who had no sense of justice, no kindness, no ruth for slaves. For men thus oppressed and hopeless there would be an infinite comfort in the thought that God, the Great Ruler and Disposer, knew them altogether, saw all their struggles to maintain his worship and to acquaint themselves with his will, took note of every wrong they suffered, "was afflicted in all their afflictions," and would one day call both them and their oppressors to the bar at which all wrongs are at once righted and avenged. Would it affright them to hear that "God taketh cognizance of all things," and has "appointed a judgment for every secret and every deed"? Would not this be, rather, their strongest consolation, their brightest hope? Would they not do their duty with better heart if they knew that God saw how hard it was to do? Would they not show a more constant kindness to their neighbours, if they knew that God would openly reward every alms done in secret? Would they not carry a blither and more patient spirit to all their labours and afflictions if they knew that a day of recompenses was at hand? The Preacher thought they would; and hence he bids them "rejoice," bids them "banish care and sadness," because God will bring them into judgment, and incites them to "keep the commandments" because God's eye is upon them, and because, in the judgment, He will not forget the work of their obedience, the labour of their love.

This, to some of us, may be a novel view whether of the present or of the future judgment of God. For the most part, I fear, we speak of the Divine judgments as terrible and well-nigh unendurable. We would escape them even here, if we could; but, above all, we dread them when we shall stand before the bar at which the secrets of all hearts will be disclosed. Now we need not, and we must not, lose ought of the awe and reverence for Him who is our God and Father which, so far from impairing, deepens our love. But we need to remember that fear is base, that it is the enemy of love; that so long as we anticipate the Divine judgments only or mainly with dread, we are far from the love which gives value and charm to obedience; and that, if we are to be good and at peace, we must "shut out fear with all the strength of hope." What is it that we fear? Suffering! But why should we fear that, if it will make us perfect? Death! But why should we fear that, if it will take us home to our Father? God's anger! But God is not angry with us if we love Him and try to do his will; He loves us even when we sin against Him, and shows his love in making the way of sin so hard to us that we are constrained to leave it. Ought we, then, to dread, ought we not rather to desire, the judgments by which we are corrected, purified, saved?

"But the future judgment--that is so dreadful!" Is it? God knows us as we are already: is it so very much worse that we should know ourselves, and that our neighbours should know us? If among our "secrets" there be many things evil, are there not at least some that are good? Do we not find ourselves perpetually thwarted or hindered in our endeavours to give form and scope to our purest emotions, our tenderest sympathies, our loftiest resolves? Do we not perpetually complain that, when we would do good, even if evil is not present to overcome the good, it is present to mar it, to make our goodness poor, scanty, ungraceful? Well, these obstructed purposes and intentions and resolves, all the good in us that has been frustrated or deformed, or limited, by our social conditions, by our lack of power, culture, expression, by the clogging flesh or the flagging brain,--all these are among "the secret things" which God will bring to light; and we may be sure that He will not think less of these, his own work in us, than of the manifold sins by which we have marred his work. We are in some danger of regarding "the judgment" as a revelation of our trespasses only, instead of every deed, and every secret, whether good or bad. Once conceive of it aright, as the revelation of the whole man, as the unveiling of all that is in us, and mere honesty might lead us to desire rather than to dread it. One of the finest and most devout spirits of modern France [59] has said: "It seems to me intolerable to appear to men other than we appear to God. My worst torture at this moment is the over-estimate which generous friends form of me. We are told that at the last judgment the secret of all consciences will be laid bare to the universe: would that mine were so this day, and that every passer-by could read me as I am!" To seem what we are, to be known for what we are, to be treated as we are, this is the judgment of God. And, though this judgment must bring even the best of us much shame and much sorrow, who that sincerely loves God and truth will not rejoice to have done at last with all masks and veils, to wear his natural colours, and to take his true place, even though it be the lowest?

> "In the corrupted currents of this world
> Offence's gilded hand may shove by justice,
> And oft 'tis seen the wicked prize itself
> Buys out the law: but 'tis not so above;
> There is no shuffling, there the action lies
> In its true nature, and we ourselves compell'd
> Even to the teeth and forehead of our faults
> To give in evidence."

To have got out of "the corrupted currents" of which audacious and strong injustice so often avails itself to our hurt; to be quit of all the shuffling equivocations by which we often pervert the true character of our actions, and persuade ourselves that we are other and better than we are; to be compelled to look our faults straight and fairly in the face; to have all the latent goodness of our natures developed, and their fettered and obstructed virtue liberated from every bond; to see our every "secret" good as well as bad, and our every "deed" good as well as bad, exposed in their true colours: is there no hope, no comfort for us, in such a prospect as this? It is a prospect full of comfort, full of hope, if at least we have any real trust in the grace and goodness of God; and if, through his grace, we have set ourselves to do our duty, to love our neighbour, and to bear the changes and burdens of life with a patient cheerful heart.

Now that we have once more heard the Preacher's final conclusion, we shall have no difficulty in fitting into its place, or valuing at its worth, the partial and provisional conclusion to which he rises at the close of the previous Sections of the Book. In the First Section he describes his quest of the Chief Good in Wisdom and in Mirth; he declares that, though both wisdom and mirth are good, neither of them is the supreme good of life, nor both combined; and, in despair of reaching any higher mark, he closes with the admission (ch. ii., vv. 24-26) that even for the man who is both wise and good "there is nothing better than to eat and to drink, and to let his soul take pleasure in all his labour." In the Second Section he pursues his quest in Devotion to Business and to Public Affairs, only to find his former conclusion confirmed (ch. v., vv. 18-20): "Behold, that which I have said holds good; it is well for a man to eat and to drink, and to enjoy all the good of his labour through the brief day of his life; this is his portion; and he should take his portion and rejoice in his labour, remembering that the days of his life are not many, and that God meant him to work for the enjoyment of his heart." In the Third Section, his quest in Wealth and in the Golden Mean conducts him by another road to the same bright resting-place which, however, for all so bright as it looks, he seems to enter every time with a more rueful and dejected gait (ch. viii., ver. 15): more and more sadly he "commends mirth, because there is nothing better for man than to eat and to drink and to rejoice, and because this will go with him to his work through the days of his life which God giveth him under the sun." To my mind there is a strange pathos in the mournful tones in which the Preacher commends mirth, in the plaintive minors of a voice from which we should naturally expect the clear ringing majors of joy. As we listen to these recurring notes, we feel that he has been baffled in his Quest; that, starting every day in a fresh direction and travelling till he is weary and spent, he finds himself night after night at the very spot he had left in the morning, and can only alleviate the unwelcome surprise of finding himself no farther and no higher by muttering, "As well here perhaps as elsewhere!" No votary of mirth and jollity surely ever wore so woebegone a countenance, or sang their praises with more trembling and uncertain lips. What can be more hopeless than his "there is nothing better, so you must even be content with this," or than the way in which he harps on the brevity of life! You feel that the man has been passionately seeking for something better, for a good which would be a good not only through the brief hours of time but for ever; that it is with a heart saddened by the sense of wasted endeavour and cravings unsatisfied that he falls back on pleasures as brief as his day, as wearisome as his toils. Yet all the while he feels, and makes you feel, that there is a certain measure of truth in his conclusion; that mirth is a great good, though not the greatest; that if he could but find that "something better" of which he is in quest, he would learn the secret of a deeper mirth than that which springs from eating and drinking and sensuous delights, a mirth which would not set with the setting sun of his brief day.

This feeling is justified by the issue. Now that the Preacher has completed his circle of thought, we can see that it is well for a man to rejoice and take pleasure in his labours, that God did mean him to work for the enjoyment of his heart, that there is a mirth purer and more enduring than that which springs from knowledge, or from the gratification of the senses, or from success in affairs, or from the possession of much goods,--a mirth for this life which expands and deepens into an everlasting joy. Throughout his Quest he has held fast to the conviction that "it is a comely fashion to be glad," though he could allege no better reason for his conviction than the transitoriness of life and the impossibility of reaching any higher good. Before he could justify this conviction, he must achieve his Quest. It is only when he has learned to regard our life--

> "as a harp,
> A gracious instrument on whose fair strings
> We learn those airs we shall be set to play
> When mortal hours are ended,"

that his plaintive minors pass into the frank, jocund tones appropriate to a sincere and well-grounded mirth. Now he can cease to "trouble heaven with his bootless cries" on the indiscrimination of death and the vanity of life. He can now say to his soul,

> "What hast thou to do with sorrow
> Or the injuries of to-morrow?"

for he has discovered that no morrow can any more injure him, no sorrow rob him of his true joy. God is with him, observing all the postures and moods of his soul, and adapting all his circumstances to the correction of what is evil in him or the cultivation of what is good. There is no dark impassable gulf between this world and the next; life does not cease at death, but grows more intense and full; death is but a second birth into a second and better life, a life of ampler and happier conditions, and yet a life which is the continuation and consummation of that we now live in the flesh. All that he has to do, therefore, is to "fear God and keep his commandments," leaving the issues of his labour in the Hands which bend all things to a final goal of good. What though the clouds drop rain or the winds blew bitterly, what though his diligence a charity meet no present recognition or reward? All that is no business of his. He has only to do the duty of the passing hour, and to help his neighbours do their duty. So long as he can do this, why should he not be bright and gay? In this lies his Chief Good: why should he not enjoy that, even though other and lesser goods be taken from him for a time--be lent to the Lord that they may hereafter be repaid with usury? He is no longer "a pipe for fortune's finger to sound what stop she please:" he has a tune of his own, "a cheerful tune," to play, and will play it, let fortune be in what mood she please. He is not "passion's slave," but the servant and friend of God; and because God is with him and for him, and because he will soon be with God, he is

> "As one, in suffering all, that suffers nothing,"

and can take "fortune's buffets and rewards with equal thanks." His cheerful content does not lie at the mercy of accident; the winds and waves of vicissitude cannot prevail against it: for it has two broad and solid foundations; one on earth, and the other in heaven. On the one hand, it springs from a faithful discharge of personal duty and the neighbourly charity which hopeth all things and endureth all things; on the other hand, it springs from the conviction that God takes note of all things, and will bring every secret and every deed into a judgment perfectly just and perfectly kind. The fair structure which rises on these sure foundations is not to be shaken by ought that does not sap the foundations on which it rests. Convince him that God is not with him, or that God does not so care for him as to judge and correct him; or convict him of gross and constant failures in duty and in charity; and then, indeed, you touch, you endanger, his peace. But no external loss, no breath of change, no cloud in the sky of his fortunes, no loss, no infirmity that does not impede him in the discharge of duty, can do more than cast a passing shadow on his heart. Whatever happens, into whatever new conditions or new worlds he may pass, his chief good and therefore his supreme joy is with him.

The Expositor's Bible: Ecclesiastes

> "This man is freed from servile bands
> Of hope to rise or fear to fall:
> Lord of himself, though not of lands,
> And, having nothing, yet hath all."

Now, too, without fear or favour, without any prejudice for or against his conclusion because we find it in Holy Writ, we may ask ourselves, Has the Preacher satisfactorily solved the problem which he took in hand? has he really achieved his Quest and attained the Chief Good? One thing is quite clear; he has not lost himself in speculations foreign to our experience and remote from it; he has dealt with the common facts of life such as they were in his time, such as they remain in ours: for now, as then, men are restless and craving, and seek the satisfactions of rest in science or in pleasure, in successful public careers or in the fortunate conduct of affairs, by securing wealth or by laying up a modest provision for present and future wants. Now, as then,

> "The common problem, yours, mine, everyone's,
> Is not to fancy what were fair in life
> Providing it could be,--but, finding first
> What may be, then find how to make it fair
> Up to our means--a very different thing."

That the Preacher should have attacked this common problem, and should have handled it with the practical good sense which characterises his Poem, is a point, and a large point, in his favour.

Nor is the conclusion at which he arrives, in its substance, peculiar to him, or even to the Scriptures. He says: The perfect man, the ideal man, is he who addresses himself to the present duty untroubled by adverse clouds and currents, who so loves his neighbour that he can do good even to the evil and the unthankful, and who carries a brave cheerful temper to the unrewarded toils and sacrifices of his life, because God is with him, taking note of all he does, and because there is a future life for which this course of duty, charity, and magnanimity, is the best preparative. He affirms that the man who has risen to the discovery and practice of this ideal has attained the Chief Good, that he has found a duty from which no accident can divert him, a pure and tranquil joy which will sustain him under all change and loss. And, on his behalf, I am bold to assert that, allowing for inevitable differences of conception and utterance, his conclusion is the conclusion of all the great teachers of morality. Take any of the ancient systems of morality and religion--Hindu, Egyptian, Persian, Chinese, Greek, or Latin; select those elements of it in virtue of which it has lived and ruled over myriads of men; reduce those elements to their simplest forms, express them in the plainest words; and, as I believe, you will find that in every case they are only different and modified versions of the final conclusion of the Preacher. "Do your duty patiently; Be kind and helpful one to another; Shew a cheerful content with your lot; Heaven is with you and will judge you:"--these brief maxims seem to be the ethical epitome of all the creeds and systems that have had their day, as also of those which have not ceased to be. It is very true that the motive to obedience which Coheleth draws from the future life of man has been of a varying force and influence, rising perhaps to its greatest clearness among the Egyptians and the Persians, sinking to its dimmest among the Greeks and the Romans, although we cannot say it did not shine even upon these; for, though the secret of their "mysteries" has been kept with a rare fidelity, yet the general impression of Antiquity concerning them was that, besides disclosing to the initiated the natural and moral truths on which the popular mythology was based, they "opened to man a comforting prospect of a future state." I am not careful to show how the Word of Inspiration surpasses all other "scriptures" in the precision with which it enunciates the elementary truths of all morality, in its freedom from admixture with baser matter, in its application of those truths to all sorts and conditions of men, and the power of the motives by which it enforces them. That is no part of my present duty. The one point to which I ask attention is this: With what an enormous weight of authority, drawn from all creeds and systems, from the whole ethical experience of humanity, the conclusion of the Preacher is clothed; how we stand rebuked by the wisdom of all past ages if, after duly testing it, we have not adopted his solution of the master-problem of life, and are not working it out. Out of every land, in all the different languages of the divided earth, from the lips of all the ancient sages whom we reverence for their excellence or for their wisdom, no less than from the mouths of prophet and psalmist, preacher and apostle, there come to us voices which with one consent bid us "fear God and keep his commandments;"--a sacred chorus which paces down the long-drawn aisles of Time, chanting the praise of the man who does his duty even though he lose by it, who loves his neighbour even though he win no love in return, who breasts the blows of circumstance with a tranquil heart, who by a wise use and a wise enjoyment of the life that now is qualifies himself for the better life to be.

***

This, then, is the Hebrew solution of "the common problem." It is also the Christian solution. For when "the Fellow of the Lord of hosts," instead of "clutching at his equality with God," humbled Himself and took on Him the form of a servant, the very ideal of perfect manhood became incarnate in this "man from heaven." Does the Hebrew Preacher, backed by the consentient voices of the great sages of Antiquity, demand that the ideal man, moved thereto by his sense of a constant Divine Presence and the hope of God's future judgment, should cast the bread of his charity on the thankless waters of neighbourly ingratitude, give himself with all diligence to the discharge of duty whatever clouds may darken his sky, whatever unkindly wind may nip his harvest, and maintain a calm and cheerful temper in all weathers, and through all the changing scenes and seasons of life? His demand is met, and surpassed, by the Man Christ Jesus. He loved all men with a love which the many waters of their hostility and unthankfulness could not quench. Always about his Father's business, when He laid aside the glory He had with the Father before the world was, He put off the robes of a king to don the weeds of the husbandman, and went forth to sow in all weathers, beside all waters, undaunted by any wind of opposition or any threatening cloud. In all the shock of hostile circumstance, in the abiding agony and passion of a life "short in years indeed, but in sorrows above all measure long," He carried Himself with a cheerful patience and serenity which never wavered, for the joy set before Him enduring, and even despising, the bitter cross. In fine, the very virtues inculcated by the Preacher were the very substance of "the highest, holiest manhood." And if we ask, What were the motives which inspired this life of consummate and unparalleled excellence? we find among them the very motives suggested by Coheleth. The strong Son of Man and of God was never alone, because the Father was with Him, as truly with Him while He was on earth as when He was in the heaven from which He "came down." He never bated heart nor hope because He knew that He would soon be with God once more, to be judged of Him and recompensed according to the deeds done in the body of his humiliation. Men might misjudge Him, but the Judge of all the earth would do Him right. Men might award Him only a crown of thorns; but God would touch the thorns and, at his quickening touch, they would flower into a garland of immortal beauty and honour.

Nor did the Lord Jesus help us in our quest of the Chief Good only by becoming a Pattern of all virtue and excellence. The work of his Redemption is a still more sovereign help. By the sacrifice of the Cross He took away the sins which had rendered the pursuit of excellence a wellnigh hopeless task. By the impartation of his Spirit, no less than by the inspiration of his Example, He seeks to win us to the love of our neighbour, to fidelity in the discharge of our daily duty, and to that cheerful and constant trust in the providence of God by which we are redeemed from the bondage of care and fear. He, the Immanuel, by taking our flesh and dwelling among us, has proved that "God is with us," that He will in very deed dwell with men upon the earth. He, the Victor over death, by his resurrection from the grave, has proved the truth of a future life and a future judgment with arguments of a force and quality unknown to our Hebrew fathers.

So that now as of old, now even more demonstrably than of old, the conclusion of the whole matter is that we "fear God and keep his commandments." This is still the one solution of "the common problem" and "the whole duty of man." He who accepts this solution and discharges this duty has achieved the Supreme Quest; to him it has been given to find the Chief Good.

Footnotes:

55. As the main ethical, literary, and historical interest of the whole Book is gathered up into this brief Epilogue, I offer no apology for the comparative length of my treatment of it.

56. In the Introduction, however, I have tried to give what is known of the history of this period. Roughly speaking, I believe the Jews owed their literary advance mainly to contact with the inquisitive and learned Babylonians, and their religious advance mainly to the sorrows of the Captivity and their contact with the pure faith of the primitive Persians.

57. Emmanuel Deutsch, whose premature death is still lamented by many as an irreparable loss. The passage will be found in his celebrated article on The Talmud in The Quarterly of October 1867. "The Quest of the Chief Good" was published at the close of that year. And at this point in it, while Deutsch was still alive, but before I knew him personally, I gently complained of the loss he had unwittingly inflicted on me. I had for ten years been collecting the gnomic sayings of the Talmud from any quarter open to one to whom the Talmud itself was a sealed book, and had indeed printed some two score of them in the Christian Spectator for 1866. And here came one who "out of his profuse wealth carelessly flung down most of my special treasures." Only half-a-dozen of the sayings I had collected now had any stamp of novelty on them to the thousands who had revelled in the wit and learning of that famous article in The Quarterly. And of these I ventured to call special attention to four which seemed to me of special value and beauty; viz., those on the four kinds of students, on new and old flasks, on not serving God for the sake of reward, and on doing God's will as if it were our will: they will all be found in this Section. But if I lost something, I also gained much by the appearance of that article, as

The Expositor's Bible: Ecclesiastes

those who read what follows will discover, although it only came into my hands as I was correcting the proofs of the final pages in my Book.

58. This partial anticipation of the Golden Rule will be found in the Confucian Analects, book xv., chap. xxiii. "Tsze-kung asked, saying, 'Is there one word which may serve as a rule of practice for all one's life?' The Master said, 'Is not reciprocity such a word? What you do not want done to yourself, do not do to others.'" The same rule is given in another form in book v., chap. i of the Analects. The other phrases put into the sage's mouth are quoted from Dr. Legge's translation of this work.

59. Maurice de Guérin in his Journal.

www.ingramcontent.com/pod-product-compliance
Lightning Source LLC
Chambersburg PA
CBHW031940110426
42744CB00028B/148